WRITING HISTORY AND MAKING POLICY

The Cold War, Vietnam, and Revisionism

Richard A. Melanson

With an Introductory note by

Kenneth W. Thompson

UNIVERSITY
PRESS OF
AMERICA

LANHAM • NEW YORK • LONDON

University Press of America,® Inc.

4720 Boston Way
Lanham, MD 20706

3 Henrietta Street
London WC2E 8LU England

Printed in the United States of America

Co-published by arrangement with
The White Burkett Miller Center of Public Affairs
The University of Virginia

Library of Congress Cataloging in Publication Data

Melanson, Richard A.
Writing history and making policy.

(American values projected abroad ; v. 6)
Includes bibliographical references,
1. United States—Foreign relations—1945-
Historiography. 2. World politics—1945-
—Historiography. I. Title. II. Series.
JX1417.A74 1982 vol. 6 [E744] 303.4'8273s 83-10362
ISBN 0-8191-3352-3 327'.009045
ISBN 0-8191-3353-1 (pbk.)

All University Press of America books are produced on acid-free paper which exceeds the minimum standards set by the National Historical Publications and Records Commission.

AMERICAN VALUES PROJECTED ABROAD

VOLUME VI

A SERIES FUNDED BY THE
EXXON EDUCATION FOUNDATION

FOUNDATIONS OF AMERICAN VALUES

Vol. I Western Heritage and American Values: Law Theology and History, *By Alberto Coll*

Vol. II Political Traditions and Contemporary Problems, *Edited by Kenneth W. Thompson*

Vol. III Institutions for Projecting American Values Abroad, *Edited by Kenneth W. Thompson*

Vol. IV Essays on Lincoln's Faith and Politics, *By Hans J. Morgenthau and David Hein*

Vol. V The Predicament of Human Rights: The Carter and Reagan Policies, *By Nicolai N. Petro*

Vol. VI Writing History and Making Policy: The Cold War, Vietnam, and Revisionism, *By Richard A. Melanson*

Vol. VII Traditions and Values: American Diplomacy, 1790 to 1865, *Edited by Norman Graebner*

Vol. VIII Traditions and Values: American Diplomacy, 1865 to 1945, *Edited by Norman Graebner*

Vol. IX Traditions and Values: American Diplomacy, 1945 to the Present, *Edited by Kenneth W. Thompson*

AMERICAN VALUES VIEWED THROUGH OTHER CULTURES

Vol. X The Elements of International Strategy: A Primer for the Nuclear Age, *By Louis J. Halle*

Vol. XI Nationalism and Internationalism: European and American Perspectives, *By Erich Hula*

Vol. XII Diplomacy and Values: The Life and Works of Stephen Kertesz in Europe and America, *Edited by Kenneth W. Thompson*

Vol. XIII Islamic Values and World View: Khomeyni on Man, the State and International Politics, *By Farhang Rajaee*

Vol. XIV Culture & Democracy: Anthropological Reflections on Modern India, *By R.S. Khare*

Vol. XV An Ambassador's Journey: An Exploration of People and Culture, *By Charles Baldwin*

Vol. XVI Selections From *The New American Commonwealth,* *By Louis Heren*

Vol. XVII African and American Values: Liberia and West Africa, *By Katherine Harris*

Vol. XVIII United States Foreign Policy Towards Sub-Saharan Africa: Change, Continuity, and Constraint, *By David A. Dickson II*

Vol. XIX Latin American Values: Their Influence on Political Decisions and Processes, *By Julie Bunck*

Vol. XX The Primacy of Freedom in Development, *By Ambassador Soedjatmoko*

TABLE OF CONTENTS

INTRODUCTORY NOTE

Professor Richard Melanson has written a study of theories of the Cold War which represents a decade of serious research and study. Like a scientist in his laboratory, Melanson has proceeded step by step to understand and analyze the differing approaches of leading individual thinkers and schools of thought. He has discussed the orthodox version of the struggle derived from the views of major figures such as Herbert Feis and John Spanier. He has delved into the foundations of thought of revisionists such as William Appleman Williams and his successors. Indeed it would be difficult to discover a more illuminating essay than Melanson's analysis of Williams' approach. Melanson has also examined the contributions of those he calls "realist revisionists" whom I have called "interpreters and critics," such as George F. Kennan, Hans Morgenthau and Walter Lippmann. Melanson goes beyond these schools to consider Vietnam revisionists, neo-conservatives, the interdependence school and the Reagan approach. Thus he has taken a more comprehensive view of Cold War thinking than anyone writing about these theories.

Moreover, Melanson keeps his eye primarily on the underlying values and core principles of the thinkers he discusses. For this reason, his book is appropriately a part of the Miller Center series on American values projected abroad generously funded by the Exxon Education Foundation. While he grapples with policy issues, it is the underlying question of values that shape policies which preoccupies Melanson above all else. The Center is pleased to have been able to assist his research and writing.

Finally, Richard Melanson stands on the threshold of a brilliant career as a student of international politics. He has already made a substantial addition to the literature both in individual studies and edited volumes. But the intellectual power he has displayed guarantees a long and creative role as an interpreter. We shall all benefit from his penetrating analysis and work.

INTRODUCTION: REVISING THE PAST

In June 1981 Robert Darnton, the Warsaw correspondent of *The New York Times,* wrote

> Having come face-to-face with the blank spaces of their history [the Poles] could not get enough. Someone had written "Bandits" under a photograph of Giereck and other members of the Politburo. A visitors' book contained a host of similar comments. One read, "Next time Katyn." For the regime, the massacre of 10,000 or more Polish troops, mainly officers, in the forest of Katyn is the greatest taboo subject in Poland today. According to official history, the Germans killed the troops after capturing them in 1941. According to discussions held in hushed tones with glances over the shoulder, the Russians did the killing while grabbing their share of the Hitler-Stalin partition in 1940.
>
> Try telling a Pole that events don't matter, that diplomacy and politics are epiphenomena, that one can neglect dates in order to study structures. He will reply that the difference between 1940 and 1941 is a matter of life and death; that nothing could be more important than the secret provisions of the Ribbentrop-Molotov pact; that the whole meaning of Poland can be strung out on dates. . . . The events of August [1980] transformed the world for him. For the rest of us they suggest that history can play tricks on itself, and that it can go back to work at its old task, teaching lessons and shaping a national consciousness. In Poland that consciousness will determine the future as well as the past.[1]

Six months later, after General Jaruzelski had imposed martial law and jailed the leaders of Solidarity, the Soviet government accused the United States of seeking to revise the "political results of World War II" by allegedly preventing the "speedy consolidation" of the pro-Soviet forces in Poland. In contrast to the 1970s, when the United States was supposedly interested in European "security," Soviet officials claimed that Reagan's policy toward Poland had ushered in "dangerous adventurism when anything can be expected from the United States, including a nuclear war."[2] In short, President Reagan had apparently forgotten the Soviet understanding of the "lessons of Yalta."

As these two examples demonstrate history and policy rarely stand in isolation from one another, and both private and official recollections of the past help to determine attitudes toward the present and plans for the future. The policy-maker, necessarily immersed in daily routines, does not often articulate an historical outlook, yet almost all policies are informed in some way by judgments about the past, however camouflaged or implicit.

Revisionist history (i.e., historical interpretations that contradict the prevailing orthodoxy) is almost as old as history itself and contains impulses "as varied and full as the full range of human motivation."[3] Frequently, history is rewritten "because perspectives have changed or new sources of information have been discovered" or "because a younger generation has become bored" or otherwise dissatisfied with the dominant explanation.[4] But in its more extreme manifestations, as in Solidarity's efforts to redate the Katyn massacre, revisionism may directly assault the authority of regimes whose legitimacy rests partly on a particular rendition of the past. Modern historical revisionism, it will be recalled, surfaced most dramatically after World War I over the issue of war guilt in the Versailles Treaty, and its very existence threw into question the status of the Weimar republicans who had signed that document.

While the cleavage between those who make policy and those who unofficially interpret its roots has not always been as wide as in Weimar Germany or Communist Poland, politically charged revisionist controversies have scarcely been unknown in the United States. During the interwar period, for example, Charles Beard and several other historians challenged the conventional view that the United States had entered World War I to protect the principles of neutral shipping rights and to make the world safe for democracy. Instead, they suggested that special interests had maneuvered Wilson into support for Allies whose war aims were at least as extravagant as those of Germany. Not surprisingly, this revisionism became deeply enmeshed in the domestic political debate over isolationism, and some of its proponents even testified before Congress on behalf of mandatory neutrality legislation designed to prevent the United States from recommitting the alleged mistakes of 1917. The revisionist cause gained an impressive (if temporary) ally in 1936 when President Roosevelt defended the "traditional American principle of non-intervention" and pledged that "if we face the choice of profits or peace, the nation will answer—must answer—'we choose peace.' "[5] As the events in China, Czechoslovakia, and Poland threatened to again draw the United States into war, however, the World War I revisionists could not sustain their claim that the Axis posed no greater threat to American security than had the Central Powers.

Public attitudes toward foreign policy during the interwar years cannot be primarily attributed to the political influence of these professional historians. Novelists and poets like Hemingway, Dos Passos, Remarque, and Pound expressed the same disenchantment about the war and reached a much wider audience. But revisionist historiography, particularly in the academic community, had a considerable political impact and certainly played an important role in articulating the isolationist outlook.[6]

World War II, of course, thoroughly discredited its arguments, and many scholars seemed eager to blame Beard and his colleagues for allegedly crippling American foreign policy in the 1930s. For example, Dexter Perkins complained in 1947 that these historians had "assisted the rise of Hitler and the loss of the first peace,"[7] while Edward Mead Earle suggested that "a good deal of [this] historical writing was the direct cause, if not the only cause, of the cynicism and intellectual nihilism which determined the climate of our university campuses for twenty years."[8]

* * * * *

This book presumes that ideas, and, in this case, historical ideas, have consequences. More specifically, it presumes that history is not written in a political vacuum: *it is both affected by and it affects events in the policy world.* Historical scholarship, and particularly diplomatic history, is sensitive to the prevailing "climate of opinion," and the scholar finds it exceedingly difficult to escape fully the influence of the political environment. Furthermore, the relationship between the historian and the climate of opinion is reciprocal: "Precisely because the historian is so integrally related to his society's intellectual temper, he influences it even as it influences him. The historian informs his contemporaries of their historical development and in so doing provides them with a memory extending back before their own lives. . . ."[9] We have already touched on the influence of the World War I revisionists in the 1930s, yet there have been at least three significant challenges to the dominant postwar historical interpretations of American foreign policy. This book examines these historiographical challengers—the "realist" revisionists of global containment, the Cold War "radical" revisionists, and the "neo-conservative" revisionists of Vietnam—and assesses their political consequences.

That is, in addition to evaluating these historical revisionisms on their own terms, we also consider the degree to which American foreign policy-makers, especially those in the Carter and Reagan administrations, have employed historical analogies informed by revisionist arguments. This second point needs amplification. As we suggested earlier policy-makers frequently depend on historical "lessons" to provide them with relevant analogies. For example, Western leaders in the 1930s, aware of the presumed "lessons" of 1914, when diplomatic inflexibility had allegedly caused a war that no one wanted, hoped that a willingness to "compromise" with Hitler would head off a new conflict. After World War II the Truman Administration, in searching for a response to what it interpreted as Soviet provocations, repeatedly cited the "lessons" of Munich in support of its strategy to contain "Communist aggression." Many professional historians have worried about the ways in which policy-makers use and misuse history and have claimed that historical "lessons" have often trapped them in misleading, simplistic, or wholly false analogies. Ernest R. May's "LESSONS" OF THE PAST[10] represents the most explicit effort to indicate how recent American foreign policy-makers have abused history. In order to reduce the incidence of these errors some scholars have proposed that professional historians be attached to appropriate agencies as "historical watchdogs." Yet, as we will see, for most of the Cold War American officials and American diplomatic historians interpreted Soviet-American relations in very similar ways. Policy-makers may have employed "simplistic" historical analogies, but their academic counterparts tended to rely on identical interwar "lessons" to explain the Cold War.

Given these circumstances we wish to discover if the historical interpretations offered by the realist, Cold War, and Vietnam revisionists were embraced, however simplistically, by American policy-makers, especially those in the Carter and Reagan administrations.

* * * * *

In chapter one, "American Diplomatic Historians and the Cold War Consensus," we review the "orthodox" historical understanding of the Cold War and argue that this academic interpretation provided important support for postwar U.S. foreign policy. Chapter two, "The Realist Revisionists," examines an early and persisting challenge to orthodoxy's account of the Cold War (particularly after 1947) and speculates on the political influence that realists like George F. Kennan, Walter Lippmann, and Hans J. Morgenthau may have possessed during the high Cold War. In chapter three, "The Cold War Revisionists," we look at leftist scholars like William Appleman Williams, Gar Alperovitz, Gabriel Kolko, Richard J. Barnet, and Walter LaFeber who rejected the historical arguments and policy consequences of both orthodoxy and realist revisionism. We also focus on the political implications of their Cold War theories. Chapter four, "Cold War Revisionism Subdued?" recalls the most prominent attempts to discredit the arguments of the Cold War revisionists and reviews several subsequent "post-revisionist" interpretations that synthesized, to one degree or another, orthodox, realist, and Cold War revisionist accounts. In chapter five, "The Realist Revisionists and Vietnam," we suggest that members of the foreign policy "establishment" who turned against the Vietnam War owed a substantial (if selective) intellectual debt to older realist revisionists like Kennan, Lippmann, and Morgenthau. We further argue that the Nixon-Kissinger "reformulation" of 1969 relied, in part, on a realist revisionist historical framework. Chapter six, "Carter, the Cold War, and 'World Order Politics'," examines the historical thinking (such as it was) of the Carter Administration and looks, in particular, for evidence of Cold War revisionism's influence on younger, "Vietnam generation" officials. In chapter seven, "Carter, Reagan, and the Vietnam Revisionists," we evaluate the "orthodox" understanding of the Vietnam War (which was developed in FOREIGN POLICY during the early 1970s) and assess its impact on the Carter Administration. We also describe the "neo-conservative" challenge to this orthodoxy and speculate on this revisionism's impact on the Reagan Administration. Chapter eight, "Revisionist History and American Foreign Policy," summarizes our arguments and offers some concluding observations about the reciprocal relationship between American diplomatic historiography and American foreign policy.

In 1979 I received a Small Grant from the Penrose Fund of the American Philosophical Society; in 1980-81 a Research Fellowship for College Teachers from the National Endowment for the Humanities; and in 1981-82 a Research Fellowship from the White Burkett Miller Center for Public Affairs at the University of Virginia. This book could not have been written without this generous financial assistance.

Finally, I would like to thank four people who helped to bring this work to fruition: John Lewis Gaddis, Ohio University, who first broached the idea of this book and who read an early draft of it; Nicholas X. Rizopoulos, the Lerham Institute, who offered several important suggestions; Robert W. Tucker, The Johns Hopkins University, who allowed me to expose some of these notions to his graduate seminar in American foreign policy; and especially to Kenneth W. Thompson, University of Virginia, who provided me with warm and unflagging support throughout the enterprise.

CHAPTER 1: AMERICAN DIPLOMATIC HISTORIANS AND THE COLD WAR CONSENSUS

For a democratic polity to sustain a coherent foreign policy, a relatively broad and stable domestic consensus is essential. A democratic consensus can impart authority and legitimacy to foreign policy by sharing and supporting its premises, purposes, and values. While such a consensus cannot guarantee enlightened diplomacy, an effective foreign policy is probably impossible without it.

There have been two periods of consensus in the post-World War II era of American foreign policy. The first, loosely termed containment, began to form in 1947, was fully operative by 1954, flourished until the mid-1960s, and was moribund by 1968. The second epoch, even more loosely dubbed détente, emerged between Nixon's "silent majority" speech of November 1969 and the last great anti-war march in May 1971, prevailed from mid-1971 until late 1973, and was floundering by early 1975. Neither Gerald Ford nor Jimmy Carter could construct a new consensus, and it is still unclear if Ronald Reagan will be any more successful. While dissimilar in many respects, each consensus was characterized by a focus on Soviet-American relations, specific diagnoses of Soviet capabilities and intentions, and relatively clear prescriptions for American responses to Moscow. What had helped to give the earlier consensus much greater strength and longevity was the presence of a remarkably cohesive and articulate elite responsible for shaping, sustaining, and ultimately destroying it and an academic community which generally supported the main outlines of American foreign policy.

An establishment may well be a permanent feature of American diplomacy.[1] Constitutional requirements, general public passivity, and the recondite nature of foreign policy expertise combine to render participatory democracy unworkable in America's international relations. A reasonably democratic establishment which articulates policy, educates (and listens to) the attentive public, builds consensus and avoids major foreign policy disasters is the most to which America can realistically aspire. In other words, an American foreign policy establishment is more or less inevitable.

The establishment which molded and maintained the Cold War or containment consensus possessed several characteristics. Although a disproportionate number of its members (particularly among the older generation) came from privileged East Coast backgrounds featuring Harvard and Yale educations, the establishment's uniqueness did not depend on sociology or education, and still less on genealogy, but on a history, a policy, an aspiration, an instinct, and a technique.[2] Its origins can be traced back to the small group of advisers which Colonel House gathered around him at Versailles to help lay plans for a democratic post-war world under American leadership. When the treaty was defeated in 1920, these businessmen and academics, now joined by a handful of international bankers and corporation lawyers, continued to press for a liberal internationalist foreign policy. Through meetings and seminars at the Council on Foreign Relations and articles published in FOREIGN AFFAIRS this group was able to survive the "normalcy" of the 1920s and the economic nationalism of the 1930s even if it was unable to convert many to its cause. World War II provided this would-be establishment with the opportunity to implement its vision, and many of its members gained valuable governmental experience, particularly in the OSS. The war imparted to them a sense of power, accomplishment, destiny, and political involvement which gave them the confidence and stature to eagerly seek key roles in post-war American foreign policy.

Seeing themselves as bipartisan counterweights to an anticipated isolationist resurgence (especially in Congress), members of this influential group were convinced that America's reluctance to exert its power during the interwar years had helped to trigger World War II, and so were determined to employ the Presidency to build an internationalist consensus at home. Certain that the United States possessed the material resources to achieve world leadership, the establishment believed that it had to supply the missing moral and spiritual ingredients necessary to transform crude power into international authority. Though they themselves rarely stood for election, these men had an instinct for the political center—an instinct which buttressed their aspiration to serve as educators to an America whose traditional tendency was to vacillate dangerously between self-righteous isolation and evangelical exhortation. And, while members of this establishment feared international Communism as a mortal threat to western values and institutions, they were unsympathetic to those who wished to ferret out "subversives" at home.

These men were, moreover, eager to defend the internationalist foreign policy record of postwar America against isolationist attacks, and they quickly articulated an interpretation of the Cold War that reigned supreme until well into the 1960s. And, as we will see shortly, American diplomatic historians of the day helped to fashion and propagate this explanation. According to this view, which received its most elaborate treatment in George F. Kennan's "The Sources of Soviet Conduct,"[3] the Soviet Union had triggered the Cold War through its refusal to respect the norms of international life. Variously cursed by Russian history and geography, Marxist-Leninist doctrine, and a pathologically insecure political leadership, the Soviet Union required expansion to survive. The United States had vainly tried to prolong the life of the Grand Alliance with the help of the United Nations Organization and other devices, but Soviet intransigence made such cooperation impossible. Confronted with dangerous Russian threats to Western Europe and the Middle East, the United States had no choice but to contain the further spread of Soviet power. If pursued with vigilance and patience such a strategy would eventually result in either the positive transformation or the collapse of the Soviet regime.

Kennan, Harriman, Acheson, and other American officials argued that the United States could not have prevented Soviet domination of Eastern Europe or the defeat of Chiang Kai-shek without an enormous expenditure of resources. According to Harriman,

> It is my belief that Stalin was influenced by the hostile attitude of the peoples of Eastern Europe toward the Red Army and that he recognized that governments established by free elections would not be "friendly" to the Soviet Union. In addition, I believe he became increasingly aware of the great opportunities for Soviet expansion in the post-war economic chaos. After our rapid demobilization I do not think that he conceived that the United States would take the firm stand that we have taken in the past five years.[4]

Kennan suggested that

> If it cannot be said that the Western democracies gained very much from these talks [Moscow, Teheran, and Yalta], it would also be incorrect to say that they gave very much away. The establishment of Soviet military power in eastern Europe and the entry of Soviet forces into Manchuria was not the result of these talks; it was the result of the military operations during the concluding phases of the war. There was nothing the Western democracies could have done to prevent the Russians from entering these areas except to get there first, and this we were not in a position to do. . . .[5]

Similarly, in the China White Paper and elsewhere the Truman Administration and its supporters claimed that the very nature of the Kuomintang had doomed American efforts to save it.

Yet in spite of the significant congruities that framed the outlook of the Cold War establishment, important disagreements and ambiguities persisted within it, especially before 1951 and after 1964. For many years commentators have noted a tension among the cornerstones of containment: the universalist implications of the Truman Doctrine, the more modest proposals of Mr. "X"—made even more so by George Kennan's subsequent disavowals—and the regional and economic foci of the Marshall Plan. Policy divisions persisted within the Truman Administration even after the firing of Henry Wallace, as is made clear by reviewing the recently declassified memoranda and follow-up papers circulated by the Policy Planning Staff, the National Security Council, and the Joint Chiefs of Staff between 1947 and 1950.[6] Significant differences existed over issues like the nature of Soviet capabilities and intentions, the character of international Communism, the consequences of Mao's triumph in China, and the limits, if any, of America's security interests. The establishment envisioned a world of freely-trading states bound together in peace by the rule of law, but it could not, in the immediate aftermath of World War II, decide what policies were needed to realize its aspiration. Indeed, the policy centerpiece of the Cold War consensus—containment—remained an ambiguous and much debated notion until after the outbreak of the Korean War. These disagreements can, perhaps, be expressed most vividly by juxtaposing the views of George Kennan, Paul Nitze, Kennan's successor as the head of the Policy Planning Staff, and Dean Acheson.

While some critics[7] have suggested that Mr. "X" faithfully reflected Kennan's outlook of the late 1940s, the analysis offered by John Lewis Gaddis[8] seems more persuasive, because it seeks to understand the complexity of Kennan's thought by focusing on his most comprehensive statements. According to this account, Kennan believed that the chief danger of the Soviet Union was the psychological malaise which afflicted the states bordering Russia—not the Soviet military threat or the appeal of international Communism. Accordingly, Kennan's strategy of containment was primarily psychological in nature. As a first step toward creating a stable and hospitable international environment, he asserted that the self-confidence of those borderlands, particularly the European ones, had to be restored. It was essential that America lend economic and political support—but not military commitments—to help ensure the survival of these threatened states. After self-confidence had been restored and after the Soviets had suffered a consequent loss of influence in these areas, the West could expect that Moscow would gradually modify its approach to international relations, so that negotiations might eventually become feasible. Made paranoically insecure by its history and its regime's ideology, this neurotic Bear might eventually "mellow" if it was constantly frustrated by a patient and steady American policy. The ultimate goal of Kennan's containment was not a *Pax Americana* but the reemergence of independent power centers in Europe and Japan, the eventual domestication of Soviet power, and the growth to maturity of American diplomacy.

In short, Kennan's strategy was more or less traditional, but it had to deal with a world temporarily dislocated by World War II, and it was to be implemented by what he feared was a most untraditional nation. It was skeptical of permanent and global alliances, military commitments, and ideology, and favored instead the creation of an international order based on diplomacy, limit, and balance. Events like the Berlin blockade, the Czech coup, the successful Soviet testing of the atomic bomb, and Chiang's defeat in China provided additional evidence for those in the Administration like Paul Nitze and James Forrestal who suspected that the Soviet Union was both a revolutionary state bent on world domination and the director of a unified, international Communist movement. The Neurotic Bear, while undeniably disturbed, remained a quasi-traditional power with whom negotiations might in the future be possible, but by 1949 a more extreme Soviet metaphor—the Great Beast of Revolution—grew increasingly persuasive. Diplomacy with such an adversary, except perhaps from a position of overwhelming military superiority, had no chance for success. Furthermore, a series of bureaucratic changes and maneuvers during 1949 and 1950 gradually encouraged the emergence of a more ambitious strategy of containment, one that would be fully articulated in NSC-68. It was this more extensive notion of containment which prevailed and which would do so until the late 1960s. And it was *this* containment, anticipated in tha ringing words of the Truman Doctrine, which received ratification in the form of the Cold War consensus.

These bureaucratic shifts included the "retirement" of Kennan, the transfer of State Department Counsellor Charles E. Bohlen to Paris, and the resignation of Secretary of Defense Louis Johnson.[9] Yet despite the "shocks" of 1948 the Truman Administration was extremely reluctant to respond militarily to Soviet expansionism. Truman

> had set an arbitrary $15 billion ceiling on defense spending, and a blue-ribbon panel declared in 1948 that even the proposed $14.2 billion budget for fiscal 1950 was "unduly high," given "the ability of the economy to sustain" such high costs.[10]

This more cautious conception of containment was not unanimously shared by Truman's advisers, as can be sensed by reading "Measures Required to Achieve U.S. Objectives with Respect to the U.S.S.R.,"[11] a top secret NSC paper completed on March 30, 1949. Among its ten major recommendations were a sharp escalation of the defense budget, significant increases in Western force levels, a global propaganda campaign, and an economic policy which would encourage domestic dissent in the Soviet Union.

This document, which anticipated the major thrust of NSC-68, was attacked by Bohlen and Kennan as "hysterical"[12] and "dangerous."[13] But as the "shocks" of 1948 were replaced by those of 1949, Bohlen, Kennan, and Johnson increasingly found themselves part of a losing coalition. Their defeat was assured by the replacement of Edwin Nourse, a fiscal conservative, with a Keynesian, Leon Keyserling, as Chairman of the Council of Economic Advisers.

Soon after Kennan stepped down as Director of the Policy Planning Staff, the new Secretary of State, Dean Acheson, recommended that the President create a special joint committee to study American objectives and strategic plans in light of the Soviet atomic test. This committee, officially known as the State-Defense Policy Review Group, took advantage of Kennan's presence in Latin America to draft a report during February and March 1950 which eventually became NSC-68. During its deliberations this group called in only one outside witness, James B. Conant, who questioned the report's basic assumptions. Furthermore, Secretary of Defense Johnson was "deliberately kept out of the picture"[14] until the document was virtually complete.

Authored mostly by Paul Nitze, NSC-68 was melodramatically written and in stark contrast to the more measured and calm prose of his immediate predecessor at the PPS. But perhaps the rhetoric was appropriate, for it had to support a set of recommendations which sharply escalated America's responses to the Soviet Union. NSC-68 was declassified in 1975, but its contents had been rather well-known since the 1950s. It agreed with Kennan that the Soviet Union was basically unsatisfiable, but it perceived Russia as indistinguishable from a world-wide Communist revolutionary movement, newly capable of initiating a war against the West and intent on world domination. To counter this global threat to our security and values, Nitze and his associates counselled "a rapid build-up of political, economic, and military strength in the Free World."[15] While no specific budget figures were suggested, "State Department officials were privately tossing around figures like $40 billion"[16] at a time when plans were being made for a fiscal 1951 defense budget of $13.2 billion.

NSC-68 was presented to President Truman on April 7, 1950. Although he seemed impressed with the diagnosis provided by the report, lingering "doubts about the fiscal wisdom of massive boosts in defense spending persisted."[17] These doubts were shared by others in the Administration, including William Schaub of the Budget Bureau, but the outbreak of the Korean War in June gave to NSC-68 the psychological impetus needed to gain its acceptance.[18] Finally, fiscal opponents of NSC-68 were muted by a December 1950 memorandum by Leon Keyserling which argued that the American economy could easily support significantly higher defense spending.[19]

These two versions of containment, Kennan's and Nitze's, and the accompanying images of the Soviet Union—Neurotic Bear and Great Beast—formed the parameters within which the Cold War consensus crystallized.[20] Acheson's position fell between these two. Because he tended to agree with Kennan that the primary threat to world stability was the Red Army and not the appeal of international Communism, Acheson supported Kennan's efforts to find ways to sow discord within the Soviet empire. But the Secretary was more impressed than Kennan with the adverse psychological consequences that would be produced by the fall of relatively unimportant areas to the Communists, and he thus agreed with Nitze that military commitments might be necessary to further bolster the morale of American allies. Foreign policy debates, particularly after 1954, occurred within the parameters set by Kennan and Nitze. While fringes of the wider public (and Congress) might long for a new Henry Wallace or for a policy to "roll back" the Russians from Eastern Europe, establishment debates (such as they were) took place within this much narrower framework.

But the NSC-68 version of containment did not simply replace Kennan's as the prevailing American strategy. While the principles of NSC-68, emphasizing ideology, credibility, dominoes, globalism, and military commitment became official American policy after 1950, Kennan's diagnoses and prescriptions were never completely discredited. In particular, some members of the establishment were periodically supportive of this earlier and now recessive strain of containment. Kennan's version, which stressed concepts like nationalism, regional autonomy, diplomacy, and a non-zero sum view of the world, remained dormant for most of the 1950s but became more influential again when America's intervention in Vietnam split the foreign policy elite in the late '60s.

All three variants of containment, but particularly the most ambitious one, argued implicitly for the necessity of a domestic consensus. Global containment theorists perceived a world full of conflict and danger and called on Americans to respond to these challenges with discipline, patience, vigilance, toughness, and unwavering loyalty, but each version implied that a domestic consensus was both prudent and moral.

However, the strength and resiliency of the Cold War consensus should not be exaggerated, for it depended on a number of rather peculiar conditions. First, the defense outlays anticipated by NSC-68 required a domestic economy healthy enough to support both domestic spending and a large defense budget. The unprecedented prosperity during most of the 1950s and 1960s, plus the Eisenhower Administration's decision to save money through its doctrine of "massive retaliation," meant that "guns and butter" were provided without chronic inflation until the mid-'60s. In retrospect, it is also clear that cheap and abundant energy, America's technological supremacy, and the temporary weakness of other industrial economies gave to this prosperity an illusion of permanence which tended to institutionalize the otherwise tenuous assumptions of NSC-68. Second, although the Truman and Eisenhower administrations concluded a series of bilateral and multilateral defense arrangements (e.g., ANZUS, Japan, SEATO, Baghdad Pact, and CENTO), they remained essentially putative until Vietnam. As long as they remained "paper" promises that did not require expensive U.S. commitments (except NATO), these alliances enjoyed general domestic support. But when SEATO was activated to help justify our Vietnam involvement, they became a good deal less popular. Third, many of the victories achieved by the United States during these years (e.g., in Iran, Guatemala, Lebanon, and the Congo) were obtained "on the cheap" through reliance on covert foreign policy instruments. Until Vietnam, the depth and resiliency of the Cold War consensus had never been seriously tested.

But why did the Korean War not fragment the foreign policy establishment and destroy the domestic consensus? The answer involves several unusually helpful factors. First, Acheson and others suspected that the North Korean attack was a prelude to a Soviet assault on the West. Thus, the heart region of containment, Europe, could be invoked as an important reason to intervene in Korea. Second, the United Nations had authorized and supported Washington's protection of the Rhee Government and hence lent to our actions additional legitimacy. And finally, the generally enthusiastic assistance from Western allies made our actions in Korea appear even less unilateral. Yet despite all of these favorable circumstances, the public attitude toward the war was more one of grudging toleration than enthusiastic support. But while the establishment did back Truman's Korean strategy, the same cannot be said of Congress, where important Republican voices urged "unleashing" Chiang and crossing the Yalu.

This controversy highlighted a more fundamental problem with the bipartisan Cold War consensus. All three versions of containment had always featured a certain ambiguity about the character of American security interests in Asia. It is important to remember that the establishment was comprised of men who considered themselves "Europeanists" in varying degrees.[21] They presumed that for a combination of strategic, historical, cultural, economic, political, and psychological reasons Western Europe could not be allowed to fall under Soviet domination. Kennan was very clear; he considered the Rhine Valley and Great Britain to be two of the world's five strategically crucial areas (the others being Japan, the Soviet Union, and the United States). The rest of the establishment agreed with Kennan's appreciation of the importance of Western Europe. Indeed, this region was deemed so vital to American interests that it was consistently cited by the Truman Administration as a primary reason for the Korean intervention. The problem was that many in Congress, especially conservative Republicans, deeply resented containment's implicit subordination of Asia to Europe. Disgusted by the allegedly immoral and disastrous history of European statecraft, these critics perceived Asia as a potentially rich and friendly area in need of American political and religious values. This struggle faded in importance after 1955, but it did lead to the gradual "de-Europeanization" of the establishment in the late 1950s and early 1960s, and the clear primacy given to European defense and Russian aggression by Kennan (and more ambiguously by Acheson and Nitze) were largely discarded by Rusk and Rostow. Johnson's lieutenants were neither Europeanists nor Asia Firsters but "globalists" who spoke as if the entire world was of equal strategic value to the United States.

By defining America's interests in an interdependent and undiscriminating manner and by redefining China as the chief target of containment, the foreign policy establishment of the 1960s pushed the Cold War consensus beyond its limits. Instead of providing something for everyone (the credibility argument for the Europeanists and the SEATO rationale for the Asianists), this variant of containment (a logical, if not necessary, extension of NSC-68) shattered the domestic consensus. The foreign policy establishment rapidly fractured along a fault line which ran from Walt Rostow to Daniel Ellsberg.

* * * * *

In addition to a confident Presidency, an articulate and unified foreign policy elite, a generally docile and bipartisan Congress, and an ideology which extolled the virtues of discipline, patience, and sacrifice, the Cold War consensus was faithfully supported by the overwhelming majority of contemporary American diplomatic historians. These scholars almost unanimously subscribed to the values and assumptions of containment and authored books which, while not always celebrations of American foreign policy, were rarely very critical of it. One could find in some of them an America that exhibited a

> . . . strange combination of a naive sense of power and virtue with a sense of powerlessness against invisible enemies. The United States was a young Siegfried magically strong, yet at the same time an orphan, surrounded by potential enemies in an unrecognizable world.[22]

In any event, almost everyone accepted Arthur M. Schlesinger, Jr.'s later verdict that containment had been the "brave and essential response of free men to Communist aggression."[23] The importance of this general academic affirmation of American foreign policy in the 1950s should not be underrated, for its later fragmentation removed a crucial symbol of legitimacy from Lyndon Johnson's effort in Vietnam.

The most important service rendered to the Cold War consensus by American diplomatic historians lay in their unrelenting refutation of rightist attacks on Roosevelt, Truman, Marshall, and Acheson. Ever since Yalta conservative revisionists like John T. Flynn, William Henry Chamberlin, George N. Crocker, James Burnham, and several prominent Republican Senators and Congressmen had lamented the "surrender" of Eastern Europe to Stalin.[24] As the rigors of the Cold War seized the United States in the late forties and early fifties, "frustrated and anxious Americans sought scapegoats for the rise of the communist menace,"[25] and these right-wing writers argued that the Cold War had been caused by FDR's "appeasement" of the Soviet Union during World War II. Through a combination of ignorance, naiveté, and perhaps even treachery, Roosevelt, they claimed, had "fought the war and conducted American diplomacy in a manner that insured the postwar expansion of Communism."[26] General Patrick J. Hurley's testimony at the MacArthur hearings in 1951 neatly summarized this outlook:

> America was in a position at Yalta to speak the only language the Communists understand, the language of power. The President . . . at Yalta was in command of the greatest land, navy, and air force ever assembled on earth. One quiet sentence to Marshal Stalin in that language could have indicated that America would require him to keep his solemn agreements. That one sentence would have prevented the conquest of all the Balkan states, the conquest of Poland, and the conquest of China. The sentence was not forthcoming. On the contrary, your diplomats and mine surrendered in secret every principle for which we said we were fighting. They talk about Stalin breaking his agreements, gentlemen. He never had to break one. We cowardly surrendered to him everything that he had signed and we did it in secret. President Roosevelt was already a sick man at Yalta.[27]

These revisionists, playing on isolationism's traditional distrust of foreign aid, singled out lend-lease as a particularly pernicious aspect of Roosevelt's legacy, and, by inflating its significance to the Soviet war effort, contended that this program had helped create "that monstrous military power that would cast a lengthening shadow over Europe and Asia throughout the following decades."[28] In 1949 one former lend-lease administrator suggested that Roosevelt and his "pro-Communist" advisers "had given the Russians the raw materials and technical information necessary to produce an atomic bomb."[29] The revisionists made much of Alger Hiss' presence at Yalta, and in its rather desperate need to "explain" Roosevelt's conduct during the later stages of the war, the John Birch Society even speculated that Soviet agents, at the Teheran Conference in 1943, had abducted the President and put a Russian double in his place until the lookalike's death in 1945! After the defeat of the Kuomintang the Truman Administration, and especially Dean Acheson, came under similar attack for "losing" China, and several State Department experts paid for this setback with their careers. Containment, itself, was portrayed as appeasement by these critics, and the Republicans, after Dewey's refusal to make foreign policy a campaign issue in 1948, fought the 1952 election with the assistance of "rollback," while their Vice Presidential candidate named Acheson "dean of the college of cowardly communist containment."[30]

Most American diplomatic historians rejected such revisionist arguments about lend-lease, Yalta, China, and "treason in high places" as factually groundless. Moreover, these scholars, with very few exceptions, shared a liberal internationalist outlook and feared that public acceptance of revisionist "myths" would encourage a dangerous resurgence of isolationism and xenophobia. In that case, they warned, not only would the United States once again abandon Western Europe, but pressures could easily build for a preventive nuclear strike against the Soviet Union.[31] These historians feared that America's ability to wage the Cold War would be seriously damaged if this right-wing revisionist history gained widespread support. In other words, scholarly doubts about revisionist interpretations dovetailed with liberal anti-Communist sentiments to produce the "orthodox" explanation of the origins and evolution of the Cold War.

What made the explanation "orthodox" was quite simply its historiographical dominance and its close adherence to official Washington's defense of postwar American foreign policy. College diplomatic history textbooks faithfully echoed and frequently simplified that defense, and writers like Thomas A. Bailey, Dexter Perkins, John Spanier, Richard Leopold, Julius Pratt, Foster Rhea Dulles, and Samuel Flagg Bemis[32] disseminated the highlights of the Cold War consensus to several generations of American students.

These texts, in reaching young members of the "attentive public" at an impressionable age and in stamping American foreign policy with a scholarly imprimateur, provided an invaluable service to the cause of liberal internationalism. Furthermore, as befitted books that worried about the contemporary civic and spiritual health of America, they frequently leavened historical narrative with moral exhortation.

A quick glance at three of these textbooks should help to illustrate these points. Foster Rhea Dulles' AMERICA'S RISE TO WORLD POWER complained about the naiveté and impatience with which the American people approached foreign relations. Dulles admitted that "the very fact of American power, as well as certain aspects of American postwar policy, may have accounted in part for what often seemed to be Soviet intransigence," but he agreed with Harriman that "as time went on, . . . what might originally have been a defensive position for the U.S.S.R. inspired by fear seemed to the western world increasingly characterized by imperialist ambition."[33] Like most of his peers Dulles dealt uncritically with the Truman Doctrine and applauded it as "a broad and challenging conception of America's new world role . . . which necessarily involved intervention and entanglement on a heretofore unimagined scale."[34] Reflecting the establishment's ambivalence toward Asia Dulles warned that "the temporizing with colonialism in Indo-China had not strengthened confidence in the West" nor was "a policy of anti-communism . . . enough to assure the friendship and support of the Asiatic world."[35] Firmly within the liberal internationalist consensus Dulles staunchly defended Acheson and Truman against "new isolationists," Asia Firsters, "partisan" Congressional critics, and domestic "red baiters."

Julius Pratt's A HISTORY OF UNITED STATES FOREIGN POLICY similarly chastized Hoover, Taft, MacArthur, and other conservative critics of containment.[36] The paramount question was whether "the United States could successfully fill the role of leader in the struggle with Communist imperialism."[37] While reasonably optimistic that it could, Pratt cautioned that much would depend on the American people's willingness to bear high taxes and to elect moderate leaders who would, on the one hand, refuse to "promise easy and cheap success in an all-out, go-it-alone war against Communism" and, on the other, would spurn a return to the false safety of Western Hemisphere isolationism.[38] Pratt concluded by issuing a set of suggestions to American policy-makers that crisply summarized the values they already held (at least rhetorically). In this familiar list Pratt included consultation with allies, bipartisanship in Congress, an independent Foreign Service, a "combination of skepticism and open-mindedness toward the Soviet Union," and the toleration of domestic diversity.[39]

Finally, there was the most popular of these university American diplomatic histories, Thomas A. Bailey's A DIPLOMATIC HISTORY OF THE AMERICAN PEOPLE, first published in 1940 and currently in its tenth edition. Fully accepting the conventional accounts of Cold War origins Bailey's text was noteworthy for its unsparing criticism of the American public's foreign policy attitudes.[40] Characterizing them as naive, grossly uninformed, adolescent, and short-sighted, he added selfishness to the list in his 1955 edition:

> Not all Americans are bearing their new burdens cheerfully and responsibly. Not all of them are prepared to recognize that their very way of life is jeopardized by the Communist menace. Many are grumbling over defense expenditures, not realizing that to Moscow the most eloquent language is that of force. Many are blindly determined to have business as usual, profits as usual, Cadillacs as usual.[41]

The implication was clear: the American people needed an enlightened elite to educate them and to prevent a resurgence of isolationist sentiment. Fortunately they were blessed with one: the foreign policy establishment. These sorts of admonitions ran in varying degrees through many of these books, and they surely reflected a concern shared by many Americans that the will of the United States was gradually being sapped in its seemingly endless struggle with international communism.

* * * * *

As we suggested earlier the contemporary climate of opinion inevitably exerts influence on historians' treatment of past events. The textbooks of the Cold War were no exception. Here we will briefly consider the manner in which John Spanier's description of the early Cold War evolved over two decades. His text, AMERICAN FOREIGN POLICY SINCE WORLD WAR II,[42] has appeared in nine editions since its publication in 1960, but we will confine our comparison to the second (1962), the sixth (1974), and the eighth (1980).

The first chapter of the 1962 edition, "The Liberal Approach to Foreign Policy," captured the essence of the Cold War establishment's outlook. Beginning with sobering words from Halford J. Mackinder and Nicholas J. Spykman, Spanier warned that

> The Soviet Union and Communist China now occupy most of the Heartland; surrounding them along a 20,000-mile periphery lie the exposed and weaker Rimland nations. . . . It is the Communists' aim to extend their control to these nations. This would leave the United States and the Americas—the Western Hemisphere—a lone island in a totalitarian sea. . . . The ability of the United States to ensure its own security—indeed, its survival—under these circumstances depends upon its capacity to establish a balance of power in Eurasia in order to prevent the Communists from expanding into the Rimland or neutralizing these nations.[43]

By 1974 Spanier had eliminated all references to these geopolitical maxims and started the first chapter, now entitled "The American Approach to Foreign Policy," with a much less apocalyptic analysis. He still advised the United States to recognize the importance of the balance of power, but he now explained its significance in markedly different terms:

> American foreign policy since World War II is the story of the interaction between the state system and the American style of conducting foreign policy. In this state system, each member—especially the Great Powers . . . —tends to feel a high degree of insecurity. . . . Self-protection is the only protection in an essentially anarchical system; understandably, states tend to regard each other as potential adversaries, menaces to each other's territorial integrity and political independence. In short, the very nature of the state system breeds feelings of insecurity, distrust, suspicion, and fear.
>
> It is this atmosphere that produces a constant scramble for power.[44]

This considerably blander description of postwar world politics reflected, at least in part, the emergent Sino-American and Soviet-American détentes of the early 1970s and the simultaneous dampening of ideological passions.

According to Spanier, America's peculiar history and domestic structure raised questions about its ability to defend the "Rimland"

(1962) or to patiently engage in the timeless game of "power politics" (1974 and 1980). That is, such allegedly unique American phenomena as an isolationist past, a consensus about basic values, a tendency to fight total wars and to seek total peace, a distrust of politics, and a periodic urge to reform the world had combined to render more difficult the achievement of a consistent and pragmatic foreign policy. By 1974, however, Spanier had identified an additional symptom of "America's national style:" revisionist diplomatic history.[45] These revisionist histories, whether of World War I, World War II, or the Cold War had allegedly shared a common theme—the presumption that America's engagements in all of these conflicts had been mistakes:

> . . . they were really unnecessary or evil, if not both. The evil enemy of yesterday identified as the aggressor and provocateur thus apparently did not represent a threat to American security at all; to the contrary, the threat turns out to have been from within, not from without. In brief, but for certain *domestic forces,* the United States could have continued to isolate itself from international politics.[46]

The 1980 edition was even more explicit: "Revisionism, then, was essentially an argument for continued isolation from world politics."[47]

In chapter two (called "The Beginning of the Cold War" in all editions) Spanier presented a thoroughly orthodox account of the events of 1945-1947. Interestingly, his discussion of the Truman Doctrine in 1974 was considerably longer and somewhat more qualified than his earlier evaluation. For example, in the 1962 edition Spanier had written:

> All the other major powers of the world had collapsed—except the Soviet Union, which was the second most powerful nation in the world and wedded to an expansionist ideology. The cold fact of a bipolar world suddenly faced the United States. The country could no longer shirk the responsibilities of its tremendous power.[48]

But in the sixth and eighth editions, Spanier was content to be less dramatic: "All the other major powers of the world had collapsed—except the Soviet Union. A bipolar world suddenly faced the United States."[49] Moreover, in 1962 Spanier observed that "If Greece collapsed . . . it would only be a question of time until Turkey and Iran would crumble before Soviet power."[50] But in the later editions, Spanier was more tentative: "If Greece collapsed . . . *it was thought in Washington* that it would only be a question of time before Turkey and Iran would crumble before Soviet power."[51] Similarly, whereas in the second edition Spanier claimed simply that "What was at stake in Greece was America's survival itself,"[52] in 1974 he modified his rhetoric: "*What was felt to be* at stake in Greece was America's security."[53] By 1980 the entire paragraph about the apparently dire consequences of American inaction in the Eastern Mediterranean had been removed and replaced with: "Consequently, the United States felt it had no choice but to act in this situation."[54]

Spanier also altered his evaluation of the Truman Doctrine itself. In 1962 he had offered this inspirational assessment:

> History had once more shown that when a great and democratic people is given decisive and courageous leadership, the people will respond quickly and wisely. Under Truman's leadership, the American public had made a decisive commitment. The United States was now a full participant in the international arena. There could no longer be any retreat. The survival of freedom was dependent solely on the United States. The only question was how responsibly and honorably this country would bear its new burden of world leadership.[55]

In the 1974 edition, however, Spanier eliminated this passage entirely and instead attempted to answer some of the criticisms that had been provoked, in part, by Vietnam. Spanier stressed four points about the initial course of containment. First, he insisted that while the United States after World War II "would have much preferred to concentrate on domestic affairs" as demonstrated by the massive postwar demobilization, "the Soviet threat to the balance of power left the United States with no choice but to adopt a countervailing policy." That is, "the bipolar distribution of power molded the nation's policy course."[56] Second, "anti-Communism was not a major ingredient of American policy during and immediately after World War II."[57] The United States, Spanier protested, had "constantly sought to overcome the Kremlin's suspicions of the West in order to lay the foundation for postwar harmony and peace." When World War II ended American policy-makers were principally concerned "to forestall a complete return to the historic position of isolationism."[58] The United States did not desire to overthrow the Bolsheviks or to push the Soviets out of Eastern Europe, and it was not until 1947—

after two more years of "continued Soviet pressure, denunciations, and vilifications"—that containment was finally launched. Third, Spanier claimed that "the role of anti-Communism in American policy was essentially to mobilize Congressional and public support for the policy once it had been decided upon. A nation that had historically condemned power politics as immoral . . . needed a moral basis for its new use of power."[59] Finally, "despite the universalism of the Truman Doctrine, its application was intended to be specific and limited, not global. American policy-makers were well aware that the United States . . . was not omnipotent."[60]

This firm, but considerably less exuberant defense was further modified in the 1980 edition. In Western Europe, Spanier argued, "America's strategic and power considerations were compatible with its democratic values. The containment of Russia could be equated with the defense of democracy."[61] But in other regions the incompatibility of strategy and values confronted the United States with a classic dilemma: "to protect strategically located undemocratic regimes might fortify containment (in the short run, at least) but stain America's reputation and weaken the justification for United States policy."[62] This dilemma, Spanier noted, was to "make the declared aim that the United States was seeking to protect the democratic way of life appear as hypocritical."[63]

Spanier's account of the early Cold War remained "orthodox." But, as we have seen, Spanier had altered his interpretation in at least four significant ways since 1962. First, whereas he had originally characterized the Soviet Union as a totalitarian state enslaved by an expansionistic ideology and relentlessly determined (with its Chinese Communist ally) to rule the "Rimland" as well as the "Heartland," by 1974 he had implicated all states in a ceaseless "scramble for power" and blamed international insecurity, fear, and distrust on the nature of the system rather than on the domestic character of the Soviet Union. Spanier continued to worry about the fitness of the United States to effectively participate in this "great game," but unlike 1962 when he described the Soviet "threat" as an unprecedented challenge to the balance-of-power, the later editions of his text stressed the allegedly timeless features of Great Power ambitions. Second, in both 1974 and 1980 Spanier introduced certain phrases to depict the Truman Administration's response to Soviet provocations which had the effect of making that reaction appear somewhat more like subjective perception and slightly less like incontrovertible truth. Spanier did not hide his own approval of that perception, even in the more recent editions, but terms like "it was thought in Washington" and "what was felt to be at stake" did modify the rather absolutist tone of the earlier version. Third, the thunderous emergence of a Cold War revisionist literature in the late 1960s (as we will see in chapter three) forced Spanier by 1974 to at least acknowledge its existence. While it is true that he dismissed Cold War revisionism as but another symptom of America's tragic infatuation with isolationism, Spanier felt obliged to make his defense of containment more explicitly analytical and less exhortational. Again, the overall result was to erode the self-confident mood of the 1962 edition. Finally, although Spanier's text continued to leave little doubt about the identity of good and evil in the world, some of the more extreme rhetoric of the earlier edition had been deleted by 1974. Now the account of American foreign policy since World War II was couched in slightly less heroic terms, and the "power politics" dimension of U.S. conduct given somewhat more emphasis.

In short, Spanier haltingly and grudgingly adjusted to a changed climate of public and historiographical opinion. Whereas in 1962 his interpretation of the Cold War was essentially *the* account (at least in the United States) by 1974 and 1980 a variety of explanations contested for dominance. It should also be noted that most of the changes Spanier made in the text occurred between 1962 and 1974—that is, during the Vietnam War. In view of the public's more assertive foreign policy mood of the late 1970s and early 1980s one wonders if Spanier's future editions will return to the greater truculence found in his earlier versions.

* * * * *

Herbert Feis, whose monumental studies of wartime and early postwar diplomacy stood in contrast to the rather heavy-handed chauvinism of many contemporary textbooks, nevertheless offered a comprehensive vindication of Roosevelt's and Truman's foreign policy records. Feis, as his critics in the 1960s delighted in publicly reminding him, was well-suited to present "the State Department's interpretation" of these events.[64] Born in New York City in 1893 Feis received his B.A. in 1916 and his Ph.D. in economics in 1921 from Harvard. After devoting a decade to university teaching at Harvard, Kansas, and Cincinnati he joined the State Department in 1931 as an economic adviser to Henry Stimson. During the 1920s Feis had intermittently advised the International Labor Organization on American industrial relations and at Geneva made the acquaintance of the United States observers to the League of Nations. He played an important role in the 1933 London Economic Conference and was outraged by Roosevelt's last-minute decision to scuttle it. Feis subsequently concentrated on inter-American affairs and attended the conferences in Buenos Aires (1936), Lima (1938), and Panama (1939). Throughout this period he frequently functioned as a conciliator of State, War, and Treasury department views. In 1943, after briefly chairing an interdepartmental committee on Strategic and Critical Raw Materials, Feis went to the War Department to serve as personal adviser to his old boss, Stimson. When Stimson retired Feis remained to work as a special consultant to his successors, Robert Patterson and Kenneth C. Royall. In 1947 Feis retired to the Institute for Advanced Study but returned to Washington for a year (1950-51) as a member of the State Department's Policy Planning Staff.[65] Feis returned to Princeton, and two years later moved to New York where he sublet Averell Harriman's Park Avenue apartment.[66]

Although he never held a senior policy-making position, Feis maintained close relations with several key Roosevelt and Truman advisers. Harriman granted him personal custody of his wartime papers, Acheson enthusiastically encouraged Feis' historiographical efforts, and he carried on a long and voluminous correspondence with his intimate friend, Felix Frankfurter.[67] On occasion Feis did personal favors for Acheson and Harriman. For example, in 1948, during the Alger Hiss affair, Feis tried to obtain medical information about Whitaker Chambers for Acheson,[68] and in October 1954, when Harriman was the Democratic candidate for governor of New York, he asked Feis to review his personal wartime correspondence in order to find favorable references about him from General Eisenhower. Feis obliged and also, as Harriman requested, searched Soviet and Communist Chinese press archives at the Council on Foreign Relations for unfavorable statements about the former ambassador's conduct.[69] In the same year Feis helped John Paton Davies, the "China Hand," prepare his defense to the charges presented by the State Department for his alleged misbehavior in China during World War II.[70] In short, Feis' long tenure in the State Department enabled him to befriend many leading members of the foreign policy establishment.

Upon his retirement from government service in 1947 Feis decided to write a reminiscent account of his experiences as economic adviser to the State Department and asked to review certain relevant (but classified) Department documents in order to "refresh his memory." Such requests were standard on the part of former officials, and Feis was granted permission under the "old boy rule" of the Department.[71]

After AS SEEN FROM E.A.[72] was published Feis further requested access to classified material unrelated to his own government experience in order to write a book on Japanese-American relations in the 1930s. Such petitions, though less numerous than those covered by the "old boy rule," were scarcely unprecedented. Several years earlier Secretary Hull had allowed William L. Langer to read Department files in the preparation of OUR VICHY GAMBLE,[73] a book that Hull believed would exonerate the Roosevelt Administration.[74] Langer, who had been named the State Department's Director of Intelligence in late 1945, and S. Everett Gleason were subsequently granted special privileges to study FDR's diplomacy on the eve of World War II.[75] In short, established scholars with State Department connections were generally afforded favors during these years, so Feis' request was granted. Even so, most of the materials reviewed by Feis for THE ROAD TO PEARL HARBOR[76] were "restricted" rather than "closed." That is, they were in the process of being declassified.[77] But when Feis' good friend, Dean Acheson, became Secretary of State in early 1949 Feis asked permission to study the wholly closed files of wartime Sino-American relations. Acheson granted the favor enthusiastically and instructed Lucius Battle to ask the appropriate officials to cooperate with Feis.[78] The arrangement took the form of a "gentleman's agreement" whereby Feis promised to avoid publication of materials that might damage or embarrass current American foreign policy. The State Department also interceded with indifferent success on Feis' behalf to gain the cooperation of other governmental agencies. Feis' assistant, Arline Van Blarcom Pratt, a former State Department employee familiar with its complicated filing system, did most of the actual research, and in 1953 THE CHINA TANGLE[79] appeared. This arrangement, despite the Democrats' defeat in 1952, continued under Eisenhower, although Dulles was probably not aware of it.[80] Rather, Feis worked directly with the Department's Chief Historian, G. Bernard Noble. Gradually, however, he apparently found it increasingly difficult to review wholly closed files, and by the time of his research for the Potsdam Conference[81] Feis' privileges lay only in his ability to see the galley proofs of the relevant FOREIGN RELATIONS volumes shortly before their publication.[82]

When Kennedy became President Feis evidently hoped that the more extensive favors shown him by Acheson would be resurrected by another old Department friend, Dean Rusk. In December 1960 Feis wrote Rusk a long congratulatory letter on his appointment and reported that the Department of the Army, after a long delay, had granted him access to the pertinent sections of the Manhattan Project files. He also told Rusk that he was about to begin a study of foreign aid and offered to serve the State Department "in that realm of action" in the United States or abroad.[83] But when Feis subsequently asked Rusk for access to the closed files[84] for the 1945 to 1948 period, the Secretary refused, and did so on highly inaccurate grounds: "[R]equests by unofficial researchers for permission to examine political files prior to release of the appropriate FOREIGN RELATIONS volume have regularly been denied."[85] Feis appealed the decision several times, but Rusk remained firm. Thus rebuffed Feis began to champion the cause of "all serious scholars" in their efforts to accelerate the declassification of State Department documents. His last book, FROM TRUST TO TERROR,[86] which dealt with the onset of the Cold War, was forced to rely on materials equally available to all private researchers. It was not without irony that Feis' last official letter to Rusk constituted a heart-felt plea to quickly end the Vietnam War before "more men and more money" were senselessly squandered.[87]

Three additional points deserve mention. First, Feis' friendship with Roosevelt and Truman advisers not only helped him gain access to official documents, but it also enabled him to have exclusive or nearly exclusive use of the personal papers and diaries of several of these men. Sumner Welles, Joseph Grew, Henry Stimson, Eugene Dooman, George Kennan, J. Robert Oppenheimer, and, most crucially, W. Averell Harriman, all provided Feis with material unavailable to most scholars. Second, although William Franklin, who succeeded Noble as the State Department's Chief Historian in 1962, refused to continue his predecessor's policy of affording research privileges to an "intellectual elite,"[88] Feis' earlier special treatment nevertheless proved very valuable to him in his declassification efforts. That is, Franklin, in his "negotiations" with the relevant State Department officers, was able to gain the declassification of some materials for the FOREIGN RELATIONS series by arguing that Feis had already hinted at their substance in his published works. It was in this wholly unintended way that Feis' privileges ultimately assisted other historians to view documents that might otherwise have remained secret. Third, the political dimensions of the entire issue of special access are difficult to state precisely, but they cannot be ignored. Even sympathetic scholars in the 1950s were troubled by the Department's policy of affording privileges to the lucky few. While there is no evidence to suggest that Acheson wanted Feis to whitewash the foreign policy records of the Roosevelt and

Truman administrations, he can hardly have expected Feis to deal harshly with them. The burning (and partisan) historical questions of the day were "Who lost China?" and "Why did FDR sell us out at Yalta?", and Acheson probably felt that a dispassionate telling of these episodes by a trusted scholar with access to the records would constitute effective replies. On the other hand, many Republicans in Congress were eager to implicate Alger Hiss in the Yalta accords and despite their fiscal conservatism regularly appropriated more funds to the Historical Office than it had requested in order to expedite the release of the Yalta record. They were especially anxious that the Yalta volume of the FOREIGN RELATIONS series be published before the 1954 elections, but after the Historical Office complained that more time was needed to ensure a high quality product, Dulles allowed the staff to proceed at its own pace.[89] Thus, while it would be unfair to claim that the Democrats simply used Feis to answer Republican critics of Roosevelt and Truman, the issue of special access to documents and the timing of their general release possessed inescapable political implications. A further irony lay in the fact that although Feis' books primarily responded to conservative revisionist charges about "appeasement," his interpretations were most harshly criticized a decade later by left-wing revisionists who claimed that U.S. behavior toward the Soviet Union had been excessively provocative.[90]

How, then, did Feis treat the American diplomatic record in China, at Yalta, and with the Soviet Union? He did not deny that the American effort in China had evidently failed to prevent the victory of a Soviet puppet. Feis' main burden in THE CHINA TANGLE was to show that the failure had been caused by an enormously complex constellation of reasons and not because of Communist dupes and sympathizers in the White House and State Department. He argued that the United States had "made great exertions in behalf of China" to realize a policy "bent to four connected ends: to uphold the Chinese people in the war against the common enemy; to restore China as a whole and independent country; to secure for China a place of great authority among the nations; and to bring to an end the grave social struggle among the Chinese people."[91] In pursuit of those goals Feis protested that

> Our friendship was firm, rejecting every chance to benefit by compromise with those who wanted to reduce or rule China. The call for help was made upon us while we were engaged in great battles elsewhere for freedom and justice in the Western world.

> These rival necessities caused us to limit the means and measures which we devoted to the struggle in China. In retrospect, we may have done less in and for China while the war for Europe was being fought out than we might safely and wisely have done. We thought we were only deferring the greater aid until that part of the worldwide struggle against tyranny was won. And then the unexpected happened: the war in the Pacific ended abruptly before our effort in behalf of China reached its planned fullness.[92]

In short, although events interceded to diminish postwar assistance to China, reasonable observers could not claim that the United States had betrayed Chiang.

Feis persistently refuted the charges of the "China Lobby" and its conservative revisionist allies. For example, he emphasized the corrupt and fragile nature of the Kuomintang; he chastized Chiang for demanding that the United States treat China like a Great Power while failing to take the steps necessary to realize his ambition; he suggested that if any American official had been "duped" by the Soviets, it had been General Patrick Hurley at his April 1945 talks with Stalin and not George Marshall; he generally defended the reporting of the China Hands, although he admitted that their use of "back channels" understandably aroused Ambassador Hurley's suspicions; and he consistently sided with Stillwell and against Chenault.

THE CHINA TANGLE, however, did not constitute merely a partisan Democratic defense of the American effort in China. Rather, it conveyed the impression of a largely dispassionate account of an incredibly complicated episode. Feis apparently presumed that if the documentary record were revealed in a straightforward manner, most reasonable people would reject revisionist claims of conspiracy, betrayal, and treason. In this sense, THE CHINA TANGLE represented another attempt to produce a convincing China White Paper.

Feis dealt with Yalta in this volume and in CHURCHILL, ROOSEVELT, STALIN: *The War They Waged and the Peace They Sought.* On balance, he offered a qualified, empathetic defense of Roosevelt's conduct. Feis argued that the Far Eastern accords suffered from only two important faults: They "hardened the decision, proclaimed at Cairo, to reduce Japan to a dependent power in the Pacific," and they "did not give conclusive form to one of the main, if not the main, justifying purposes of the [agreements]—to secure

Soviet cooperation with the Chinese government."[93] The first flaw, in effect, created a power vacuum in the Far East to be eagerly filled by the Soviet Union, while the second left Moscow "free to bargain about both the cost and the value of its friendship" with Chiang.[94] But Feis also suggested that "if at the time of the Japanese surrender, the [Chinese] government armies had been in better shape, the Yalta Accord might have worked out as Roosevelt thought it would."[95] Moreover, he placed heavy blame for the unreadiness of the Kuomintang forces on Chiang and his lieutenants. Feis even directly confronted the anti-Roosevelt revisionists:

> The Yalta Agreement has since been condemned in many moods and ways. The President's action in signing this accord has been indicted by many as having hurt China, and the more extreme as having betrayed it. Some, with an excited lack of proportion, have named it as the cause of the downfall of the Chiang Kai'shek regime and the Communist triumph in China.[96]

And in response to a Nationalist official who in 1952 had called Yalta a "disastrous mistake" Feis lamented that "Defeat and pain smother and twist. They write harsh and poor history. But when Roosevelt accepted the role of mediator, of mutual friend between the Soviet Union and the Chinese . . . Government, he accepted the chance that someday such words would be spoken."[97] If Roosevelt had not died just two months later, "perhaps . . . he could have turned the Yalta Accord into the triumph of compromise which he conceived it to be."[98]

In regard to the Declaration on Liberated Europe Feis admitted that it was "hard to judge whether either Soviet or British governments shared the sense of the American formulators that its principles might govern events. Its loose net of phrases allowed easy passage to any determined purpose."[99] But "the effort to enthrone principle at Yalta and subsequently," Feis cautioned, "ought not to be dismissed as futile," for it "may have served to sustain the resistance of democratic elements in Central Europe."[100]

Did FDR cede Eastern Europe to Stalin at Yalta? Feis doubted it: "If the President had been more stubbornly patient and more patiently stubborn it may be that certain agreements would have been more clear and more favorable to the Western aims. But would this really have affected later events . . . ?"[101] Not unless the United States had been willing to militarily contest the Soviets in Poland and the other disputed territories, and the American public, Feis repeatedly observed, clamored for a rapid and almost total demobilization. They were unprepared to garrison Western Europe; they certainly opposed any U.S. invasion of Poland (or Manchuria). In sum, Feis argued that at Yalta Roosevelt carried out the wishes of the American electorate, and it was rather unfair for parts of it to retrospectively condemn him for his conduct there.

In CHURCHILL, ROOSEVELT, STALIN, BETWEEN WAR AND PEACE, and (much later) FROM TRUST TO TERROR, Feis chronicled the disintegration of the Grand Alliance and the onset of the Cold War. From his perspective blame for the rupture and ensuing tension rested squarely with Moscow. He portrayed Stalin as a cold, purposive revolutionary tirelessly devoted to the exploitation of Western goodwill and the expansion of Soviet influence. Despite Roosevelt's patient efforts to build a relationship of trust, Stalin remained shockingly skeptical of virtually every American action. Feis presumed—he did not argue—that America's intentions were benign, unprovocative, and designed to construct a postwar world of peace, freedom, and justice. While at times Feis seemed troubled by Roosevelt's penchant for declarations of principle geared to postpone hard decisions until after the war,[102] he neither questioned these principles' desirability nor doubted their universal applicability. Perhaps the following observation best expresses Feis' attitude toward the Cold War:

> Roosevelt and his colleagues were right: the nations needed moral law and freedom. Churchill was right: the nations needed magnanimity and balance of power. Stalin was sullying a right: the Russian people were entitled to the fullest equality and protection against another assault upon them. But under Stalin they were trying not only to extend their boundaries and their control over neighboring states but also beginning to revert to their revolutionary effort throughout the world. Within the next few years *this was to break the coalition* and, along with the spread of nationalist passion in the hitherto passive parts of the world, create the turbulence in which we are all now living.[103]

In short, the Soviets desired considerably more than simply security from future attack. The United Nations Organization and a new balance of power could provide that. Feis suggested that in their twin rejections of Roosevelt's and Churchill's visions of the postwar world, the Russians mutated a legitimate right of self-defense into a boundless lust for empire and revolution. This wholly unacceptable conduct had triggered the Cold War for Feis.

This rendition constituted the core of the orthodox case about the origins of the Cold War, but a few final points should be mentioned. First, this account of American diplomacy frequently betrayed an air of defensiveness. Despite the apparent strength of the Cold War consensus during these years, the liberal internationalist establishment nevertheless felt vulnerable to charges that it was (and had been) "soft on Communism." And, as we have seen, Acheson and other policy-makers hoped that Feis and other sympathetic historians would expose the alleged meanness and injustice of this brand of revisionism by emphasizing that Roosevelt and Truman had merely implemented the wishes of the American people. But when Feis published his final book in 1970 the climate of opinion had shifted significantly, and a rather different kind of revisionism had emerged. As a result, in FROM TRUST TO TERROR Feis now self-consciously defended America's early Cold War record against those who claimed that FDR and Truman had actually provoked conflict with the Soviet Union by aggressively attempting to construct a liberal-capitalist international order dominated by the United States.[104] Second, although Feis' account of wartime and postwar American foreign policy was generally supportive, he did not write "heroic" history. His bland, rather crabbed, writing style reduced the global drama of the Grand Alliance to almost claustrophobic dimensions wherein Roosevelt, Truman, and their small circle of advisers received nearly exclusive attention. Feis all but ignored the influence of domestic politics on decisions (save for his reminders that the American people had demanded rapid postwar demobilization), and he also hesitated to speculate on the broader motives and outlooks that may have animated the coalition members. He seemed content to "let the record speak for itself" (or at least the American part of it) without supplying much explicit interpretation. Nevertheless, Feis left little doubt about his conclusion: the American treatment of the Soviet Union had been consistently reasonable, generous, goodwilled, and benevolent, whereas the Russians had reciprocated with mistrust, deceit, intransigence, and unrestrained ambition. But his reluctance to explicitly stress the moral dimension of U.S.-Soviet relations disappointed some former American policy-makers who had evidently wanted Feis to present a more vivid drama of good versus evil.[105] Finally, there remains the issue of Feis' special access to State Department records. One cannot escape the conclusion that, on balance, Feis' credibility was undermined by Acheson's decision to open these files to a privileged few. In the short run, Feis' ability to view classified documents lent an aura of authority to his work and certainly cast doubt on those who had hinted at secret conspiracies and treason in high places as the explanation of Roosevelt's behavior. Yet even otherwise sympathetic historians maintained ethical qualms about the State Department's practice of showing special consideration to "responsible" senior scholars, and when in the 1960s a new generation of revisionists hostile to Cold War orthodoxy arose, Feis was hard-pressed to defend his former privileges. Their claim that he had functioned as the State Department's "court historian" cast further doubt on the objectivity of orthodoxy's substantive interpretations, and Feis' very belated attempts to accelerate the declassification process in the interests of "all serious scholars" were greeted with a good deal of skepticism.

* * * * *

Diplomatic historians obviously did not monopolize scholarly explanations of the Cold War. By the early 1950s a new industry—Sovietology—manned primarily by political scientists, strategists, economists, and East European emigrés had become a major source of foreign policy information and advice. Prior to that time the few Soviet experts America possessed tended to be Foreign Service Officers who had been attached to the East European section of the State Department during the interwar period. But the new centrality occupied by the Soviet Union in American diplomacy inevitably spurred the rapid growth of public and private research centers dedicated to the study of Communist affairs. One of the most prominent (and notorious) was the Foreign Policy Research Institute at the University of Pennsylvania. Through its sponsorship of seminars, research projects, the journal ORBIS, and a variety of publications dealing with the Soviet Union and international Communism, this Center quickly became a bastion for those who supported an assertive and spiritually uplifting foreign policy. Perhaps the Institute's best-known book was PROTRACTED CONFLICT,[106] the product of a long-term study involving such luminaries as Henry Kissinger, William Y. Elliott, and William R. Kintner but chiefly authored by Robert Strausz-Hupé. Several works of this nature appeared during the high tide of the Cold War consensus,* including Elliot R. Goodman's THE SOVIET DESIGN FOR A WORLD STATE, Anthony T. Bouscaren's SOVIET FOREIGN

*The historical interpretations of the Cold War offered by these books frequently verged on the "Yalta sell-out" brand of revisionism.

POLICY, and Bertram D. Wolfe's COMMUNIST TOTALITARIANISM,[107] but PROTRACTED CONFLICT certainly attracted the most public attention.

Strausz-Hupé's primary thesis was that Communists, in seeking "total victory" in the world, perceived their relationship to others as one of limitless and endless conflict occurring in many dimensions and phases or as "protracted conflict." Furthermore, Marxist-Leninist doctrine laid down operational principles toaid in making strategic and tactical choices in Communism's global struggle: the use of proxies or third parties; deception and distraction; seizing and maintaining the initiative; and the sowing of discord among its enemy's allies. By pursuing these principles international Communism had won many significant victories and had embroiled the West in a crisis which held all humanity in the balance. Strausz-Hupé and his colleagues conceived of the Soviet Union as the architect of an incredibly subtle, patient, and far-reaching strategy ultimately aimed at world domination. Driven by an insatiable lust for power the Soviets were held responsible for every major crisis since at least 1945: Berlin, Korea, Lebanon, Jordan, Guatemala, Algeria, the Suez, Indonesia, and Iran.

What could the United States do in these bleak circumstances? Like Bailey, Pratt, and other diplomatic historians these students of Communism feared that because of "material plenty and a happy history" the American people were "ill equipped for the task of promoting a modern world order."[108] Yet

> . . . history has cast the United States in the inevitable and unenviable role of leader of the Free World. Against the pseudo-universal and long-range goals of Communism, the United States must proclaim unabashedly its genuine universal goals and unveil a sustained program for attaining them. Our first task—to give spiritual and political content to the many specific actions we must take—requires that we unfurl a banner to which the just aspirations of all peoples can rally. Only the vision of a new world order—a new universal system capping the systemic revolution of our times—will have the power to draw diverse humanity to our cause.[109]

In this mortal conflict with Communism for control of the ongoing world revolution "peaceful coexistence" was not possible, for it would simply be exploited by Moscow as a means for furthering its purposes. Only by achieving total victory over Communism in the newly independent countries could America's goal of an international order under the rule of law be realized.

It subsequently became fashionable to dismiss books like PROTRACTED CONFLICT as the empty-headed ravings of the reactionary Right, but while these analyses may have appeared ludicrous from the perspective of the 1960s, they fell well within the boundaries of the Cold War consensus and represented widely shared American views about the nature of the Soviet Union and the responsibilities of the United States. This outlook, as we will see, would evidently become much more reasonable again by the late 1970s and early 1980s when a new right-wing revisionism reemerged.

* * * * *

Samuel Flagg Bemis offered an interpretation of the Cold War which, while sharing much with 1950s orthodoxy, nevertheless departed from it. Bemis had been regarded as a distinguished student of American diplomatic history since the publication of JAY'S TREATY in 1923.[110] After World II his efforts focused more on recent American foreign policy, and he produced several essays dealing with the geopolitics of American security. Typical was his Presidential address to the 1961 meeting of the American Historical Association. Bemis began it with an unflattering portrait of Roosevelt:

> Our great miscalculation, if one may so presume to say, . . . came . . . from Roosevelt's . . . misjudgment of the nature and forces of Soviet policy, from his naive assumption that he could cooperate with Russian revolutionary power once the Soviet Union no longer had need for such cooperation, once it stood victoriously on the World Island of Eurasia. The hunchful and hopeful President relied on the policy of Teheran and Cairo, already antiquated by the rush of events in Europe and Asia. After Yalta, traditional policy toward China collapsed on the continent of Asia. Where is the Open Door now?[111]

Moving to the Truman and Eisenhower administrations he questioned the sufficiency of containment and the regional security pacts it had spawned:

> . . . would not history since ancient times lead its votaries to question whether money, however massively, helpfully, and generously bestowed, can be substituted for foresight, for work, pride, sacrifice, courage, or valor, either in the giver or the taker? And does not a policy of containment by its very nature yield the

> initiative to the revolutionary aggressor? Really it has not contained all around the World Island of Eurasia.[112]

Bemis concluded with stern words:

> A great and virile people, Theodore Roosevelt's characterization of the American people, can also waste away when it turns to massive self-indulgence. . . . During the letdown of the last fifteen years we have been experiencing the world crisis from soft seats of comfort, debauched by mass media of sight and sound, pandering for selfish profit to the lowest level of easy appetites, fed full of toys and geegaws, our military preparedness held back by insidious strikes for less work and more pay, our manpower softened in will and body in a climate of amusement.[113]

These precepts had formed the core of conservative Republican opposition to the emerging Cold War consensus in the late forties and early fifties. In his treatment of Roosevelt's Russian diplomacy, China, containment, foreign aid, and the character of American society, Bemis clearly echoed the attitudes of Taft and MacArthur.

Dean Rusk heard Bemis' speech and responded to it the following day at the AHA convention.[114] Applauding his remarks as a "lucid review of the course we have traveled" and noting "the sharpness and relevance of the questions" he had posed,[115] the Secretary refused to challenge either Bemis' account of the origins of the Cold War or his claim that China had been "betrayed." In addition, Rusk agreed that the United States had been on the defensive in its struggle with international Communism, particularly with regard to wars of "national liberation," and he tried to reassure Bemis that the Kennedy Administration was determined to take the initiative in the Third World with the help of a variety of new techniques.

The Kennedy Administration's return to a strategic doctrine ("flexible response") that had been sanctioned by NSC-68 but abandoned by Eisenhower, its fascination with "brush fire" wars and "nation building," and its implicit renunciation of the heretofore crucial distinction between Europe and Asia (now simply termed "Eurasia") largely fulfilled the universalist and unilateralist connotations of the Truman Doctrine. Walt Rostow had anticipated much of this in his then widely respected THE UNITED STATES IN THE WORLD ARENA.[116] Rostow's explanation of the origins of the Cold War largely reflected the dominant historiographical orthodoxy, yet there was a hint of condescension in his defense of Roosevelt:

> Since wartime American policy in Europe toward the postwar world was made neither by knaves nor fools but by men of both political parties representing the best the nation could then mobilize, it is important to reconstruct with sympathy the elements and forces that entered into it and to establish why the perspective now afforded by hindsight was not then self-evident.[117]

More startling were his assertions that between 1947 and 1950 the Administration had taken insufficient advantage of the wider implications of the Truman Doctrine, and that NSC-68 had been "a sluggish reaction to new threats."[118] Instead of immediately applying to Asia the "lessons of limited war" learned in Greece, Truman and his advisers had allegedly neglected

> to appraise the extent to which the nation's main strength—strategic air power—left open an area of vulnerability not merely to limited wars conducted at one remove by Moscow's agents but also to situations where the imperatives of Western morality and the alliance system to which the United States was deeply committed would make extremely difficult the employment of the nation's main strength.[119]

When the "challenge in Eastern Eurasia" came in June 1950, the United States found itself unprepared.

Rostow further criticized the Truman Administration for not pursuing a more flexible diplomacy after the Korean War became stalemated. Although "Communist strategy and tactics began to change about June 1951 to concentrate on alternative and less overtly military means for advancing the power of Moscow and Peking," Truman "took as his central task in the following two and a half years the problem of building a structure of alliances calculated to prevent another Korean War."[120]

Faced with the "crisis of 1956-1958" the Eisenhower Administration responded even less effectively than had its predecessor. Obsessed with the fear of budget deficits, Eisenhower was

> unresponsive to the bipartisan internationalist coalition which, in a sense, he was chosen to lead and which certainly elected him. He was sluggish in response to new problems defined within the Executive Branch, and he virtually rejected the President's role of personal leadership and innovation in the political process until inescapable circumstances and strong pressures within his staff persuaded him to act.[121]

By these actions Eisenhower had ungratefully abandoned the foreign policy establishment which, Rostow claimed, had helped to elect him and then offered to give him advice. Cowed by tight-fisted fiscal conservatives and unable to tap the dynamic potential of the Presidency, Eisenhower had betrayed the elite by steadfastly defending a strategic doctrine ("massive retaliation") that ought to have been repudiated in 1950. It was a great tribute to the power of the Cold War establishment that Rostow sought to discredit Eisenhower by banishing him from it.

Although few recognized it at the time, Rostow had pushed the foreign policy consensus to its breaking point. Leaving Kennan far behind, and Acheson only a bit less so, he had not only accepted the premises of NSC-68 but had driven its implications further than most of its framers had intended.

* * * * *

Rostow had fashioned an interpretation of American Cold War policy that was revisionist in its attacks on Roosevelt, Truman, and Eisenhower. Roosevelt had been naive, Truman had responded hesitantly and with confusion to Communist aggression, and Eisenhower had suffered from timidity and budgetary myopia. Whereas the orthodox historians had lavished praise on these presidents, Rostow accused them of bungling Soviet-American relations. Rostow's purposes were no doubt partly partisan, for he was an enthusiastic supporter of John Kennedy's candidacy, but his revisionism also captured the spirit of many members of the foreign policy establishment, who by the late 1950s had become bored and frustrated with the sluggishness and empty rhetoric of the Eisenhower Administration. The Communist world seemed dynamic, bursting with energy, and eager to expand into Africa, Latin America, and Southeast Asia. In view of these contemporary circumstances it was easy to believe that the Roosevelt and Truman administrations had also missed opportunities to act with vigor in these areas. In short, Rostow's analysis helped to lend historical credence to the assertive programs of the New Frontier. The United States, despite its vast strength and virtually unlimited resources, had been unable to arrest Communist advances. In place of the failed promises of the Republicans, Kennedy would "get the country moving again" by rolling back the Soviets from their beachheads in the Third World. Rostow was convinced that the Soviet Union had retained its ideological commitment and had imparted a dangerous zealotry to the Red Chinese as well.

Not everyone in the Kennedy Administration rushed to embrace these strictures, and many considered Rostow to be a rather intemperate visionary. Nevertheless, his books were widely read, they were clearly attuned to the outlook of many Kennedy intimates, and they captured the dynamic (and arrogant) spirit of the New Frontier.

CHAPTER 2: THE REALIST REVISIONISTS

The orthodox account of the origins of the Cold War rested on three chief contentions: (1) that Soviet ambition and intransigence had by 1945 triggered the Cold War; (2) that the American reaction, though perhaps belated, was "the essential response of free men to communist aggression;" and (3) that the United States committed no major avoidable foreign policy mistakes in meeting the Soviet challenge. Yet these historians worried that the American people, unused to the burdens of world leadership, would tire of their international responsibilities and escape again into the illusion of isolationism.

This interpretation simultaneously reflected and contributed to the contemporary "climate of opinion," and it accurately expressed the outlook of the foreign policy establishment. American diplomatic historians may have resented Feis' privileged access to archival records, but very few challenged his explanations of World War II diplomacy, the atomic bomb decision, or the origins of the Cold War. As we have seen, in those rare instances when academic dissent occurred, it usually focused on FDR's Yalta "folly," the Chinese "fiasco," and the allegedly amoral, incomplete, and static nature of containment. Overall, however, most scholars doubtless agreed with the author of a much used diplomatic history text who complained that "we are too little astonished at the unprecedented virtuousness of U.S. foreign policy, and at its good sense."[1]

Yet from the time of the Truman Doctrine's enunciation there had been a handful of critics who had maintained serious reservations about America's conduct of the Cold War and the orthodox interpretations that defended it. These "realist revisionists" were more interested in the Cold War's evolution after 1947 than in its origins, but they were nevertheless troubled by Feis' account of the Big Three's disintegration. William Hardy McNeill's AMERICA,

BRITAIN, AND RUSSIA[2] represented the most detailed realist revisionist explanation of the origins of the Cold War until the 1960s. Although written at the height of Soviet-American tensions, its tone of Thucydidean detachment distinguished it from the heroic story told by so many contemporary historians. Rejecting the orthodox tendency to see the Cold War as a nearly unique confrontation between good and evil, McNeill argued that it had been the more or less inevitable result of the fragmentation of the powerful, yet fragile, Grand Alliance that had lost its *raison d'être* by 1946. Careful to avoid placing "blame" on either Russia or America for initiating the Cold War, McNeill found "a potential contradiction between Stalin's purposes in Eastern Europe and his hope of remaining on good terms with America and Britain." They "might have well agreed to Stalin's program if he had been able to persuade Poles, Rumanians, and others to accept the role he had assigned to them . . . without resort to high-handed intervention and brutal disregard of the niceties of democratic government,"[3] but in the end,

> As between the friendship of the Western Powers and a secure politico-military position on his western frontier, Stalin chose the latter. He probably never made the choice in any deliberate and cold-blooded manner. Rather, insisting upon the security of his frontiers, he little by little sacrificed the sympathy of Britain and America.[4]

This portrait of Stalin as an improvisational, incremental, opportunistic figure caught in a tragic contradiction bore little resemblance to the purposive world revolutionary described by many writers in the early 1950s.

Equally iconoclastic was McNeill's recognition of the potentially explosive consequences of Roosevelt's vision of the postwar world. Although

> Wilson and after him Roosevelt became prophets and teachers, able to conjure up in the minds of millions a hope and a confidence that they sorely needed . . . , but self-righteousness and moral indignation may not be perfectly reliable guides to national policy in a multi-national power system. They are, indeed, *fundamentally subversive* of any such system.[5]

This notion of Wilson and Roosevelt as moral revolutionaries ill-equipped for the conduct of a steady foreign policy devoted to the national interest was clearly at odds with the mainstream of the post-NSC-68 Cold War consensus, but it lay at the heart of the realist revisionist critique of global containment. Not surprisingly, McNeill's book, despite its originality, remained in "decent obscurity . . . on a few library shelves"[6] until rediscovered by opponents of the Vietnam War in the 1960s:

> . . . in 1953 the Cold War had been well and truly joined in Asia as well as in Europe, and Americans, at least, were less interested in how it began than in how to carry it toward some kind of (dimly conceived) victory while still escaping nuclear disaster.[7]

Significantly, McNeill, who was not a professional diplomatic historian, researched and wrote AMERICA, BRITAIN, AND RUSSIA while a fellow at the Royal Institute of International Affairs, somewhat shielded from the fervently anti-Communist atmosphere of Eisenhower's America.

* * * * *

Led by George F. Kennan (after 1947), Hans Morgenthau, and Walter Lippmann, the realist revisionists were less impressed with Soviet revolutionary claims than with the reality of the Red Army in Eastern and Central Europe. They accepted the orthodox assertion that the United States had no choice but to oppose Soviet expansion there, but they believed that Truman and Acheson had mistaken traditional Russian imperialism for totalitarian Communist aggression. Furthermore, they criticized the apparent ease with which the Truman and Eisenhower administrations fashioned iron laws from highly questionable historical analogies. Not only had the "lessons of Munich" been extravagantly invoked to justify the sweeping terms of the Truman Doctrine, but the alleged lessons of Azerbaijan and Greece subsequently became the model for the general American approach to the Soviet Union. For example, they objected to Truman's characterization of South Korea as "the Greece of the Far East" and to Eisenhower's claim in 1957 that the "lessons" of Greece required American aid to South Vietnam. The realist revisionists cringed at this official proclivity to apply specific European or Middle Eastern "lessons" to vastly different situations.

While they remained fearful that a return to isolationism constituted an ever-present possibility, they disputed the orthodox contention that American foreign policy since 1945 had broken decisively with the narrow xenophobia of the past. Instead, they warned that the logic of the Truman Doctrine was but the other side of the isolationist coin.[8] That is, the United States, still largely in the grip of Wilsonian illusions and pretensions, had correctly responded to the Soviet Union by shoring up the economies of its Western European allies through the Marshall Plan, but characteristically and unfortunately the Truman Administration had felt compelled to cloak these regionally specific and pragmatically self-interested actions in the lofty speech of abstract and universal moral obligation. This initial error had then been compounded by Acheson's and Dulles' determination to create "situations of strength" before negotiating with Moscow. And far from limiting this principle to Europe—the real stake in the Cold War—both administrations came to gird the globe with a plethora of regional military pacts which condemned the United States to a future of unlimited containment.

The realist revisionists sought to provide American foreign policy with real and distinctive alternatives. Indeed, the assumptions, values, and concepts of these critics have exerted a substantial, if fitful, influence over postwar American diplomacy. More specifically, the pre-NSC-68 version of containment, the so-called "limitationist" critique of the Vietnam War, certain aspects of both the Nixon and Carter foreign policies, and proposals offered in the early 1980s for a "selective" containment and a "solvent" foreign policy by Robert W. Tucker and James Chace[9] all owe intellectual debts of one magnitude or another to these older critics of global containment. At the same time, despite the enormous academic attention paid to Cold War revisionism (as we will see in the next chapter), its impact on actual American foreign policy has been rather negligible.

Lippmann, Kennan, and Morgenthau did not possess identical views of American diplomacy: they had sharp disagreements on issues ranging from the rearmament of western Germany in the 1940s and the utility of military power in the 1950s to the nature of an acceptable settlement in Vietnam in the 1960s. Nor were the positions taken by these men over the course of thirty-five years always consistent or unambiguous. Nevertheless, a review of their writings from the late forties and early fifties reveals that they shared a broadly similar outlook characterized by a restrictive conception of foreign policy goals. At its core lay the rule of priorities, choice, and discrimination in the employment of American power.[10] Lippmann's idea of "solvency," which he originally elaborated in U.S. FOREIGN POLICY: *Shield of the Republic* in 1943, best expressed its essence.

There he argued that America had been without a real foreign policy since the Monroe Doctrine completed the consistently wise diplomatic initiatives of the Founders. From 1823 until 1898 Britain's command of the seas and its success in maintaining a European balance-of-power gradually led Americans to believe incorrectly that their safety depended on their alleged moral superiority. This chauvinistic delusion did not, however, become fatal until the acquisition of the Philippines and the relative decline of British power in the 1890s dangerously extended an exposed America's overseas commitments. The United States, however, failed to formulate a foreign policy that was responsive to these changed conditions. The reason, Lippmann suggested, was that during the long period of British protection Americans had forgotten

> the compelling and, once seen, the self-evident common principle of all genuine foreign policy—the principle that alone can force decisions, can settle controversy, and can induce agreement. This is the principle that in foreign relations, as in all other relations, a policy has been formed only when commitments and power have been brought into balance.[11]

Thus

> Without the controlling principle that the nation must maintain its objectives and its power in equilibrium, its purposes within its means and its means equal to its purposes, its commitments related to its resources and its resources adequate to its commitments, it is impossible to think at all of foreign affairs.[12]

But, given the preponderance of American power at the end of World War II, wouldn't these maxims, if rigorously applied, have directly justified the doctrine of global containment or, perhaps, a preventive strike against the Soviet Union? No, because Lippmann was acutely aware of the finiteness of the American resource base. For example, he argued that

> To encourage the nations of Central and Eastern Europe to organize themselves as a barrier against Russia would be to make a commitment that the United States could not carry out, [for] . . . the region lies beyond the reach of American power, and therefore the implied commitment would be unbalanced and insolvent.[13]

On the other hand, he emphatically rejected any drastic diminution in the obligations already accumulated in the western hemisphere, western Europe, and the western Pacific, for the abandonment of these areas would eventually endanger America's physical security. In place of the Truman Doctrine Lippmann recommended a concentration of American resources on the members of the Atlantic Community and the mutual withdrawal of Soviet and Anglo-American troops from Europe. Furthermore, he feared that any attempt to transform western Germany into part of an anti-Soviet coalition would constitute a provocative intensification of the Cold War.

Yet Lippmann's hopes for a newly solvent American foreign policy in the postwar world were only partly realized. In ISOLATION AND ALLIANCES (1952) he condemned Cordell Hull and other officials enslaved by Wilsonian ideology for their identification of "the international order with the existence of a universal society composed . . . of theoretically equal and entirely separate national states."[14] This "isolationism of the internationalists" had led to the temporary repudiation of the Atlantic Community in the futile and desperate search for Asian allies. Lippmann was hopeful that projects like the Marshall Plan signified that the United States had begun to recognize the naturalness, appropriateness, and wisdom of giving priority to the Atlantic Community, but he remained concerned lest America fail to articulate a compelling foreign policy alternative to Wilsonianism or isolationism.

Hans Morgenthau's POLITICS AMONG NATIONS[15] had reintroduced the concept of power to the American vocabulary. In particular his assertion that the struggle for power is universal in time and space"[16] had produced widespread criticism. According to Kenneth W. Thompson,

> Power politics at the time was a questionable and controversial phrase at the University of Chicago [where Morgenthau then taught]. It epitomized the evil that world government and public administration were to eradicate so that people could live in a civilized world. American political theorists condemned Morgenthau's "Germanic way of looking at things." Practical politicians . . . were quick to dissociate themselves, publicly at least, from his definition of politics.[17]

But if Morgenthau was critical of the rationalism and moralistic excesses of Cordell Hull and other American Wilsonians, he was equally skeptical of those who seemed unaware of the limitations and proper use of power. While America's purposes necessarily involved more than simply continental defense, he ridiculed the "crusading notion that any nation, however virtuous and powerful, can have the mission to make the world over in its own image," and warned that because "no nation's power is without limits, . . . its policies must respect the power and interests of others."[18] Like Lippmann, he located the Cold War in Europe and supported aid to Greece and Turkey on the ground that Britain could no longer fulfill its traditional role of maintaining a European balance-of-power. Morgenthau discovered in the Truman Doctrine that special blend of sentimentalism, moralism, and utopianism which had so frequently characterized American foreign policy:

> In so far as the Truman Doctrine defines the objectives and method of American policy with respect to the concrete conditions prevailing in Greece and Turkey, it is sound doctrine upon which, as the results have shown, a successful foreign policy can be built. In so far as the Truman Doctrine defines its objectives and methods in terms of a world-embracing moral principle, it vitiates its consideration of the national interest and compels a foreign policy derived from it as the results have shown, to be half-hearted and contradictory in operation and threatened with failure at every turn. As a guide to political action, it is the victim, as all moral principles must be, of two congenital weaknesses: the inability to distinguish between what is desirable and what is possible, and the inability to distinguish between what is desirable and what is essential.[19]

The Doctrine's thrust, Morgenthau suggested, was a "message of salvation to all the world, unlimited in purpose, unlimited in commitments, and limited in its scope only by the needs of those who would benefit."[20]

What was needed, he concluded, was a clearer and more prudent understanding of the American national interest. Indiscriminate anticommunism could not provide a solid basis for such a redefinition, because it would inevitably involve over-commitment, a moralistic approach to the world, and the threat to democracy at home. Writing at the height of the Korean War Morgenthau noted with sadness how Dean Acheson had been unable to maintain his originally sober and flexible attitude toward the Soviet Union in the face of the Truman Doctrine's uniquely American logic.[21] In his speech before the National Press Club in January, 1950 Secretary Acheson observed that "I hear almost every day someone say . . . that the real interest of the United States is to stop the spread of Communism. Nothing seems to me to put the cart before the horse more completely than that. . . ."[22] The primary task, rather, was to employ a variety of military, economic, technical, and political instruments to oppose Russian imperialism. Such a strategy might mean that certain countries could not be defended. According to Morgenthau,

> such subtlety and discrimination is a far cry indeed from the sweeping generalizations of the Truman Doctrine. Yet nothing could illuminate more strikingly the depth of our sentimental illusions than the fact that the Secretary of State who [in this speech] . . . understands the realistic requirements of American foreign policy, has been responsible for policies, at least in Asia, that have been marred and frustrated by those very sentimental considerations he refutes so convincingly . . . .[23]

In short, the United States, despite the best efforts of some of its leaders, had misperceived the character of its adversary and formulated a foreign policy deeply flawed by intellectual error. Fox had been wrong to suggest that the French Revolution was the exclusive concern of the French nation. But Burke had erred in urging Britain to fight the Revolution in the name of moral principle. It was Pitt's advice, Morgenthau asserted, that America should heed in its contest with the Soviet Union: "The hon. gentleman defies me to state, in one sentence, what is the object of the war. In one word, I tell him that it is security. . . ."[24]

George F. Kennan had been a critic of global containment from its very inception, although his "X" article appeared to be an enthusiastic endorsement of the Truman Doctrine. In fact,

> He objected strongly both to the tone of the message and the specific action proposed. He was in favor of economic aid to Greece, but he had hoped that military aid could be kept small, and he was opposed to aid of any kind to Turkey. It was . . . to the tone and ideological content of the message, the portraying of two opposing ways of life, and the open-end commitment to aid free peoples that he objected to most.[25]

Kennan, whose "long telegram" of 1946 had led directly to his appointment as the first director of the State Department's Policy Planning Staff, gradually lost influence, until in early 1950 Acheson sent him on an extended tour of Latin America "to get his sometimes adversary out of his hair."[26] The memorandum which issued from this journey could hardly have satisfied those who saw in Latin America the next battleground of Communism and democracy. He discovered everywhere "an exaggerated self-centeredness and egotism and a pathetic urge to create the illusion of cleverness and virility and the fiction of extraordinary human achievement."[27] Furthermore, "Latin America lives, by and large, by a species of make-believe: not the systematized, purposeful make-believe of Russian communism, but a highly personalized, anarchical make-believe, in which each individual spins, like a cocoon, his own little world of pretense."[28] This memorandum, heavy with melancholy and pessimism, was quietly buried in the archives, and copies made of it were destroyed.

His usefulness in Washington apparently ended, Kennan moved to Princeton to concentrate on historical scholarship. Unlike orthodox diplomatic historians who emphasized the virtuousness and idealism of American foreign policy, Kennan's interpretation focused on the disastrous consequences of its legalistic-moralistic tradition. American diplomacy, he argued, had been poorly served by a pervasive legalism which sought to translate the domestic rule of law into a universal one.[29] Largely satisfied with the international status quo, America's lawyer-diplomats could not conceive that aggrieved states might wish to use force to create a more congenial world order. Instead of seeking accommodation through realistic diplomatic bargaining Americans had traditionally looked for formal legal criteria to preserve peace. To make matters worse American foreign policy had also been characterized by a wide and often overbearing streak of moralism. Rather than employing the diplomatic arts to persuade or discourage potential adversaries, Americans were much more fond of the stern lecture and the indignant sermon. The Hay Open Door Notes, the Kellogg-Briand Pact, and the doctrine of unconditional surrender were all expressions of this uniquely American penchant.

Kennan, like Lippmann, looked to the Founders for guidance. Washington, Madison, and the Adamses correctly realized that there were but two basic purposes of American foreign policy: the defense of its territory from military and political intrusion and the protection of private American citizens abroad.[30] Yet these modest and limited goals were later abandoned by American leaders determined to bestow the American dream on the rest of the world. The unfortunate result was a pervasive conviction that the United States possessed a moral obligation to remake the world in its own image. Kennan counseled a return to the older conception of the national interest which relied on the power of quiet example at home to contribute to international peace.

During the high Cold War Kennan made several specific policy recommendations which, largely because of his former influence, received widespread publicity. He gradually accepted most of Lippmann's original objections to containment, Mr. "X" version, and in 1957 called for the mutual withdrawal of all foreign forces from Europe. But whereas Lippmann's critique of "globalism" depended primarily on the circumstantial fact that America lacked the resources to successfully conduct such a policy, Kennan had principled doubts as well. To a much greater degree than either Lippmann or Morgenthau, he questioned the efficacy of military force in the contemporary world. Haunted from his youth by the indecisive carnage of World War I and by what he believed was a tragic determination of the West to destroy its civilization, Kennan remained deeply disturbed by the apparent inability of modern societies to employ military power with any degree of judiciousness. For this imprudence Kennan blamed the pernicious power of public opinion (as Lippmann had done), which clamored for total victory and total virtue, and the military-industrial complex, which inevitably led to swollen defense budgets and runaway arms races. But unlike the Cold War revisionists, who, paradoxically, had reached very similar conclusions by following quite different paths, Kennan had no solution to a problem which he viewed as endemic to technologically advanced democracies. He did suggest, however, that the United States could not reasonably expect to serve as a relevant international model until it seriously looked at itself:

> To the extent that we are able to divise and implement programs of national action that look toward the creation of a genuinely healthy relationship both of man to nature and of man to himself, we will then for the first time have something to say to people elsewhere of an entirely different order than the things we have had to say to them hitherto. To the extent that we are able to develop a social purpose in our society, our life and our experiences will become interesting and meaningful to peoples in other parts of the world.[31]

Three final points deserve mention. First, the historical revisions undertaken by these men served as the base on which they constructed their analyses of postwar American foreign policy. Unlike their orthodox colleagues they were at least as concerned with the persisting dangers of "Wilsonian internationalism" in American diplomacy as they were fearful of a new wave of isolationism. Because they believed that the Cold War had originated and *remained* in

Europe, and because they claimed that the American response to Soviet provocations had been inappropriate to the extent that it had been unsteady, couched in the rhetoric of universal anti-Communism, and too eager to involve international organizations in a moralistic campaign against "aggression," Lippmann, Kennan, and Morgenthau were revisionists by the standards of the 1950s. While conventional historians confined their criticisms of American conduct to the alleged complacency of the citizenry in the face of the Communist "threat," these commentators focused on the inability of political leaders to provide that citizenry with a carefully articulated foreign policy which would avoid the verbal excesses so characteristic of American diplomacy since the nineteenth century.

Second, it is difficult to assess the impact of these critics on American foreign policy during the high Cold War. That they remained members in good standing of the foreign policy establishment cannot be gainsaid. Some observers have even contended that their precepts were quietly heeded by Truman and Eisenhower:

> Declarations of policy intentions to the contrary notwithstanding, American foreign policy quite consistently avoided extravagant or overambitious undertakings, manifesting a sense of balance and proportion [yet] undiscriminating verbal anti-Communism overshadowed actual restraint in the public mind, creating in turn pressure for a more "dynamic" foreign policy.[32]

According to this view the presumed need to mobilize and sustain public and Congressional support for what was in reality a rather modest foreign policy forced both Administrations to speak the universalist language of the Truman Doctrine and NSC-68. But many contemporary observers, including Lippmann, feared that this strategy would backfire:

> this [disingenuous] method of dealing with our people has . . . established no political and moral foundation for a settled and steadfast policy. The great Utopian promises have too often turned out to be dust and ashes, and they no longer arouse the fervor and the ardent hopes of 1918 and of 1945.[33]

Several "Utopian promises" in the form of (non-European) bilateral and multilateral security treaties were subsequently concluded by Truman and Eisenhower. Whether or not American policy-makers really believed in their "Utopian" rhetoric ultimately proved irrelevant, for it clearly possessed serious policy consequences. By the mid-1960s diplomatic deeds had expanded to fit the size of the Presidential words. Hans Morgenthau ruefully noted that "What in the past we said we were doing or would do but never did, we are now in the process of putting into practice: to stop the expansion of communism on a global scale by force of arms."[34]

This conclusion leads to a final point. The axioms of Morgenthau, Kennan, and Lippmann may or may not have served as the real basis for American policy during these years, but it is clear they were never completely forgotten by students of American foreign policy. If they remained dormant (at least rhetorically) in the confident years between Korea and Vietnam when a variety of Asian "promissory notes" were issued, they were quickly remembered by many members of the establishment when the Vietnamese note came due. By 1965 all three realist revisionists had come to oppose American intervention there on grounds very reminiscent of their earlier criticisms of the Truman Doctrine.

* * * * *

In chapter one we suggested that the anti-Communist consensus was in no small measure strengthened by the spate of highly visible Cold War history college texts written by orthodox diplomatic historians like Bailey, Pratt, Dulles, and Richard Leopold. From the late forties until the late sixties these books enjoyed a virtual monopoly in American college and university classrooms, and several generations of students were exposed to the study of American foreign relations primarily with their assistance.

The realist revisionists, with two major exceptions, declined to challenge this aspect of orthodoxy's supremacy. Morgenthau's POLITICS AMONG NATIONS, of course, achieved incredible popularity, but neither he nor Kennan nor Lippmann ever wrote a textbook devoted exclusively to a diplomatic history of the United States or the Cold War. In 1962, however, Norman A. Graebner published COLD WAR DIPLOMACY: *American Foreign Policy, 1945-1960* and fifteen years later offered a second edition.[35] Let us look briefly at the Foreword to the 1977 update in order to observe his faithful articulation of limitationist axioms. According to Graebner, instead of accepting the infinite variations of national interest in world politics, the United States after World War II "attempted to reduce the globe to more easily manageable proportions by remaking it in the American image with ample projections of power and influence."[36]

The early postwar programs of international stabilization and economic expansion in Europe constituted limited objectives and did not exceed the capabilities of the United States. "The existence of internal tyranny, defended with ideological rationalizations, was neither proof of external Soviet expansionism nor necessarily a workable guide to Western policy," yet "for such devotees of toughness as Dean Acheson and John Foster Dulles, analytical subtleties were synonymous with softness."[37] Graebner sorrowfully noted that "anticommunism proved from the beginning to be a deceptive standard for United States relations with the USSR, for *it weakened the traditional restraints of American conservatism* and propelled the nation into objectives it could not achieve."[38] He concluded that Lippmann had been correct in his observation that " 'we flowed beyond our natural limits and the cold war is the result of our meeting the Russians with no buffers between us. The miscalculation . . . falsified all our other calculations—what our power was, what we could afford to do, what influence we had to exert in the world.' "[39] In time, he concluded, this program of indiscriminate anti-Communism bequeathed Vietnam to America.

CHAPTER 3: THE COLD WAR REVISIONISTS

For more than a decade after the crushing defeat of Henry Wallace in 1948 the American Left did little to challenge the dominant historiography of the Cold War. Traumatized by McCarthyism and smothered by a pervasive anti-Communist consensus, it suffered silently through the Eisenhower years. The Left's limited energies remained occupied with domestic issues like school desegregation and the anomic consequences of modern suburban living. Virtually no one questioned the orthodox or realist explanations of the Cold War, and those very few like Carl Marzani and Vera Michels Dean[1] who did offer direct dissents either labored in obscurity or were publicly vilified.

Yet by the early 1960s a full-fledged New Left or Cold War revisionism had emerged to fundamentally attack the historiography, priorities, values, and policy recommendations of orthodox scholars and their realist revisionist critics. Fathered by William Appleman Williams and supported in varying degrees by Gar Alperovitz, Gabriel Kolko, Walter LaFeber, Richard J. Barnet and a dozen or so other diplomatic historians,[2] by the late sixties Cold War revisionism had shattered the academic anti-Communist consensus. In effect, it argued that (1) American ambition and economic requirements (real or imagined) had brought on (or at least escalated) the Cold War; (2) the Soviet reaction was essentially defensive and reasonable; and (3) America's "Open Door imperialism," while brilliantly successful for several decades, had been gradually frustrated by a variety of revolutionary movements and non-capitalist states. These historians claimed that the notion of an American isolationist tradition represented a self-serving myth and warned that drastic domestic changes had to be undertaken if the United States was to survive and the world spared nuclear disaster. Their interest in the origins of the Cold War rested on the contention that it was during this period that American plans for a capitalist world order had been both largely realized and effectively challenged. Postwar history could best be understood, therefore, as the working out of this struggle between the American empire and its revolutionary and socialist antagonists. The origins of the Cold War, they suggested, stood as a symbol of both American aspirations and American frustrations, not only (or even primarily) in its relations with the Soviet Union but with the developing world as well. The policy of containment was but a technique designed to defend and extend the Open Door, and this strategy had remained basically unchanged since the days of Woodrow Wilson.

* * * * *

Because of Williams' seminal role in developing Cold War revisionism we will examine his work at some length. Like several of these revisionists Williams was born and raised in the rural Midwest. He graduated from Annapolis in 1944, but was medically discharged from the Navy in 1947, and thereafter entered graduate school at the University of Wisconsin where he studied under Fred Harvey Harrington. Williams published his first book, AMERICAN-RUSSIAN RELATIONS, 1789-1947,[3] in 1952 but remained largely unknown until the appearance of THE TRAGEDY OF AMERICAN DIPLOMACY[4] seven years later. In this volume and in THE CONTOURS OF AMERICAN HISTORY (1961),[5] THE GREAT EVASION (1964),[6] and THE ROOTS OF THE MODERN AMERICAN EMPIRE (1969),[7] he created an elaborate interpretive framework to explain the development of American foreign policy.

Williams' understanding of American diplomacy ultimately rested on his dualistic view of human nature.[8] Depending on whether property relations were private or social either man's egoistic or social half would triumph. This fundamental dualism meant that a society's choice of economic systems had significant consequences; but because ideas possessed a more or less independent existence, individuals living under capitalism could occasionally transcend class interests and work for the general welfare by forming a "national class." But any national class was hard-pressed to rebut the claim that economic regulations were merely transparent devices that unfairly advanced the interests of special groups. These circumstances made the formulation of a true national interest virtually impossible. Thus the national class was constantly confronted by an ultimately insoluble dilemma: how to achieve an ethical community without placing severe restrictions on private property.[9]

In order to *avoid* this dilemma, American leaders had traditionally opted for marketplace expansion. Yet although enlightened American leaders like Madison had hoped that expansion would reduce the tension between man's egoistic and social halves by "providing enough resources and opportunities to satisfy the demands of the ego and enough space to absorb the demagogic energies of would-be dictators,"[10] Williams claimed that it actually served to strengthen capitalism's impoverished conception of community as a competitive marketplace dedicated to narrow self-interest.

Very occasionally American leaders had squarely faced this dilemma and had attempted to achieve a community at home without resorting to an expansionist foreign policy. For example, Herbert Hoover wished, without explicitly denouncing capitalism, to move to a transitional form of political economy wherein the federal government would function as umpire of the actions of capital, labor, and the public to encourage cooperation without lurching toward fascism or bureaucratic statism.[11] Moreover,

> Hoover was against the Empire. He was willing to work toward a largely self-contained economy, and he was consistently opposed to the assumptions and attitudes that produced the cold war.[12]

This benign portrait of Hoover directly challenged the assumptions of liberal internationalism embraced by the containment establishment and anticipated a favorite device later used by other radical historians: the resurrection of conservatives like Hoover, Robert Taft, and Henry Stimson who almost certainly would have had little appeal but for their opposition to extensive overseas commitments.[13]

Yet Williams contended that despite the efforts of Hoover and other nationalist class leaders, capitalism had always demanded (or seemed to demand) economic expansion. He noted that after gaining independence from England, "Americans . . . launched a sustained drive to win and hold a preponderant position in world shipping and overseas markets," and "simultaneously opened a militant and determined campaign to acquire territory." During the mid-nineteenth century, "the world became the potential American frontier," for "*laissez faire* was the seminal fountain of one-worldism, and Americans erupted in a wave of entrepreneurial activity that crashed into every shore around the globe." In the post-Civil War period

Americans realized that agricultural exports were needed to enlarge their markets and to guarantee their prosperity. With the closing of the continental frontier by 1890 American urban leaders came to share the agrarians' view and adapted it to include industrial exports. Convinced of the ultimately supreme economic might of the United States, American officials issued the Open Door Notes. These were "designed to establish and maintain open access and fair competition in the markets of the world by placing the power of America publicly and formally on the line in support of the principles of self-determination and equal opportunity."[14] The Open Door worked brilliantly for half a century, and an American empire of unprecedented scope was established and maintained. This empire was not the traditional kind, however, for it did not rest upon overseas colonial possessions. Rather, American imperialism was of an "informal" nature whose strength derived from American economic access to investment in all areas of the globe.

But by the middle of the twentieth century this empire had been attacked by lesser industrial states like Japan and Italy, and by poverty-stricken non-industrialized regions whose development was controlled or restricted by the United States. Furthermore, the rise of the Soviet Union and China to major power status after World War II and the proliferation of situations in which the United States apparently had to intervene to maintain its conception of order eventually made the Open Door Policy self-defeating. If the United States persisted in its expansionist outlook, Williams warned, it would face nuclear war, total isolation, or a renewed competition of unlimited dimensions in outer space. Because capitalism subordinated the social dimension of human nature to grasping, acquisitive, narrow self-interest, respectful and non-manipulative human relations were extremely difficult and perhaps impossible to sustain. The behavior of capitalist America consistently reflected this fact, for it had failed to establish creative, symbiotic relationships with other nations. Even such apparently altruistic instruments as the Marshall Plan and the Alliance For Progress were disguised forms of economic coercion. The Open Door, which preached the virtues of equal opportunity for all, had been based on the expectation that American economic power would effectively close that door to others or create a set of dependencies helpful to the United States. Far from denoting cooperation and equality, the Open Door Policy mirrored America's predilection for competition, self-interest, and hypocrisy.

Drawing inspiration from Marx, Charles Beard, and John Hobson, Williams' notion of an informal American empire rationalized by a deceptive Open Door Policy had an enormous impact on a generation of American historians reaching maturity in the early 1960s. Orthodox and realist revisionist historians had explained American foreign policy in terms of idealism and an isolationist tradition, but Williams argued instead that these concepts served as hypocritical disguises for the obvious reality of overwhelming American power. Many young scholars were deeply impressed with an interpretation that seemed so aware of the contemporary fact of a *Pax Americana.*

The theme of American expansion became the single most influential aspect of Williams' work. Scholars who otherwise might have found his writings eccentric seized upon his explanation of overseas growth. Yet at the heart of the explanation lay a fundamental ambiguity which Williams never squarely confronted: an uncertainty about the ultimate reasons for American expansionism. It was unclear whether the United States had expanded (1) because of a persistently mistaken conviction by American officials that the continued integrity of domestic institutions required expansion; or (2) because these institutions actually did require expansion to insure their continued well-being; or (3) because the habits of capitalism had gradually planted in the collective American psyche a belief that the health of domestic institutions depended on sustained growth. Williams offered each of these interpretations at different times: first, the explanation of honest but mistaken conviction—"The key to understanding the American empire is found in comprehending how the economically natural or easy or desirable came to be considered the economically necessary. . . .";[15] second, the explanation of objective necessity—"The never-ending necessity to accumulate additional surplus value, or capital, a process which was essential for the system as well as to the individual businessman, meant that this market 'must, therefore, be continually extended',";[16] and third, the explanation of psychic necessity—"[By 1900] . . . the interests of the political economy (and hence of the nation) were already involved, and the psychology of the situation was always weighted against withdrawal."[17]

This ambiguity made it difficult for Williams to make policy recommendations. He wanted the United States to conduct a non-expansionistic diplomacy, but on the basis of his own analysis it was not clear how that could be done. Did America's economic institutions need to be radically transformed so that they would no longer require expansion? Or was it enough to put trust in leaders who could rid themselves of the mistaken conviction that expansion was necessary? Or could the American people be expected to withdraw support from the expansionist consensus if they could be taught that continued growth was merely a "psychic" necessity? Because Williams never came to grips with this issue, his influence on American foreign policy-makers was much less than it otherwise might have been.

* * * * *

Williams' interest in portraying twentieth century international relations stemmed solely from his desire to trace the growth of America's informal empire, and his description of recent world politics clearly betrayed this bias. The twentieth century international dialectic had been simple: The United States expanded and other nations contracted (Spain, England, France), fell under American hegemony (the Third World), or mounted counterattacks to this Open Door imperialism (Germany, Japan, the Soviet Union). No doubt in his zeal to revise the orthodox view of the United States as a passive, reactive nation Williams exaggerated, and yet the members of the containment establishment also shared part of his misconception, for they asserted that constant American pressure on the periphery of Soviet power would lead to its ultimate modification or collapse. In both instances there was a faith in the ability of the United States to influence events in other societies while at the same time remaining immune from them. The difference, of course, was that while the foreign policy establishment celebrated this power, Williams viewed it as a disaster.

Since Williams contended that diplomacy was largely a reflection of domestic institutions (or convictions about their requirements) it followed that he treated international politics in much the same manner as domestic politics: a consequence of the ego's triumph over the social self. Williams found international relations as presently constituted to be distasteful and necessary only until truly human communities were established. And because of this transitory nature he assumed that any discussion of the "eternal verities" of world politics would be irrelevant. He attempted to smooth the way for a mostly peaceful domestic socialist revolution by emphasizing the consensual character of American politics, yet despite the pandemic violence of twentieth century international relations, Williams did not concede that the peaceful establishment of a universal true community was impossible. Instead, by his frequent references to the good intentions which characterized the foreign relations of capitalist America, Williams implied that a socialist America, which continued to display benevolence as well as its new-found attributes of true love and democratic participation, would encourage through action and example the peaceful passage into a world of genuine communities. International relations in its traditional form would expire as war, exploitation, and greed were replaced by a system of inter*community* relations based on altruism and equity. Since real socialism would allow people to fulfill themselves through acts of love and participation, all would be treated equally, and contemporary, but chimerical, concerns like national defense would disappear. Furthermore, an isolationist posture, which Williams seemed to claim was the only short-run policy open to a capitalist America, would be precluded under a socialist regime, for while a capitalist America must define freedom in terms of an ever-expanding and exploitative marketplace, a socialist America would replace domination with symbiosis. An isolationist and socialist America would be a contradiction in terms—a conceptual impossibility.[18]

* * * * *

Williams' historical figures reflected ideas and behaved with perfect steadiness and consciousness to achieve a clearly defined goal. His decision-makers (at least the Americans) were never hemmed in by events, were never lacking in overall strategies, were never more than momentarily puzzled, and were only constricted by the inherent deficiencies of their capitalist outlook. Even unexceptional men like Chester A. Arthur, James G. Blaine, and William Howard Taft were able to engage in remarkably subtle analyses upon which they proceeded to act. The effect of Williams' treatment was to reduce historical actors to minds, unassailed by doubt, infirmity, or idiosyncrasy.

Within this rationalistic framework policy-making became a deceptively simple process. Because Williams discounted the possibility that foreign policy decisions might have involved such elements as genuine misunderstandings of situations, the lack of conscious or coherent goals, or the influence of unarticulated but compelling social myths (save, perhaps, for a mistaken notion about the real needs of American capitalism), the formulation of policy was affected and determined by a sharply limited number of factors: the decision-maker's outlook which derived ultimately from the property arrangements of society which framed and limited the range of choices to be seriously considered;[19] an analysis of the policy-maker's domestic socioeconomic structure undertaken to understand what should be done to sustain (or, on rare occasions, to reform) those institutions;

and the formulation of long-term goals and shorter-run strategies and tactics to achieve a congruity between personal outlook and social analysis. Williams had described a decision-maker who was deeply aware of his own assumptions about the world and able to work consistently (indeed, obsessively) to realize a clearly seen yet distant end. The result was a parade of rather wooden historical figures marching to a clear, even, and inexorable drumbeat.

His policy-making model represented, on the one hand, a rejection of the "power elite" thesis, popularized in America by C. Wright Mills and later to be embraced by Gabriel Kolko, and, on the other, an attack on "group theorists" like David Truman who claimed that American foreign policy was the outcome of an elaborate process involving serious conflict among competing politico-economic constellations. Because Williams believed that American politics was based on a broad consensus reflecting a set of quite specific values, he, unlike many American radicals, did not emphasize the influence of a "military-industrial complex" (or some similar anti-democratic concept of American foreign policy). But neither did he pretend that genuine domestic clashes over significant issues informed the character of American diplomacy, for Williams asserted that our foreign relations had been consistently formulated on the basis of a nearly pervasive consensus about diplomatic aims and purposes.

* * * * *

Williams' understanding of the Cold War and his evaluation of the postwar foreign policy establishment were derived from his more general framework. He discovered the roots of the Cold War in America's response to the Bolshevik Revolution. Instead of challenging Americans to rethink their historic "evasion" of private property's ultimate dilemma, the Bolshevik Revolution terrified them. The Wilson Administration helped to mount an intervention against Lenin, led an hysterical anti-Communist campaign at home, refused to extend diplomatic recognition to the Soviet regime, and sought to isolate Moscow while pressing the Open Door to its very borders. This basic pattern was repeated by succeeding administrations. After entering World War II to prevent the Axis from denying American goods and investments access to large areas of the globe, the United States used its power in 1945 to coerce the Soviets into accepting its vision of the postwar world. When Stalin refused to expose his security zone to the logic of the Open Door, Washington embarked on another anti-Communist crusade designed to quarantine the Soviets and to expand America's economic preeminence to Eastern Europe. The Cold War, Williams concluded, originated in the narrow, capitalist outlook of American officials—a *Weltanschaaung* fully shared by the vast majority of the American public. This consensus encouraged the United States to pry open every global nook and cranny to exports and investments. As he put it,

> America's postwar programs and policies were based on the confidence that the economic power of the United States, deployed in keeping with its traditional ideas and practices of Open Door expansion, would simultaneously generate recovery in Europe and development in the colonial areas of the world. That would block further uprisings in the idiom of the Bolshevik Revolution and at the same time sustain the isolation of the Soviet Union.[20]

Unlike many of the 1960s radicals, Williams detected no hint of conspiracy in the role played by the foreign policy establishment but construed its actions as essentially reflective of the broad-based expansionist consensus. Nevertheless, Williams was incensed by its alleged cowardice, for, unlike Hoover, it had no interest in grappling with the fundamental dilemma of private property. In 1957 he offered this judgment of the establishment:

> Only sixteen years ago, supported by a chorus of enthusiastic liberal and conservative intellectuals, Henry R. Luce announced the maturity of the American Century. It was High Noon, he judged, and hence time to accept wholeheartedly our duty and our opportunity as the most powerful and vital nation in the world and in consequence to exert upon the world the full impact of our influence, for such purposes as we see fit.[21]

Furthermore, Williams argued,

> Shared by big corporation executives, labor leaders, and politicians of every ideological bent, this estimate of America's power and role in world affairs dominated policy-making decisions long after the Russians had tested their first nuclear weapons.[22]

This outlook, then, had characterized the Cold War establishment even before America's entry into World War II. It was in this context that containment was formulated:

> This pervasive sense of certainty confined whatever discussions that did arise to the issues of the means to be used, or the limits to which America should go in exerting its will and its way. What passed for debate about the policy of containment, for example, revolved not around the validity of the policy, but about whether or not it went far enough.[23]

Thus Williams shared with his more orthodox colleagues the presumption that there had been but one containment policy. But whereas orthodox historians like Bailey had discovered in the immediate postwar years a battle between internationalists and isolationists (with the former fortunately emerging victorious), Williams saw but another tactical squabble within the consensus over how best to pursue the Open Door. From his perspective NSC-68, and even the later "rollback" rhetoric of some Republicans, represented only insignificant wrinkles in the cloth woven by Kennan in 1946. And Kennan's analysis was, of course, fully consistent with an American Open Door imperialism that had characterized the outlook of such leaders as Jefferson, Madison, and the two Roosevelts.

Williams was convinced, however, that by the late 1950s the American Century was already showing signs of decay. He observed that "within the past five years it has become apparent that something is awry,"[24] and "many Americans are beginning to sense for themselves that a prosperity paid for in the coin of chicanery and collusion, inflation and inequities, aimlessness and alienation, is very apt to become an air-conditioned nightmare."[25] Yet he had no sympathy for Bailey's faith in the foreign policy elite or Bemis' program of moral rearmament. The continued growth of Soviet power, anti-American rumblings in the non-aligned world, and the sense of domestic malaise evident in the last Eisenhower years convinced Williams that the underlying rationale for the Cold War had to be abandoned: "the assumption that the United States has the power to force the Soviet Union to capitulate to American terms is the fundamental weakness in America's conception of itself and the world."[26] The lessons for the foreign policy establishment should have been obvious:

> It is essential . . . to abandon the bipartisan imperialism of Thomas Jefferson and Theodore Roosevelt. America is neither the last great hope of the world nor the agent of civilization destined to destroy the barbarians. We have much to offer, but also much to learn. And the basic lesson is that we have misconceived leadership among equals as the exercise of pre-

> dominance over others. Such an outlook is neither idealism nor realism; it is either self-righteousness or sophistry. Either is an indulgence which democracy cannot afford.[27]

In place of this arrogant and futile search for absolute supremacy Williams advised a foreign policy conducted by an American leadership shorn of its mistaken conviction about the need to dominate the world, or, if one understands him to explain American expansion on the basis of institutional necessity, a socialist diplomacy grounded in cooperative values. The result would be a continental economy grounded in decentralized domestic institutions.

More specifically, Williams warned that "American foreign policy must be changed fundamentally in order to sustain the wealth and welfare of the United States on into the future." To this end he recommended that "the frontier-expansionist explanation of American democracy and prosperity, and the strategy of the Open Door Policy, be abandoned on the grounds that neither any longer bears any significant relation to reality."[28] In its place Williams called for a foreign policy supportive of an "open door for revolutions."[29] To achieve this goal he urged "a patient and concerted effort to establish and maintain a *modus vivendi* with the Soviet Union, the People's Republic of China, and their allies" entailing significant economic agreements. This approach would "open the way for continued reform within communist countries" and make it easier for the United States to allocate its aid through the United Nations.[30] "Once freed from its myopic concentration on the cold war," Williams observed, "the United States could come to grips with the central problem of reordering its own society so that it functions through such a balanced relationship with the rest of the world, and so that the labor and leisure of its own citizens are invested with creative meaning and purpose."[31] Then, "having structured a creative response to the issue of democracy and prosperity at home," America "could again devote a greater share of its attention and energy to the world scene."[32]

But although Williams hoped for a "radical but noncommunist reconstruction of American society in domestic affairs," he acknowledged that "there is at the present time no radicalism in the United States strong enough to win power . . . through the processes of representative government."[33] Thus, "ironically," Williams admitted, his "radical analysis leads finally to a conservative conclusion," for "the well-being of the United States depends—*in the short-run but only in the short-run*—upon the extent to which calm and confident and enlightened conservatives can see and bring themselves to act upon the validity of a radical analysis."[34] If, however, "the United States cannot accept the existence of... limits" to its freedom of action in the world "without giving up democracy and cannot proceed to enhance and extend democracy within such limits, then the traditional effort to sustain democracy by expansion will lead to the destruction of democracy."[35] Needless to say, Williams' recommendations hardly constituted a philosophy of political activism, and, as we will see, it disappointed many on the Left who were more committed to direct involvement than Williams.

* * * * *

Williams' early works were received more as curiosities than as dangerous assaults on the conventional wisdom. In these last few years before Vietnam the Cold War consensus was not about to be shattered by an obscure historian's theories about an Open Door empire. Orthodox scholars like Foster Rhea Dulles were surprisingly mild in their evaluations, and although Oscar Handlin bitterly denounced Williams' interpretations, it was the political Left that was especially upset by some of his conclusions. Staughton Lynd, for instance, maligned Williams' "Hegelianism," his denigration of individualistic American radicals like the Abolitionists, and his penchant for the "sweeping statement" and the "categorical conclusion,"[36] while Robert L. Heilbroner branded THE GREAT EVASION "vulgar, self-serving, imprecise, shallow, dubious, and careless,"[37] primarily in its gross misunderstanding of Marx, and Eugene Genovese admitted that ". . . the book fails almost totally as an exposition of Marxian thought, or as a Marxian-influenced introduction to contemporary national and world politics"[38] though he still found it of "great value."

In 1969, partly in response to Lynd and others who had been critical of the lack of footnotes and other documentation in his earlier works, Williams published a massive study entitled THE ROOTS OF THE MODERN AMERICAN EMPIRE.[39] There he meticulously and exhaustively traced the manner by which the expansionist sentiments allegedly held by late nineteenth century American farmers were transmitted to corporate manufacturers. While this scholarship pleased a few critics, some erstwhile admirers felt betrayed. Howard Zinn, for example, accused Williams of abandoning "radical" for "professional" history:

> He inundates us with data to answer professionally interesting questions: who was expansionist first, the agricultural businessman or the industrial businessman? when did expansionist ideology become important, before or after 1890? But what does this do for us?[40]

Zinn concluded that the result was "to fulfill Tolstoy's definition of the historian as a deaf man answering questions no one has asked."

Michael Harrington found other reasons to object:

> . . . what bothers me about the Williams emphasis is that it tends to play down the possibilities of fighting to change American policy from within. For it describes only what is expansionist and crass in the past and omits what was genuinely anticommercial and democratic. As a result, the present configuration of American power is made to seem much more historically inevitable than it really is. And this is a strange consequence of Williams' analysis since he himself is obviously very much committed to transforming the nation.[41]

These comments from the Left indicate the paradoxical position occupied by Williams and the fragmented nature of American radical thought even during the heady days of the late 1960s. Yet despite serious doubts about his Marxism, professionalism, political tactics, and historical treatment of certain radicals, the Left was virtually united in its celebration of Williams' foreign policy revisions. His notion of Open Door imperialism proved particularly captivating, for by identifying a pervasive interventionist impulse, it provided a powerful response to those orthodox diplomatic historians who had emphasized America's anti-colonialist, anti-expansionist, isolationist tradition. Arthur M. Schlesinger, Jr. judged that Williams was

> one of the few contemporary American historians who can be said to have founded a school; and the multiplying books of his disciples have had marked impact on the way younger historians think about American foreign policy.[42]

Indeed, by the early 1960s this so-called Wisconsin school of diplomatic history had produced several young scholars who had already achieved solid reputations. One of them, Walter LaFeber, wrote a Cold War history college text which by the end of the 1970s would sell over 400,000 copies,[43] and others like Lloyd Gardner and

Gar Alperovitz soon published influential revisionist monographs.[44] Yet both Williams and his school attracted relatively few students until the Vietnam War unleashed an avalanche of domestic dissent.

* * * * *

By the late 1960s

> What had been a small, if steadily growing, body of "revisionist" literature suddenly became the inspiration for a copious outpouring of articles and books reopening historical questions once thought settled or of so little importance as to be forgotten.[45]

Older themes like the Monroe Doctrine, the expansionist program of William Seward, and the Philippine insurrection joined the Cold War issues of Yalta, Potsdam, and Hiroshima as targets of this assault. Indeed, the whole sweep of American diplomacy was subjected to searching and often searing reinterpretations. Large commercial publishing houses quickly recognized the mushrooming popularity of radical revisionism, and when Random House published Williams' THE ROOTS OF THE MODERN AMERICAN EMPIRE in 1969, THE NEW YORK TIMES lavished three glowing reviews on it.

These historical reconsiderations found an avid audience on college campuses as increasingly disillusioned students sought persuasive explanations of Vietnam and the foreign policy that had led to it. In view of the general distrust of private and public American institutions which Vietnam both triggered and reflected among large segments of this student generation, it was inevitable that the issue of the American use of the atomic bomb became a flash point in the now rapidly escalating "revisionist-orthodox" controversy.

The traditional explanation of Hiroshima and Nagasaki was apparently both clear and simple: the "decision" to employ this weapon had been a purely military one taken to save American and Japanese lives and to hasten the end of the war.[46] Yet, although this account was fully acceptable to (and partly authored by) the foreign policy establishment and was consistent with the assumptions of the Cold War consensus, there had remained a certain uneasiness among some of its left-liberal fringes that the United States had been the first and only nation to use in anger a weapon of such destructiveness and symbolic significance. These doubts, while never widespread in America, commanded much more popular and political support in Britain where massive "ban-the-bomb" demonstrations formed a noisy counterpoint to the academic dissents of scholars like the physicist P.M.S. Blackett.[47]

In 1965 Gar Alperovitz, who had studied with Williams as an undergraduate at Wisconsin in the late 1950s, published ATOMIC DIPLOMACY: *Hiroshima and Potsdam.* The book caused an immediate sensation. For two decades most Americans had been reconciled to Hiroshima because of their belief that it had been militarily necessary and had actually spared the lives of millions of American soldiers and Japanese civilians. But now Alperovitz, in a heavily documented study, argued that the United States had dropped these bombs for primarily *political* purposes in order to affect Soviet behavior in Eastern Europe, Germany, and the Far East. Claiming that the use of the bomb was the culmination of an elaborate diplomatic strategy adopted by Truman soon after Roosevelt's death, he hypothesized that "hard-line" advisers to FDR, kept largely at bay so long as he was President, rapidly won his inexperienced successor's confidence and convinced Truman to "get tough" with the Russians.[48] Until the early summer of 1945 the atomic bomb had been deemed a military necessity to force an immediate and unconditional surrender of Japan. But this situation had begun to change with the growing desire of the Japanese to find a way to terminate hostilities. Alperovitz asserted that this fact contributed to the gradual transformation of the atomic bomb into a political anti-Soviet "trump card." After vainly attempting to utilize an array of economic weapons like Lend Lease and the possibility of a postwar reconstruction loan to induce Stalin to adhere to America's interpretation of the Yalta agreements, the Truman Administration devised a complex "strategy of delay" to avoid a showdown with Moscow over Eastern Europe and Germany until after the successful employment of the atomic bomb. Since it was obvious that domestic pressure would compel the quick removal of American troops from Europe, and since America's economic muscle had not moderated Stalin, Truman and his advisers, Alperovitz suggested, decided that little could be done without the successful conclusion of the Manhattan Project. Accordingly, Truman delayed an early post-VE Day meeting with Stalin, dispatched Harry Hopkins to Moscow to pacify the Soviet leader, urged Chiang to prolong his country's talks with the Russians over the implementation of the Yalta accords, and adopted other slow-down tactics to postpone a confrontation.

No alternative explanation, Alperovitz contended, could account for the otherwise curious American handling of the Japanese attempts to surrender in July 1945. Despite the fact that Truman and other high

American officials seemingly had no firm objections to the surrender terms communicated to Moscow from Tokyo, and despite the fact that the Teheran pledge of unconditional surrender had already been breached by Eisenhower's negotiations with the Badoglio government in Italy, conventional explanations had always stressed that the atomic bomb had been necessary in order to obtain the Japanese surrender. Alperovitz argued, however, that because of the impending reality of the bomb, there was no great hurry to accommodate the Japanese until the Russian entry into the Pacific war became imminent. Then the Truman Administration attempted to end the conflict immediately by detonating two devices over Japan. Although the atomic bombs accomplished this goal, the broader diplomatic strategy failed abysmally, for instead of working to mute Stalin's behavior in Eastern Europe, the opposite effect apparently occurred in light of Molotov's intransigence at the London Foreign Ministers Conference in September.

Two points should be emphasized here. First, the conventional treatment of this theme had never denied that the American possession and use of the atomic bomb had been devoid of political intentions. Herbert Feis, for example, admitted that given the enormous capabilities of this weapon American policy-makers had quite naturally considered its probable effect on the Soviet Union. What was in dispute was the *centrality* of these calculations, for even Herbert Feis had concluded that the Japanese probably would have surrendered without the bomb and without invasion by the end of 1945.[49] Second, Alperovitz never directly accused Truman of the *commission* of an immoral act in the decision to drop the bomb. Rather, he asserted that

> . . . it appears that the natural military assumption that the bomb would be used became intermeshed with diplomatic strategy in a way so subtle it was probably not completely understood by the participants themselves. Using the bomb became so deep an assumption that, as Churchill reminds us, '. . . the decision whether or not to use the atomic bomb . . . *was never even an issue.*'[50]

Yet, Alperovitz cautioned,

> One would . . . like to believe that the sole motive of [American] officials was to save lives. It is not pleasant to think that they were so fascinated with their new 'master card' of diplomacy that they scarcely considered the moral implications of their act when they

> used it. That, however, is precisely what the evidence now available strongly suggests.[51]

The conclusion was clear: Truman and his staff, while not technically guilty of a crime, were certainly answerable to the charge of moral negligence, or at the very least, gross moral insensitivity. At a time when Operation "Rolling Thunder" was being unleashed against North Vietnam—a bombing program with overtly political aims—the appearance of ATOMIC DIPLOMACY: *Hiroshima and Potsdam* was bound to stir controversy.

This book was probably better known to the foreign policy establishment than any other "radical revisionist" work. But by 1970 Alperovitz had abandoned diplomatic history for a concern "with domestic policy matters and with efforts to transform the political economy of our domestic institutions."[52] Alperovitz announced that hereafter he would concentrate on bringing about domestic reforms:

> We shall ultimately have to get at the root of the idea of the interventionist tradition—so that the idea of expansion, of intervention—and the idea that "freedom" requires both—no longer weaves comfortably into the basic fabric of our society. . . .
>
> In short, we must find means . . . to restructure fundamentally the deepest American attitudes and institutional patterns at the core of our system of political economy. Thus, in the end, we are confronted with the challenge of change at home as well as abroad.[53]

For Alperovitz, intervention in Vietnam in 1965 no less than attempted intervention in Eastern Europe in 1945 formed part of a counter-revolutionary pattern rooted in the presumed or actual needs of American capitalism. To finally break this pattern it was necessary "to speak intelligently to the great majority of Americans, and, with patience and commitment to the long haul, to offer a creative alternative to ideas which so many have held for so long."[54]

* * * * *

The late 1960s and early 1970s witnessed a veritable flood of revisionist interpretations of recent American diplomacy by authors largely indebted to Williams. Perhaps the most challenging of these works were by Gabriel Kolko, who represented a distinct yet related variant in radical revisionist thought. In two monumental studies of wartime and postwar American foreign policy, plus a smaller book of essays on contemporary themes,[55] Kolko presented a complex, often brilliant, and sometimes indecipherable critique of the United States in world affairs. He began with the claim that World War II had utterly and irreversibly destroyed the old Eurocentric political, social, and economic order that had been tottering since 1914.[56] Because the *ancien regime* had been totally discredited by its appeasement of and collaboration with Fascism, the wartime Resistance movements in Europe and Asia fell under the influence of a Left that wished to establish postwar revolutionary governments. The United States, which had been a frequent (if somewhat aloof) participant in the Old Order, realized early in the war that it would emerge from it as the most powerful nation in the world. To ensure its supremacy Washington formulated a set of extremely ambitious and articulate economic and political aims that sought to construct a reformed liberal capitalist world order supervised by America and by 1943 had positioned itself against the primary impediments to this vision: the Left, the Soviet Union, and the British Empire. Roosevelt and Truman were fully successful in their efforts to severely restrict the imperial power of Britain. By forbidding London from exercising hegemony over Europe, and by outmaneuvering it in the Middle East and Latin America, the United States accelerated the radical diminution of British power. Yet the other goals of American diplomacy ultimately proved unachievable, partly because of the Soviet Union, but chiefly because of the uncontainable power of the revolutionary Left. Indeed, the Soviets, characterized by "pervasive, chronic conservatism,"[57]

> . . . understood the American intention and the risks of any covert aid to the Left, and they gave precious little of it during and immediately after the war, when they discovered that even an obviously conservative policy failed to blunt the American belief that behind all the world's social and economic ills, somehow, and in some critical fashion, a Russian plot and device existed.[58]

In fact, Kolko assured, Stalin frowned on both the extreme Right and the extreme Left, and ". . . it was Soviet conservatism on revolutionary movements everywhere that gave Western European capitalism the critical breathing spell during which it might recover. . . ."[59] In spite of this parallelism in American and Soviet policies, Washington nevertheless failed to realize its postwar visions, for its self-appointed tasks were beyond the ability of any state to achieve:

> The problem, which it was impossible for anyone in Washington to sufficiently perceive and appreciate, was that the kind of world emerging from the war required power beyond the factory and army, the kind of resources and inspiration that only revolutionary movements in villages and mountains can possess and generate.
>
> For insofar as world conflict was transformed from wars between states into ideological and civil wars for social transformation and liberation. . . . To succeed in that situation one had to be neither American, English, or Russian, but to be present in every village in the hungry world, or, as in the case of the Russians, to endorse an inevitability that they could neither initiate nor prevent.[60]

But in view of the insuperable obstacles blocking its path, why did America persist for almost three decades in this impossible dream? After all, in pursuing it the United States had become a counter-revolutionary power without peer and had become involved "in a deepening trauma whose effects began to weaken American capitalism far more than the attainment of its expansive, unattainable goals might ever have strengthened it."[61]

Kolko provided the answer in THE ROOTS OF AMERICAN FOREIGN POLICY. It was here that Kolko's disagreements with Williams and his disciples became clear. Whereas Williams could never quite decide whether American expansionism was rooted in mistaken conviction, psychic necessity, or institutional requirements, Kolko evinced absolutely no ambiguity: The objective needs of its capitalist system had forced America's leaders to constantly seek more exports, more foreign investments, and more raw materials to the point where only a totally subservient globe could sate its enormous appetite. For Kolko the notion of an even temporarily enlightened, mercantilist "national class" was plainly a bad joke, as was Williams' dream of a decentralized, continental economy.

Yet despite these differences Kolko's explanation of the origins and evolution of the Cold War was largely a careful elaboration of the outline originally sketched by Williams in THE TRAGEDY OF AMERICAN DIPLOMACY. Accepting Williams' central idea of an Open Door empire Kolko produced a mass of documentary evidence to support the claim that a major goal of America's World War II diplomacy had been the destruction and absorption of the old European imperial system. Kolko also agreed with Williams' characterization of the Soviet Union as a deeply conservative, defensively-minded state which threatened American security only insofar as American security needs were fundamentally unlimited. He injected a new twist into the argument by submitting that Stalin had in several instances vainly assisted the United States in its unrelenting campaign against the Left. Finally, Kolko affirmed Williams' assertion that America's attempt to make the world safe for liberal capitalism was bound to fail, but Kolko's emphasis was slightly different. According to his analysis the United States had been swimming against the vast, inexorable, and uncontrollable tides of history—tides which had swept away capitalism and traditional states (save for America)—and had sent a torrent of leftist revolution flooding over the world. With Russia's help Western Europe had been temporarily spared, but the Soviets had in turn survived only by accepting the inevitability of a triumphant Left. Kolko transformed Soviet-American rivalry into an irrelevancy—a contest between anachronisms, for the seat of ideological ferment and future political power had migrated to the Third World. And it was in the "villages and mountains"—not in the Kremlin—that America's aspirations would be destroyed.

Williams and Kolko disagreed about other issues as well.[62] Whereas Williams argued that the Open Door had become a thoroughly internalized part of the American outlook, Kolko perceived it primarily as a "tactic for restructuring the world economy and facilitating American economic penetration."[63] Williams alleged that American imperialism had frequently been motivated by intentions which unknowingly exploited others, but Kolko argued that these consequences were clearly anticipated by American leaders. Finally, although Williams was convinced of the decisive importance of an expansionistic public consensus, Kolko claimed that the monolithic quality of the foreign policy elite made grass-roots opinion largely irrelevant.

Such differences, however, were not especially significant. While it was difficult to generalize about a "radical revisionist" thesis regarding event "X," personality "Y," or doctrine "Z," the overall interpretative spectrum occupied by these scholars was comparable in breadth (or narrowness) to that filled by the orthodox historians of the 1950s.

With Kolko's writings the limits of the radical revisionist assault on conventional explanations of the Cold War had, in a sense, been reached, for they formed an almost perfect mirror image of the most exuberant defenses of American diplomacy. Where once the Soviets had been ambitious and the Americans magnanimous, the situation was now reversed; where once Russian intransigence had initiated the Cold War and had prompted a belated Western response, the opposite was now true; where once it had been the Soviet Union who had made insatiable and unappeasable security demands on an America who had sought to be accommodating, the tables had now been turned; and where orthodox historians had once made Soviet-American confrontation the central theme of world politics and the Third World the battleground for their competing "ways-of-life," Kolko viewed it as a peripheral contest between two largely atavistic entities unable to control the stateless revolutionary fervor in the southern hemisphere.

Significantly, Kolko's last inversion bore some resemblance to an increasingly prevalent outlook within the Johnson Administration and, of course, to Rostow's revisions of the Cold War. Kolko's radical downgrading of the centrality of Soviet-American relations was partly paralleled by Washington's apparent shift in emphasis from containment of the Soviet Union to containment of China. And the Johnson Administration's nearly total preoccupation with Vietnam and with other wars of "national liberation" seemed to lend credence to Kolko's claim that the locus of world power had moved south and east.

* * * * *

In 1963 Richard J. Barnet and Marcus G. Raskin founded the Institute for Policy Studies in Washington, D.C. Easy to caricature but more difficult to characterize accurately the I.P.S. has functioned for twenty years as a "left-liberal" think tank with a wide variety of social, economic, and political interests. From its inception its foreign policy concerns have been guided, shaped, and articulated most prominently by Barnet, a former State Department official who resigned during the Kennedy Administration. While not a diplomatic historian by training (he graduated from Harvard Law School), Barnet's policy-oriented analyses of the "permanent war economy," the "national security manager," multinational corporations, détente, and American military security have been informed by an understanding of the Cold War which, while distinct in some respects from Williams, Alperovitz, and Kolko, nevertheless bears a close resemblance to Cold War revisionism.

Barnet developed his historical interpretation of Soviet-American relations most fully in THE GIANTS,[64] although some of his earlier works also contain discussions of the history of the Cold War.[65] According to Barnet the Cold War originated in and has been sustained by the mutual misperceptions of the American and Soviet national security managerial elites who for various psychological and institutional reasons were each convinced of the other's aggressive intentions. While geopolitical and ideological factors probably made acute tension between the "two expanding empires" inevitable, "the crises of the past generation have been magnified by misperceptions."[66] But

> By the late 1960s the struggle of the two elites to understand each other had taken a new turn because external events had radically altered their relationship. Each nation had achieved the capability of incinerating the other. America's forward thrust through military action had been stopped. Soviet ideological hegemony over the "Soviet camp" had been challenged. Both societies were suffering from a crisis of legitimacy: in the United States the disillusionment of the Vietnam War, Watergate, domestic spying, racial tension, unemployment and the end of the boom; in the Soviet Union mounting cynicism about the shallowness of the ideology, the inefficiency of the economy, the corruption and crudeness of the bureaucracy, and the pervasiveness of repression.[67]

Yet the similarities between the two giants did not end there:

> Both are preoccupied with security problems that transcend the rivalry between them. For the United States elite the growing threat is the weakening of American control over the world economy, the uncertain access to raw materials, and the spiraling costs of running the most complex industrial civilization on earth. The Soviet Union is in a position to exacerbate America's problems if it chooses, and occasionally to profit from them, but it has very little to do with the process of decline of American power against which the managers of the American Government are seeking to develop new strategies.
>
> The managers of the Soviet Union are beset by a number of threats—the hostility of China, mounting ideological challenge from dissidents, from communist modernizers within and without. The consequences of a frozen revolution . . . add to the unresolved problem of the Russian empire—how to maintain control over a huge land mass of many nations, languages, and cultures without an idea that legitimizes the centralization of power. The United States is not the source of any of these problems.[68]

By thus casting the Soviet-American contest as a "symmetrical" struggle between two fearful, ideologically sensitive, misperceiving elites Barnet not only emptied the Cold War of all moral content but threatened to remove its more tangible stakes as well. Indeed, this "plague-on-both-your-houses" approach tended to make the Third World appear virtuous by contrast, and Barnet's writings were peppered with admiring references to "revolutionary" states and movements. Yet notwithstanding his emphasis on Soviet-American affinities Barnet concluded that the United States bore a special responsibility for the Cold War:

> For much of the last generation the United States had clearer and larger ambitions than did the Soviet Union, a *Pax Americana* backed by a preponderance of military might and economic power. . . . Until the 1970s U.S. military or paramilitary forces were involved in a foreign military operation or coup roughly once every eighteen months. But the Soviet Union has yet to send combat troops outside the empire [as of 1977!] it claimed for itself after World War II. Thus, neither in arms, money, nor influence were they a match for the United States. For much of this period the United States ran the arms race with itself.[69]

Not unreasonably, the Soviets sought to imitate American military power and by the late 1970s had achieved near equality. This circumstance, when combined with the formidable domestic problems that infected each giant, created irrestible demands for détente.

Barnet was not, however, content to settle for an armed truce as the best resolution of the U.S.-Soviet conflict. His ultimate aim, rather, was mutual disarmament to guarantee peace, and although he did not discount the obstacles to Russian disarmament, Barnet primarily emphasized the institutional impediments which stood in the path of American disarmament. For example, in ROOTS OF WAR he admitted that

> It is frustrating but true that there is no single revolutionary stroke that will cut the roots of war. They are deeply entwined around every institution, including our schools and family life. . . . The myth of competition and the glory and excitement of victory are fundamental to the American way of life. No nation honors its winners more or is more confused as to what to do with its losers. This is a country where being called "aggressive" is a compliment.[70]

Apart from this pervasive cultural imperative toward competition Barnet identified three specific roadblocks to organizing the nation for peace. The first was "the concentration of power in a national security bureaucracy which increasingly comes to play by its own rules without regard to what it does to the country it is supposed to be defending."[71] The second great root of war ostensibly lay in America's capitalist economy and the business creed that sustained it. Like Williams Barnet could not quite decide if capitalism's need to expand was real or the result of intellectual error: "The primary reason military power is projected abroad is to buy influence, which has been thought essential to the maintenance of the American standard of living."[72] Finally, war in America had been institutionalized by the "vulnerability of the public to manipulation on national security issues," so that they had become "willing to accept uncritically the myth of the national interest."[73]

Unlike many of the Cold War revisionists whose solution to the problem of the "American empire" entailed vague hopes for a socialistic future, Barnet offered a rather concrete *political* program. To break the "excessive power" of the national security bureaucracy he proposed three steps. First and most importantly, the military bureaucracies had to be shrunk in size "so that the balance of power in government once again passes to those agencies which are in the business of building and healing instead of killing and destroying."[74] Second, some form of popular control over the national security managers had to be reestablished "so that they will no longer be free to play out their imperial fantasies at the expense of the American people."[75] Specifically, "Congress must reassert the constitutional prerogatives it gave up so long ago in the area of foreign affairs," and "there should be a constitutional limit on the President's right to commit troops abroad without a declaration of war."[76] And third, the system of rewards in the national security bureaucracy had to be changed so as "to introduce the notion of personal responsibility for official acts." In short, "there must be a new operational code for the national security managers that rewards the peacemakers instead of the warmakers."[77]

But Barnet doubted that the United States could disarm significantly, lower the defense budget, or relax economic warfare against commercial competitors, nor, he suggested, could "the American businessman halt the restless, exploitative search for economic opportunity abroad unless the economy is managed in a very different way."[78] Of course, the incentive system could be changed in such a way that the capitalist "would find it profitable to invest in meeting social needs instead of stimulating and satisfying private wants, which are becoming more and more trivial and providing increasingly less satisfaction."[79] Yet "as long as the American economic imperative is growth, the pressures toward economic expansion and military presence abroad will be irresistible."[80] But

> . . . regardless of economic system, an America that continues to gobble up fifty per cent of the earth's resources each year while millions starve will never find peace. Whether such far-reaching reconstructive changes can be accomplished under some modified form of private ownership or mixed economy can only be answered by making the attempt.[81]

Finally, in order to end the public's manipulation by the national security managers, grass-roots America was obliged to ask, "Who benefits from the military bureaucracy's definition of the national interest?" Neither major political party reflected the "deep but inarticulate aspirations for peace of the American people," for "each is controlled by forces in our society which have benefited or have thought they benefited from permanent war."[82] Thus, "we can have a generation of peace only if the American people demand it and are prepared to build a society rooted in the politics of peace."[83]

But notwithstanding his skepticism Barnet's proposals did find a great deal of sympathy within the Democratic Party of the early and mid-1970s. Attacks on the "imperial Presidency," "swollen" defense budgets, the misplaced priorities of the "warfare state," and the gluttonous appetites of a self-indulgent America were all regularly made by George McGovern and his supporters, and the call for America to "come home" was fully compatible with Barnet's vision of a reformed, non-interventionist United States. Put differently, Barnet's blend of liberalism, populism, and radicalism, articulated with the assistance of an increasingly visible and well-connected Institute for Policy Studies, succeeded in cultivating a sizable political constituency, especially among Congressional Democrats of the "class of '74." While his historical interpretation of the Cold War supported and strengthened his policy recommendations, politicians could smile on Barnet's proposals without thinking much about his historiography. Cold War revisionism helped to alter the intellectual culture of American colleges and universities, but the concrete advice offered by Barnet and I.P.S. was of particular relevance to policy-makers and legislators. It was in this rather diluted and circuitous manner that Cold War revisionism initially made its way to Washington.

* * * * *

In 1963 Walter LaFeber published THE NEW EMPIRE[84] which relied on Williams' Open Door Empire thesis to argue that the United States had actually undertaken a systematic program of overseas expansion between 1865 and the Spanish-American War. At a time when America had allegedly been languishing in an isolationist trance statesmen from Seward to McKinley, LaFeber claimed, had been busy increasing the economic influence of the United States around the world. This book attained considerable popularity in the 1960s among younger American diplomatic historians, in particular, and it was widely used in both graduate and undergraduate courses.[85] The decision by the Organization of American Historians to devote an entire panel to THE NEW EMPIRE at its 1971 national meeting surely attested to the volume's sizable impact on American diplomatic historiography.

But LaFeber's AMERICA, RUSSIA, AND THE COLD WAR stands as the radical revisionist work that has probably had the greatest influence on college American diplomatic history courses since its appearance in 1967.[86] Now in its fourth very successful edition, this survey of the Cold War was no tract. Although LaFeber placed a good deal more emphasis on American foreign economic policy than either orthodoxy or realist revisionism, AMERICA, RUSSIA, AND THE COLD WAR lacked the accusatory tone of Williams and Kolko. Moreover, the economic determinism of some of the cruder revisionist accounts was scrupulously avoided.[87] His analysis rested on his claim that in 1945 American officials had built their initial postwar foreign policy on four major and related assumptions. First, they presumed that "foreign policy grew directly from domestic policy; American actions abroad did not respond primarily to pressures of other nations, but to political, social, and economic forces at home." And of these forces, "policy-makers could consider the economic the most important . . . , a not unreasonable conclusion given the national crisis endured in the 1930s." The memory of the recent Depression and widespread fears of its revival led to a second assumption: The disastrous economic dislocations of the 1930s had precipitated political conflicts which, in turn, had triggered World War II. To avoid a repetition "free flow of exports and imports were essential." Third, the United States had experienced tremendous economic growth during the war and, coupled with the damage suffered by other industrial powers, now "wielded the requisite economic power to establish this desired economic community." Finally, American officials, again mindful of the legacy of the thirties, were "determined to use this gigantic economic power," and they attempted to do so through the United Nations, the World Bank, and the International Monetary Fund. They "hoped that such agencies would minimize exclusive and explosive economic and political interchange. Of course, there was one other implication of this policy: American economic power necessarily made the United States the dominant force in these organizations."[88]

The French and the British accepted American conditions for postwar economic assistance, but the Soviet Union proved much less compliant and proceeded to drop an iron curtain around the occupied countries of Eastern Europe. For LaFeber, "doctrinal demands and neurotic personal ambition partly explained Stalin's policies in this area. But the overriding requirement dictating policy was the Soviets' need for security and economic reconstruction."[89] But "for American policy-makers dedicated to creating a Western-democratic world built on the Atlantic Charter Freedoms, Stalin's moves posed the terrible problem of how to open the Soviet empire without alienating the Soviets." According to LaFeber, "in these dilemmas lay the roots of the Cold War."[90]

American officials responded to the difficulties in Germany and Eastern Europe "by devising three tactics which, they believed, would draw back the enveloping curtain." First, "throughout the summer of 1945, the Truman Administration hoped that the American possession of atomic bombs would, in the words of . . . Stimson, result in 'less barbarous relations with the Russians.' "[91] But even after Hiroshima and Nagasaki, "Eastern Europe remained sealed off." Stimson now advised changing tactics, and in September he "urged direct, bilateral discussions with the Soviets to formulate control of atomic energy and write a general peace settlement."[92] The stalemate at the London Foreign Ministers meeting, however, convinced the State Department to try and "buckle Stalin's iron fence with economic pressure."[93] Yet this tactic also failed, and soon the Soviets were making noises in the Middle East and Asia.

LaFeber argued that these Russian thrusts "were rooted more in the Soviets' desire to secure certain specific strategic bases, raw materials, and above all, to break up what Stalin considered to be the growing Western encirclement of Russia." But American officials mistook these rather traditional motives for a revolutionary offensive by Stalin and decided that the Soviets must be stopped everywhere.[94] They eventually developed the Truman Doctrine and—"the other half of the walnut"—the Marshall Plan.

Interestingly, once LaFeber disposed of the 1945-1947 period in this manner he analyzed the birth and extension of containment with a framework borrowed, in part, from the realist revisionists. He showed great sympathy for both Kennan and Lippmann and pinpointed NSC-68 as the symbol of a globalized and militarized American policy. Unlike other Cold War revisionists LaFeber did not explicitly renounce all forms of containment nor did he emphasize the "Open Door" intentions of American officials. Yet LaFeber departed from the realist revisionist account in at least four important ways: He evinced little admiration for the balance-of-power aims of traditional diplomacy; he credited American foreign policy with a sizable amount of inner coherence (though less than Williams and Kolko had); he paid abundant attention to the domestic sources of American foreign policy—and showed even greater interest in this dimension beginning with the second edition when he made more explicit use of recent Cold War revisionist works; and he presumed that a nation's foreign economic policy is frequently the most accurate measure of its international purposes.

Taken together these five men—Williams, Alperovitz, Kolko, Barnet, and LaFeber—formed the parameters of Cold War revisionism in the 1960s. Williams articulated an elaborate interpretation of American history, part of which—his Open Door thesis—exerted tremendous influence on younger diplomatic historians. Alperovitz offered an account of America's "atomic diplomacy" that shocked orthodox historians and became especially well-known to members of the foreign policy establishment. Kolko pushed Cold War revisionism to its limits by presenting a mirror image of the Johnson Administration's defense of the Vietnam intervention. Barnet's concrete proposals found a considerable political constituency among parts of the Democratic Party in the late sixties and early seventies, while LaFeber's "moderate" revisionism reached an especially wide college audience through his best-selling AMERICA, RUSSIA, AND THE COLD WAR.

CHAPTER 4: COLD WAR REVISIONISM SUBDUED?

Not everyone welcomed the reinterpretations of the Cold War revisionists with unbounded enthusiasm. For example, Herbert Feis jousted publicly with Gar Alperovitz over the issue of the atomic bomb,[1] Arthur M. Schlesinger, Jr. deplored the whole idea of a Cold War revisionism,[2] and Eugene V. Rostow dismissed Williams' criticism of Truman's handling of the postwar Soviet loan as "fantasy."[3] Nor were the revisionists reluctant to defend themselves. Alperovitz branded Feis America's "official national historian,"[4] while Williams called FOREIGN AFFAIRS the "HOUSE BEAUTIFUL of the State Department" and condemned Schlesinger as a "global interventionist" despite his misgivings about Johnson's Vietnam policy.[5]

But more substantive critiques of Cold War revisionism did, in time, appear. Two of the most thoughtful were Robert W. Tucker's THE RADICAL LEFT AND AMERICAN FOREIGN POLICY[6] and Charles S. Maier's "Revisionism and the Interpretation of Cold War Origins." Tucker ultimately rejected most of Cold War revisionism's explanations but only after subjecting them to the most careful scrutiny. Furthermore, he was scarcely uncritical of the dominant historiography that it challenged. In particular, Tucker chastized orthodox historians for smugly presuming that America's post-World War II diplomacy had been morally superior to that of other victorious states in comparable situations.[8] He suggested that the Cold War revisionists had "forced us to acknowledge the extent to which an obsessive self-interest has been central in American foreign policy" and had compelled us to recognize a "unique disparity between ideals professed and actual diplomatic behavior." And while Tucker questioned the revisionists' facile dismissal of non-economic factors and motivations and their exaggeration of the coherence and consistency of American diplomacy, he applauded them for exposing the fallaciousness of the attempts of Schlesinger to sanguinely explain recent American foreign policy as merely the unfortunate result of intellectual error.[10]

Similarly, if Maier finally evinced misgivings about the persuasiveness and sufficiency of most of their claims, he also refused to embrace the orthodoxy of the 1950s:

> . . . traditional Cold War historians no less than the revisionists have been involved in tautologies. Historical explanations are normally tested by efforts to find and weigh contradictory evidence, but Cold War analyses on both sides have relied upon propositions that cannot be disproven. Sometimes disproof is precluded by prior assumptions, and while revisionists may believe America's capitalist economy neccesitates a voracious expansionism, Cold War theorists have similarly argued that any commitment to communism is *ipso facto* destructive of a "moderate" or "legitimate" international order.[11]

He concluded that

> Spokesmen for each side present the reader with a total explanatory system that accounts for all phenomena, eliminates the possibility of disproof, and thus transcends the usual process of historical reasoning. More than in most historical controversies, the questions about what happened are transformed into concealed debate about the nature of freedom and duress, exploitation and hegemony.[12]

These analyses were largely eclipsed, however, by a far different sort of work—a book which in itself and in the uproar it triggered testified to the growing nastiness of the "orthodox-Cold War revisionist" debate—Robert James Maddox's THE NEW LEFT AND THE ORIGINS OF THE COLD WAR.[13]

Maddox's purpose was clear: to subject seven leading examples of Cold War revisionism[14] to a "very simple test" in order to compare "the evidence as presented . . . with the sources from which the evidence was taken."[15] Complaints about the revisionists' use of evidence had been routinely registered ever since the publication of THE TRAGEDY OF AMERICAN DIPLOMACY in 1959, but until Maddox's book, they had been subordinated to criticisms of more substantive issues. Thus his decision to devote an entire book to these alleged methodological sins gave THE NEW LEFT much of its distinctiveness, and it owed its notoriety to the bold conclusion that "*without exception*" these seven books "are based upon pervasive misusages of the source materials . . ." so that "even the best fails to attain the most flexible definition of scholarship."[16] According to Maddox, the most striking characteristic of revisionist historiography had been "the extent to which New Left authors . . . revised the evidence itself," and "until this fact is recognized, there can be no realistic assessment of the elements of revisionism which can justifiably be incorporated into new syntheses and those which must be discarded altogether."[17]

Characterizing these books as "polemics" which indulged in "lamentable" practices, Maddox noted that despite their distortions, they had "earned fame and academic advancement for their authors."[18] But what of the publishers? Did the scholars from whom they sought advice "before agreeing to publish these books fail to report the methods employed in them?" Or, did these publishers ignore their complaints "on the ground that these volumes were 'controversial'," and "hence eminently salable?" These reprehensible practices may have damaged faith in the integrity of their imprimatur and undermined the assumption that the books were "subjected to (and passed) rigorous critical examination."[19]

Even less excusable was the alleged failure of other diplomatic historians writing in influential journals to call attention to such practices. Their reviews "had the effect of endorsing these revisionist works as responsible pieces of historical research, their disagreements with specific interpretations notwithstanding."[20] In short, there had been "a striking malfunctioning of the critical mechanisms within the historical profession."[21]

But why had ordinarily exacting reviewers "shown a most extraordinary reluctance to expose even the most obvious New Left fictions"?[22] Maddox suggested that some of them may simply have been so unfamiliar with the evidence that they were unable to discover any discrepancies. But a "far more intriguing possibility," was that "reviewers who were perfectly aware of the procedures employed nevertheless concluded that it was unnecessary to share this information with their readers."[23] Maddox concluded with this question: "Perhaps, after all, the New Left view of American foreign policy during and immediately after World War II can *only* be sustained by doing violence to the historical record?"[24]

Those attacked by Maddox responded in various ways. Gar Alperovitz wrote a rebuttal in THE JOURNAL OF AMERICAN HISTORY;[25] Gabriel Kolko, David Horowitz, and Lloyd Gardner circulated long refutations within the historical profession; and Horowitz supplemented his reply with incendiary remarks in RAMPARTS;[26] Horowitz accused Maddox of the basest motives: revenge, jealousy, and "personal animus"[27] and claimed that "not only Feis, but George Kennan . . . , Eugene Rostow, and Schlesinger," had pressed for the "publication of the Maddox book, despite the doubts and hesitations of more objective readers."[28]

Princeton University Press was soon involved in the storm. Had it published the book because of the "lobbying efforts of a conspiracy of Cold War liberals"? In May, 1973 Horowitz sent an open letter to the Editorial Board in which he "argued that Maddox's book 'so exceeds the limits of reasonable debate, is so systematically and relentlessly dishonest in its presentation of the work which it attacks as to deprive it of any intellectual value whatsoever and to render its impact simply pernicious'."[29] Given these circumstances, Horowitz continued, "it would have seemed an elementary caution (let alone decency) to have solicited opinions."[30] It was soon revealed that in 1971 Feis and Kennan had strongly urged Maddox to write "more articles attacking the 'revisionists'," and had subsequently "written letters of recommendation to Princeton University Press in support of Maddox's manuscript."[31]

Maddox's editor, Sanford Thatcher, claimed that the manuscript's readers had agreed "on its basic soundness" and argued that Maddox had written it solely because he had been astonished by the liberties revisionist historians were taking in their use of evidence." Thatcher complained that it was "particularly regrettable . . . that those who reviewed the book in various media largely failed to address the major historiographical question which the book raised, preferring instead to focus on peripheral issues, such as the author's style and the book's 'political implications'." "Unfortunately," he concluded, "it now seems likely that Gabriel Kolko, and perhaps others who share his views will be attempting to block submission of such [i.e., revisionist] manuscripts by engaging in some sort of boycott against the Press, in reprisal for our publication of Maddox's book."[32]

THE NEW LEFT AND THE ORIGINS OF THE COLD WAR did uncover numerous examples of questionable scholarship,[33] but it also entangled Maddox in some rather serindipidous disputes. For example, he asserted that in ARCHITECTS OF ILLUSION Lloyd Gardner had failed

> . . . to provide any real evidence that the men charged with the conduct of American diplomacy acted out of the motives and assumptions he attributed to them. If, for instance, American policies toward Eastern Europe were dictated by the fear of depression and a shift to the left (even accepting Gardner's qualification that Eastern Europe was seen as but part of a larger struggle), one would expect to find those who made policy discussing the issues in such a related way with each other if not publicly. Gardner was unable to show that any such discussion ever took place. His efforts to deflect attention from this most crucial gap in his argument were ingenious, but they cannot withstand analysis.[34]

After enumerating about twenty examples of "irrelevant evidence, misused quotations, jumbled figures, and distortions of documentary materials," he suggested that ARCHITECTS OF ILLUSION is a fitting title for a book that is in many ways itself based on illusion."[35] Maddox claimed, for instance, that Gardner had misused a quotation when he wrote that

> when Secretary of State Byrnes told Truman that the atomic bomb "might well put us in a position to dictate our own terms at the end of the war," he was referring to relations with Russia Gardner's source for this quotation, Truman's MEMOIRS, permits *no doubt* that Byrnes' remark was made in the context of dictating terms to Japan, not to Russia.[36]

Gardner replied that

> Maddox's presentation of the accusation proves we are, after all, human. First, Byrnes was not Secretary of State when this statement was made, Stettinius was. Second, that interpretation of Byrnes' remark is perfectly justified, given Byrnes' documented statements on other occasions, the context of the discussion, and Truman's quotation of Byrnes not on one point, but on two in the same paragraph:
>
> > "Byrnes had already told me that the weapon might be so powerful as to be potentially capable of wiping out entire cities and killing people on an unprecedented scale. And he had added that in his belief the bomb might well put us in a position to dictate our own terms at the end of the war. (Truman, I, Signet edition, p. 104)"[37]

But in the immediately preceding sentence in ARCHITECTS OF ILLUSION which neither Maddox nor Gardner cited, Gardner wrote: "Where Stimson only hoped there might be some way to get 'less barbarous' relations with Stalin, Byrnes seemed convinced of it."[38] And in the full paragraphs of Truman's MEMOIRS there was this passage:

> I listened with absorbed interest, for Stimson was a man of great wisdom and foresight. He went into considerable detail in describing the nature and the power of the projected weapon. If expectations were to be realized, he told me, *the atomic bomb would be certain to have a decisive influence on our relations with other countries.* And if it worked, the bomb, in all probability, would shorten the war.
>
> Byrnes had already told me that the weapon might be so powerful as to be potentially capable of wiping out entire cities and killing people on an unprecedented scale. And he had added that in his belief the bomb might well put us in a position to dictate our own terms at the end of the war.
>
> *Stimson, on the other hand, seemed at least as much concerned with the role of the atomic bomb in the shaping of history as in its capacity to shorten this war.* As yet, of course, no one could positively know that the gigantic effort that was being made would be successful. Nevertheless, the Secretary appeared confident of the outcome and told me that in all probability success would be attained within the next few months. He also suggested that I designate a committee to study and advise me of the implications of this new force.[39]

In other words, although Stimson was at least as concerned with the broader diplomatic consequences of the atomic bomb (including relations with Russia) as with its immediate impact on Japan, Truman *appeared* to say that, in contrast, Byrnes was primarily interested in the bomb's ability to end the war. Truman did not claim that Byrnes was oblivious to the bomb's political implications but, rather, inferred that Stimson was more interested in this dimension than was Byrnes. The sentence of Gardner's not cited by Maddox (i.e., "Where Stimson had only hoped there might be some way to get 'less barbarous' relations with Stalin, Byrnes seemed convinced of it") did not seem to be supported by the Truman paragraphs. Remember, Stimson was, if anything, more concerned than was Byrnes with the diplomatic ramifications of this weapon. But Maddox was not justified in asserting that "there can be no doubt" that Byrnes was referring to Japan in the sentence quoted in THE NEW LEFT, for on the basis of these paragraphs from the MEMOIRS it was impossible to be sure whether Byrnes' reference was to Japan or Russia or to a combination of both![40]

Similar exchanges among Maddox, the seven revisionists, reviewers who liked THE NEW LEFT, and those that hated it continued for some time. They often verged on the surreal.

* * * * *

Maddox's real intention in THE NEW LEFT AND THE ORIGINS OF THE COLD WAR was to create a "smoking pistol" of joint culpability by insinuating that the "political commitment" of these historians had led them to pervert their scholarship. Lacking conclusive proof that they conspired even indirectly to hoodwink their colleagues and the public, Maddox tried to involve them in a plot to sustain their theses through lies, distortions, and other unethical practices. And *he* provided the missing link—the "smoking pistol": a "New Left" yearning to overthrow the existing political (and historiographical) order by a "footnote revolution."

These motivations notwithstanding, did Maddox prove his two primary charges? On balance the answer must be no. To sustain his first point—that "New Left" history was distinguished by "pervasive misusages of the source materials"—Maddox applied "a very simple test" to "seven of the most prominent New Left works" by comparing "the evidence as presented by the revisionists with the sources from which the evidence was taken.[41] The problem with this test was that it was not so simple as Maddox believed. To be a simple test there would have to have been a relatively easy way to separate a documentary fact from a personal interpretation: does *this* fact yield *this* interpretation? But as the disscussion of the Gardner exchange revealed, it is frequently difficult to with confidence answer this question. Beyond this conundrum there lay an argument about the notion of history itself. At what point, if any, in the process of writing history, does an "imaginative leap" occur which supplements a "literal-mindedness" with something else? Maddox entered murky waters when he applied his "simple test." That he sensed a problem here may account for his quiet insertion of two additional criteria to judge the validity of the "New Left" case: the reasonableness of its interpretations and the sufficiency of the evidence offered to sustain an argument. In response to a charge that THE NEW LEFT dealt primarily with interpretations and not with the fabrication of evidence Maddox asserted:

> Professor [Warren] Kimball . . . writes as though I somewhere made a pledge to avoid *all* questions of interpretations. But I made no such statement, and felt free to discuss interpretations whenever it seemed appropriate.[42]

But Maddox had promised to confine his analysis to matters of "fact." For him to ground his entire case on a "simple test" to discover the *facts,* and then to evaluate *interpretations* (without so informing the reader) was misleading. Second, in several places Maddox argued that revisionist historians had failed "to demonstrate convincingly"[43] an assertion or to produce "the scantiest evidence"[44] to affirm a thesis. These criticisms, of course, rested on different ground from the "simple test" that Maddox claimed the "New Left" had singularly failed. In short, Maddox retreated to other tests when his simple one proved problematic without indicating that he had shifted the basis of his critique.

There were two related difficulties. With very few exceptions Maddox did not specify whether the examples of poor scholarship which he cited reflected the overall quality of the books or whether they are the most flagrant instances of "pervasive misuages." It is true that Maddox did uncover a number of glaring discrepancies between interpretations and evidence. He generally failed, however, to compare the relative importance of these "errors" with the central thesis of the book under scrutiny. Finally, Maddox's refusal to apply his "simple test" to orthodox historians of Cold War origins, while implying that the "New Left" case could *only* be sustained by unsavory practices showed questionable judgment.

Maddox claimed that certain unnamed American diplomatic historians had tried to discourage the publication of his book on the ground that no work "ought to call attention to the possibility" of compromised scholarly obligations. John J. Rumbarger, former editor of the AHA NEWSLETTER, contended that Maddox's complaints in this regard stemmed solely from two letters of rejection.[45] Rumbarger argued that although Maddox knew that the NEWSLETTER was not a scholarly journal, he nevertheless submitted an essay that had been excerpted from THE NEW LEFT AND THE ORIGINS OF THE COLD WAR. According to Rumbarger,

> . . . what cannot be dismissed or ignored is his failure to report the real reason for the rejection of his first submission to the *Newsletter* as it was reported to him. I wrote to Maddox at the end of August, 1971 that the critic to whom I had forwarded his

> manuscript (which turns out to have been virtually his entire chapter on Gabriel Kolko's THE POLITICS OF WAR) thought that although some parts were of interest and "certainly worth airing," much of what you had to say "is on a quibbling basis." I also told Maddox that this reader (and I) thought you guilty of much of what you ascribe to Kolko in attempting to generalize from THE POLITICS OF WAR to all revisionist interpretations... Finally I told him the reader considered "the whole piece quarrelsome and intemperate."[46]

Was this the sole basis of Maddox's charge that "scholars, students, and lay readers alike" had been "poorly served by what can only be regarded as a striking malfunctioning of the critical mechanisms within the historical profession"?[47] Apparently there was much more, for Maddox added that

> I used these readers' reports from the *AHA Newsletter* because they stated the case most openly—many of the comments I received directly said so in euphemistic terms. Because Mr. Rumbarger could not possibly know what comments and/or reader's reports I received from sources other than the *Newsletter,* any statement of his about what my argument was "soley based" on is necessarily uninformed. If he alleges that I misquoted from the reports, I am prepared to produce my copies.[48]

Fortunately, this dispute ended here, but its character was indicative of the general atmosphere produced by the radical revisionist-orthodox debate by the early 1970s. The publication of THE NEW LEFT and the vitriolic arguments it prompted marked the culmination of an increasingly angry controversy over Cold War origins. The very appearance of a book which searched for culprits was one sign that the substantive historical themes had been largely exhausted. Furthermore, that a critique as flawed as Maddox's could have been credited by so many historians as a sufficient anti-revisionist statement surely testified to the hostility produced by this "scholarly" disagreement.

In a masterful understatement Robert H. Ferrell admitted in 1972 that "the older generation has not been charmed by the Cold War revisionists."[49] In fact, it was "profoundly disturbing to historians who had grown up during the Cold War or had engaged in its crusading period,"[50] and it surely "provoked hostility, resentment, and fear in some segments of the profession."[51] But in some ways the frequently ad hominem character of this controversy was merely a symptom of animosities evident within the wider historical profession. Like many academic organizations in the late sixties and early seventies the American Historical Association became embroiled in a number of "political" disputes centering on the Vietnam War but touching on other social issues as well. A "Radical Caucus" led by Staughton Lynd and Howard Zinn repeatedly dueled with the Association's "establishment" and probably commanded the support of roughly forty per cent of the full membership for a few years. The annual Business Meeting provided the occasion for tumultuous confrontations which climaxed in a near riot in 1971 when courtly John K. Fairbank, a past President of the AHA, was accused by the "insurgents" of forcibly preventing a member from gaining the microphone. This unlikely event resulted in general embarrassment, and, as America continued its withdrawal from Vietnam, the Association returned to more mundane activities.

* * * * *

Why did Cold War revisionism capture the imagination of so many students and scholars in the late '60s and early '70s? No doubt its popularity in part rested on the inherent persuasiveness of its arguments. But its explanatory power cannot wholly account for the enthusiam generated in the academy by Cold War revisionism. The moral fervor and idealism of this critique certainly appealed to the young and almost young of a decade ago. Beneath the often-noted reluctance[52] of the revisionists to compare American international conduct with that of other states and the consequent tendency to set impossibly high standards for the United States, there lurked a profound desire to transform America into a universal example. If not all of these scholars described their vision with the explicitness of Williams, there was little doubt that most of them dreamed of a true city on the hill possessed of a providential mission. This inspirational message, especially when uttered in a political culture redolent with egalitarianism, was bound to carry force.

There were also at least three additional reasons for Cold War revisionism's impressive influence during these years: the extraordinary and apparently permanent nature of American power, the experience of Vietnam, and the character of the orthodox defense of American foreign policy. By the mid-sixties America's overwhelming power appeared more entrenched than ever. The intoxicating "victory" in the Cuban missile crisis, unprecedented economic prosperity in the United States coupled with a new sluggishness in Soviet growth rates, the remarkable achievements of American technology and agriculture, and the enfeeblement of China because of the Cultural Revolution, indicated to some commentators that, short of nuclear war, America's continued supremacy was virtually assured.[53] Such predictions were of no solace to those Americans who pictured the United States as an abusive, insensitive, greedy, undemocratic, racist society. But for Williams, Kolko, and many of the other Cold War revisionists, the American sun had already begun to set. The apparent invulnerability of capitalist America was, in fact, a mirage disguising a reality of untamable Third World revolutions (Kolko), powerful socialist regimes (Williams), and acute resource dependence (Harry Magdoff).[54] There was, of course, an irony here, for it was America's alleged vulnerability that formed the core of the Johnson Administration's defense of its involvement in Vietnam. According to this argument, the credibility and ultimately the security of the United States depended upon a willingness to defeat Communist aggression wherever it occurred. Kolko and Dean Rusk agreed that Vietnam stood as a symbol of America's ability and determination to act, and both men believed that a defeat in Southeast Asia would give an enormous boost to the morale of world revolutionary movements (Kolko) or to the power of international Communism (Rusk), which would, in turn, administer a devastating blow to America's vision of world order (Rusk) or to the American empire (Kolko).

Even from the perspective of the 1980s it remains difficult to guage the exact relationship between the Vietnam War and Cold War revisionism. Lloyd C. Gardner was correct in claiming that the audience for a "critical scholarship on all aspects and periods of United States foreign relations" was "stimulated and broadened by the Vietnam controversy.[55] Yet to thereby conclude that in the absence of Vietnam a radical revisionism would not have arisen, or that, once offered, it would have been unanimously dismissed would be unjustified. Robert W. Tucker, for example, saw Vietnam "as much a precipitant as a cause of the disaffection that enabled radical criticism to gain its . . . influence,"[56] and argued that

> . . . Vietnam must itself be placed against the decline in the sixties of the classic cold war. This decline could have been expected to give rise to revisionism, including radical revisionism, quite without the war, and the emergence of the radical critique may in fact be traced to the years immediately preceding Vietnam. With the decline of the cold war, forces of change within domestic society that had long been suppressed were bound to become manifest.[57]

Yet it is undeniable that many of the historical judgments reached bv the Cold War revisionists betrayed a present-mindedness directly affected by the Vietnam experience, or at the very least, by conditions which, while significant in the 1960s, were either unknown or drastically different two decades earlier. For example, Gabriel Kolko, in describing the world of 1945, emphasized forces and elements which seemed more appropriately included in a survey of the late 1960s. Kolko claimed that the global salience of Soviet-American antagonism had been vastly overrated. In fact, the United States, because of a panicky anti-Communism, had missed an opportunity to form a conservative détente with Moscow immediately after World War II, but, because of the overwhelming energy of peasant revolutionary movements, this condominium of power was never built. Similarly, Kolko discovered in the Europe of 1945 a left-wing Resistance and a revolutionary potential remarkably like those which were thought to exist in the Southern hemisphere twenty years later. According to this view, the ideological hostility allegedly evinced by the United States toward the European "Left" (consistently described as a vast, homogeneous mass) was simply a precursor of its later behavior in Africa, Asia, and Latin America. Finally, the notion of a Europe transformed by World War II from the seat of corrupt reaction into an infinitely malleable landscape ready for radical revolution resembled the picture being painted by many American liberals in the 1960s of the post-colonial world.[58]

Despite the impact of contemporary circumstances on Cold War revisionism, these scholars did not invent present-mindedness. Lloyd Gardner was correct in suggesting that "there has never been a time when the nation's political consciousness was separate and apart from its historical consciousness. It won't do to try to explain away revisionism on these grounds, unless one is prepared to do the same for other interpretations."[59] In fact both the orthodox historiography of the 1950s and the Cold War revisionism of the 1960s were significantly affected by their respective political environments. But, while the present-mindedness of radical revisionism was often maligned, virtually no one in the 1950s had called attention to this element in the conventional historiography. The failure to do so was but another manifestation of the remarkably pervasive consensus which characterized public defenses and scholarly accounts of American foreign policy during the high tide of the Cold War. Yet orthodox histories had been informed by the circumstances of the 1950s, and their judgments about the origins of the Cold War were consequently affected. For instance, it was common practice to exaggerate the power of the Soviet Union in the 1940s and to attribute to it qualities that it did not possess until at least a decade later. Likewise, orthodox historians viewed containment as a global policy sprung full-grown in 1947 designed from the beginning to combat international Communism. The fact that containment had gradually evolved into something rather more ambitious after 1950 was either unappreciated, or described as an inevitable development. Indeed, at a time when the Cold War consensus was beginning to fragment, the exaggerations, eccentricities, and seemingly anachronistic present-mindedness of orthodox historiography lent to Cold War revisionism a persuasiveness it might not otherwise have enjoyed.

Did the Cold War revisionists have a long-term effect on the writing of American diplomatic history? On balance, it would seem so. According to Robert A. Divine,

> . . . the revisionist impact has been lasting. Few today would affirm the more extreme revisionist views of the 1960s, but neither would many repeat the simplistic account of how the Cold War began that prevailed in the 1950s. The revisionists forced all diplomatic historians to reassess the factors contributing to the Cold War and to explain this historical development in a more complex and satisfactory way. There is not yet a fully-accepted synthesis on the origins of the Cold War, but one is gradually emerging, and the revisionists played an important role in bringing it about.[60]

Walter LaFeber, from a rather different perspective, agreed that Cold War revisionism brought some needed changes to the study of American diplomatic history.[61] Because of revisionism more scholars have tried to avoid writing diplomatic history "in the one-statesman-to-the-other tradition" and have instead emphasized "how we have to understand the domestic side in depth before we can understand U.S. foreign policy." Second, they cannot dismiss "the economic dimension of that policy" with nearly the same ease as the orthodox historians of an earlier generation. Third, LaFeber noted that the Cold War revisionists provided "a scholarly basis for questioning power" and for "balancing power in the U.S. political system." That is, these revisionists helped to legitimize critiques of American global hegemony and the imperial Presidency. Finally, because of Cold War revisionism more attention has been given to "how U.S. policy impacts on other peoples, especially in the Third World," while not viewing that policy "as simply a one-way street

(Washington to the U.S. official in the field). That in turn has made us more aware of Third World concerns, and also, Soviet concerns."[62]

* * * * *

Fortunately, the nadir was reached by the Cold War controversy because Maddox's attacks did not last very long. There soon appeared a spate of "post-revisionist" works synthesizing in varying measures the insights and arguments of both Cold War and realist revisionism. Among the most prominent of these interpretations were John Lewis Gaddis' THE UNITED STATES AND THE ORIGINS OF THE COLD WAR, 1941-1947; George C. Herring's AID TO RUSSIA, 1941-1946; Lynn E. Davis' THE COLD WAR BEGINS; Daniel Yergin's SHATTERED PEACE; and Bruce R. Kuniholm's THE ORIGINS OF THE COLD WAR IN THE NEAR EAST.[63] Of these books the last three possess particular interest for this study because their authors maintained extremely close ties with the Carter Administration. Davis served four years as Deputy Assistant Secretary of Defense for Policy Plans and National Security Council Affairs, Kuniholm was a member of the State Department's Policy Planning Staff, while Yergin declined two invitations to join the PPS and was highly regarded by several senior Carter officials.

Gaddis, who had been trained by Divine at the University of Texas in the mid-1960s, wrote a book which, if it had been published a decade or two earlier, would surely have been labeled a revisionist interpretation, for it challenged, or at least modified, several of orthodoxy's major arguments. Foremost was Gaddis' rejection of the claim that the Cold War had been caused by an ideologically motivated Soviet Union, in possession of a master plan for imperialist expansion and world revolution, which had forced a confrontation with an innocent and wholly benign America. Instead Gaddis suggested that the Cold War had arisen out of an extremely complex dialectic of actions, reactions, perceptions, misperceptions, capabilities, and constraints. Unlike the orthodox historians (or the radical revisionists) he was reluctant to assign responsibility for the Cold War, yet at the same time he criticized those who viewed the conflict as irrepressible,

> . . . if for no other reason than the methodological impossibility of "proving" inevitability in history. The power vacuum in Central Europe caused by Germany's collapse made a Russian-American

> confrontation likely; it did not make it inevitible. Men as well as circumstances make foreign policy, and through such drastic expedients as war, appeasement, or resignation, policy-makers can always alter difficult situations. . . . One may legitimately ask why they do not choose to go this far, but to view their actions as predetermined by blind, impersonal "forces" is to deny the complexity and particularity of human behavior, not to mention the ever-present possibility of accident.[64]

And in his assessment of American actions in 1945 and 1946 Gaddis flirted with some of the revisionists' conclusions:

> Convinced that technology had given them the means to shape the postwar world to their liking, Washington officials assumed that these instruments would leave the Russians no choice but to comply with American peace plans. Attempts to extract concessions from Moscow in return for a loan failed, however, when the Soviet Union turned to German reparations to meet its reconstruction needs. The Russians also refused to be impressed by the atomic bomb, leaving the Truman Administration with the choice of actually using it, or returning to *quid pro quo* bargaining. American omnipotence turned out to be an illusion because Washington policy-makers failed to devise strategies for applying their newly gained power effectively in practical diplomacy.[65]

Gaddis' evaluation of the Truman Doctrine was, as we will see in the next chapter, very close to that of Kennan, Lippmann, and Morgenthau, and clearly at odds with orthodox conclusions:

> By presenting aid to Greece and Turkey in terms of an ideological conflict between two ways of life, Washington officials encouraged a simplistic view of the Cold War which was, in time, to imprison American diplomacy in an ideological straightjacket almost as confining as that which restricted Soviet foreign policy. Trapped in their own rhetoric, leaders of the United States found it difficult to respond to the conciliatory gestures which emanated from the Kremlin following Stalin's death, and through their inflexibility, may well have contributed to the perpetuation of the Cold War.

Yet the preceding passage should also indicate that Gaddis was no Cold War revisionist, if only because of his refusal to portray the Soviet Union as a fully traditional, defensive Power consistently guided by *Realpolitik* considerations. Indeed, to the extent that Gaddis believed that the Cold War had been "caused" by anyone, he asserted that primary responsibility lay with Stalin, though not for the reasons given by orthodox historians:

> Little is known even today about how Stalin defined his options, but it does seem safe to say that the very nature of the Soviet system afforded him a larger selection of alternatives than were open to leaders of the United States. The Russian dictator was immune from pressures of Congress, public opinion, and the press. Even ideology did not restrict him: Stalin was the master of communist doctrine, not a prisoner of it, and could modify or suspend Marxism-Leninism whenever it suited him to do so. This is not to say that Stalin wanted a Cold War—he had every reason to avoid one. But his absolute powers did give him more chances to surmount the internal restraints on his policy than were available to his democratic counterparts in the West.[67]

Furthermore, Gaddis ridiculed the revisionists not only for their alleged economic determinism but for their inconsistent use of that dogma. He noted that they frequently took literally only official American statements of economic interest, disregarding as irrelevant whatever other explanations policy-makers gave for their actions, but instead of logically concluding that the Cold War was the inevitable result of two diametrically opposed economic systems and ideologies in conflict with each other, the revisionists asserted that the United States, "because of its military and economic superiority . . . , could have accepted Moscow's postwar demands without endangering American security.[68] This procedure, Gaddis argued,

> . . . places revisionists in the odd position of employing a single-cause explanation of human behavior, yet criticizing the subjects they deal with for not liberating themselves from the mechanistic framework which they, as historians, have imposed.[69]

Gaddis' solution was to emphasize several themes—domestic constraints, bureaucratic rivalries, and political interests—which historians had usefully employed in a variety of other contexts but which had been curiously overlooked by most interpreters of the Cold War controversy. For example, in seeking to understand Roosevelt's Polish policy he pointed to the President's perceived need to retain the support of Polish-American voters in crucial states like Illinois and Ohio in the 1944 election. Unlike many orthodox historians who enthusiastically applauded Roosevelt for his determination to apply the principles of the Atlantic Charter to Poland or those revisionists who saw in his diplomacy a provocative attempt to extend the Open Door to Eastern Europe, Gaddis asserted that Roosevelt's options had been significantly shaped and limited by domestic political realities. Cold War revisionists had frequently described American foreign policy as if it were the product of a single-minded structure, but Gaddis suggested that bureaucratic competition was often so severe that no cohesive strategy was possible. For instance, orthodox historians had claimed that Stalin had used the reparations issue as a pretext for communizing his German occupation zone. Gaddis, however, argued that rivalries among the State, War, and Treasury departments in regard to Germany's future produced several contradictory policies which exacerbated Soviet distrust of Western intentions.

> How, then, did the Cold War begin? It . . . grew out of a complicated interaction of external and internal developments inside both the United States and the Soviet Union. The external situation—circumstances beyond the control of either power—left Americans and Russians facing one another across prostrated Europe. . . . Internal influences in the Soviet Union—the search for security, the role of ideology, massive postwar reconstruction needs, the personality of Stalin—together with those in the United States—the ideal of self-determination, fear of communism, the illusion of omnipotence fostered by American economic strength and the atomic bomb—made the resulting confrontation a hostile one.[70]

By judiciously blending orthodox, realist, and revisionist explanations and by introducing important new themes, THE UNITED STATES AND THE ORIGINS OF THE COLD WAR initiated a search for a post-revisionist synthesis—a search that would continue throughout the 1970s.

* * * * *

The year after Gaddis' work appeared George C. Herring, Jr. published AID TO RUSSIA, 1941-1946: *Strategy, Diplomacy, and the Origins of the Cold War.* A graduate student at the University of Virginia in the early 1960s Herring had been Gaddis' immediate predecessor at Ohio University before moving to the University of Kentucky. According to Herring much of Cold War revisionism suffered from serious weaknesses:

> Few studies deal with the problem [of lend-lease] in any depth, and most have not taken advantage of the abundance of archival and manuscript sources that has become available to scholars only in recent years. . . . Interpretations have been highly colored by the emotions and prejudices of the times. Authors have ignored the context in which major decisions were made; they have failed to judge the diplomacy of the period on its own terms. Finally, both the [conservative] revisionists of the forties and . . . [the radicals] of the sixties and seventies share an implicit acceptance of what D. W. Brogan has termed the "illusion of American omnipotence." They assume that the United States had the capacity to prevent the Cold War. They argue that different policies on economic assistance alone might have averted or at least limited the conflict that developed after 1945.[71]

On the other hand, he argued that lend-lease aid to the Soviet Union involved something more that a simple American desire to help the Russians defeat Germany in the shortest possible time:

> . . . U.S. policy makers were keenly aware of the potential political value of economic assistance to the USSR and throughout the period they vigorously debated the tactics that should be employed to make it an effective instrument of diplomacy. This debate forms a central issue in the making of American policy toward Russia during these years; it reveals much about American attitudes toward the Soviet Union and about the goals and instruments of U.S. policy.[72]

Moreover, in contrast to Feis and other orthodox interpreters Herring (like Gaddis) was sensitive to the ways in which domestic political pressures could affect decisively American foreign policy. For example, he argued that

> Those responsible for handling assistance for the USSR had to consider the deep-seated suspicions Americans had long entertained toward the Soviet Union and communism. More important, they had to take into account the political implications of foreign aid itself. Lend-lease represented a sharp departure from past American practices in foreign relations. Americans valued its importance as an instrument of war, but because of its novelty and expense it involved they always regarded it with a suspicious eye. It depended upon annual appropriations from Congress.

> Throughout the war it remained a potentially volatile political issue, and could not be kept out of partisan politics.[73]

In order to determine the relationship between lend-lease aid and the origins of the Cold War, Herring posed questions that implicitly acknowledged a debt to the Cold War revisionists, for they probably would not have even been asked in the 1950s: [F]or what purposes and in what manner did the United States employ its economic assistance to the USSR during the years from 1941 to 1946, and what effect did its policies have on Soviet-American relations?"[74]

According to this view, in handling lend-lease to Russia, FDR "always gave top priority to strategic concerns," for he "regarded economic assistance as a principal means of holding together the uneasy alliance until the common threat could be removed" and "feared that if the United States did not provide timely assistance to the Russians, Stalin might be tempted to conclude a separate peace with Hitler."[75]

But orthodox historians had allegedly erred by contending that American officials had ignored postwar problems in their concentration on winning the war. To construct a stable, prosperous, and peaceful postwar world U.S. policy-makers "worked for a peace based on the principles of the Atlantic Charter—" free trade, self-determination, and a universal organization— "principles that squared with traditional American ideals and with tangible vital interests."[76] And to induce the Russians to participate in this world many American officials "perceived that lend-lease could be used as a political instrument. . . ."[77]

Anticipating to some degree the "Riga-Yalta" taxonomy developed a few years later by Daniel Yergin (and which we will shortly discuss) Herring claimed that during the war "there were two schools of thought on how economic assistance might best be used for political gain."[78] One group, led by former ambassador William Bullitt, ambassadors Steinhardt, Standley, and Harriman, and General John Deane shared a general pessimism about Russian-American cooperation and concluded that accommodation was only possible if U.S. aid were "conditioned on the receipt of a *quid pro quo*:"

> The Russians, they argued, could not be dealt with on any other basis. They would not understand or appreciate American generosity; they would not repay American aid in good will. Only if the United States required military, political, or economic concessions in return for its help could it be sure to protect its

own interests and establish the mutual respect and reciprocity that was essential for postwar collaboration between the two nations.[79]

The other group, whose views were most notably articulated by former ambassador Joseph E. Davies, General James H. Burns, and Harry Hopkins, were "generally sympathetic toward the Soviet Union, arguing that its extreme concern about security derived from a history of costly invasions and from the open hostility capitalist nations had displayed toward it since the revolution."[80] If treated generously the Russians might "respond in kind" and "lay a firm basis for postwar collaboration." Roosevelt, Herring suggested, consistently supported the second group, partly because he hoped that unconditional aid might contribute to postwar amity, but primarily because the President believed that such assistance would promote wartime cooperation.

Herring concluded that, on balance, Roosevelt's reasoning was "sound," for "those who advocated the use of lend-lease as an instrument of pressure exaggerated its strength."[81] The "*quid pro quo*" strategy might have wrested limited concessions from Moscow, but it would not not have compelled Stalin "to conform to American standards of behavior in international relations" nor would it have dissuaded him from establishing a "buffer zone in Eastern Europe." Indeed, had Roosevelt followed Harriman's advice, it would probably have aroused the Soviet leader's already profound anxieties and might have led him to press toward his objectives all the more rapidly and ruthlessly."[82] As it was, FDR's policies may "have contributed to later Russian-American conflict by raising hopes that could not be realized"[83] and for failing to make clear to Stalin that postwar assistance depended on public and Congressional support.

Roosevelt's handling of lend-lease convinced Herring that the Cold War revisionists' perception of an America aggressively employing its economic power to shape the world in its own image was seriously mistaken, for while the President's approach was motivated by expediency and self-interest, it also suggested how far he "was willing to go to establish a workable relationship" with the Soviet Union.[84] Herring admitted that the Cold War revisionists "correctly noted" that Truman "initiated significant changes in lend-lease policy" and that "these changes stemmed from a growing distrust of the Russians and were designed to influence Soviet policy in Europe."[85] They were also right to observe that "Truman was much less sympathetic to Stalin's security concerns than Roosevelt," and that "he regarded"

Stalin's "policies in Eastern Europe as immoral and a threat to America's aims for the postwar world."[86] But, Herring warned, "to stop there is to provide only an incomplete and distorted picture of the circumstances under which Truman acted,"[87] for the American desire to assist the USSR waned in proportion to Stalin's refusal to implement the American interpretations of Yalta's European provisions. And, in any case, domestic political pressures made it impossible for Truman to continue Roosevelt's unconditional aid policy and extremely difficult to stockpile the Russians after the German surrender.

To be sure, the Truman Administration had largely accepted Harriman's view of lend-lease as a diplomatic weapon, but because of domestic constraints and bureaucratic confusion and bungling, "the administration did not employ lend-lease *systematically* to achieve its foreign policy objectives."[88] Nevertheless, the abrupt cutback in aid after V-E Day "did contribute to the rise of Soviet-American tension" by reinforcing Stalin's fears and misgivings. Furthermore, "the evasive and ambiguous replies to Soviet overtures [for a loan], the long delay before making a formal offer, the lost request, and the conditions connected to the loan negotiations could not have been better calculated to strengthen the already profound Russian suspicions of American intentions."[89] Yet Herring suggested that it would be

> . . . naive to assume that postwar American generosity would have evoked deep gratitude and good will in the Soviet Union. The experience of lend-lease in fact suggests that postwar aid, by itself, would not have done much to allay Soviet suspicions. Economic aid could have acted as a healing force only if accompanied by an American willingness to accept, at least tacitly, predominant Soviet influence in Eastern Europe. The wisdom of such a course has much to commend it in retrospect, but history and experience had not prepared American leaders to act in this fashion.[90]

Thus, at least from early 1945 the United States had "attempted to exploit the apparent advantage offered by postwar assistance" but had done so "erratically and ineffectively, securing no tangible gain and only contributing to the rise of tension" with Moscow.[91] But these aid policies, Herring claimed, did not "cause" the Cold War. Clashing Soviet and American interests in Eastern Europe had brought on the Cold War, and the issue of economic assistance represented "as much a result as a cause" of that conflict.[92]

In essence, Herring accepted the Cold War revisionist thesis that lend-lease aid had been used politically to gain concessions from the Soviet Union. But Herring challenged the revisionists by contending that wartime assistance was primarily military in intent and that Truman's policies deepened Stalin's mistrust but did not constitute a leading cause of the Cold War. That conflict, for Herring, arose in Eastern Europe, and although he apparently concluded that the Cold War could have been avoided by an American willingness to grant to the Soviets a security zone there, he also realized that American experience, principles, and domestic opinion forbade that cession. In other words, in meeting one revisionist argument (that of economic aid), Herring opened the door on a further revisionist contention (that of U.S. intransigence in Eastern Europe) without fully confronting it.

* * * * *

The issue of Eastern Europe, however, did form the primary focus of Lynn E. Davis, THE COLD WAR BEGINS: *Soviet-American Conflict Over Eastern Europe.* She began with three questions inspired by Norman A. Graebner. First, "what was the exact importance of Eastern Europe in the origins of the Cold War?" Second, "why did the United States exhibit such a lack of concern with developments in this part of the world prior to World War II?" And finally, why did the United States continue to oppose Soviet actions in Eastern Europe after 1945 and even go so far as to call for the 'liberation' of these countries from Communist control?"[93]

Like almost all of the 1970s' post-revisionists Davis explicitly rejected the answers of both orthodoxy and Cold War revisionism:

> [Revisionist] interpretations are no more sufficient than earlier [orthodox] interpretations which characterized American policy merely as a reaction to a well-planned Soviet policy to achieve political control of Eastern Europe. These . . . historians have gone too far to the other extreme and have been equally simplistic in their descriptions of United States policy and their judgments as to responsibility for escalation of conflict. They ignore the decentralized nature of the American policy-making process. They never consider the possibility that conflict may develop over issues and interests which are not clearly thought through in

> advance or may arise through imperceptible commitments and bureaucratic momentum.[94]

In short, like Gaddis and Herring, Davis sought to invest her explanation of Cold War origins with a sensitivity to domestic political and bureaucratic dimensions.

The central question of Davis' study was "how and why did an initial commitment by the United States to the Atlantic Charter principles gradually develop into explicit confrontation between the United States and the Soviet Union over Eastern Europe?"[95] More specifically, Davis wished to discover the manner in which the United States became enmeshed in conflict over the political future of Eastern Europe and to identify those issues which escalated Soviet-American tension; she wanted to determine the degree of deliberate calculation with which the United States decided to oppose Moscow in Eastern Europe; she sought to articulate the intellectual rationale of that policy; and she wished to judge the broader global consequences of American conduct in Eastern Europe.

Davis concluded that American policy toward Eastern Europe during World War II was characterized by two somewhat contradictory concerns: maintenance of Allied unity and implementation of the Atlantic Charter principles. At first, American officials tried to achieve these goals by involving Moscow in the plans for a United Nations organization, but when the Soviets showed little enthusiasm for the project, Roosevelt at Yalta and Byrnes at Potsdam attempted to prevent a public rupture by "finessing every issue which threatened to obstruct agreement."[96] To this end American policy-makers "were continually satisfied to reach an agreement in principle without spelling out the steps in its execution."[97] At the same time, they remained committed to the implementation of the Atlantic Charter principles. According to Davis, they realized that the rhetorical abandonment of these principles would have lessened tension with Stalin,

> . . . however, prevention of conflict with the Soviet Union was never considered the most important United States objective. They refused to accept publicly Soviet unilateral determination of the political future of Eastern Europe, and as a result they failed to achieve either goal, cooperation with the Soviet Union or implementation of the Atlantic Charter principles.[98]

On the other hand, she emphasized that "American officials did not plan in advance or spend a great deal of time formulating specific responses to Soviet actions in Eastern Europe," for this area remained "very much a peripheral issue throughout the war, and what policy did exist was largely the result of an accretion of daily telegrams."[99]

According to Davis, "almost by default, responsibility for the day-to-day formulation of American responses to Soviet actions in Eastern Europe"[100] fell to five men in the State Department's Office of European Affairs—James Clement Dunn, H. Freeman Matthews, Cavendish W. Cannon, Charles E. Bohlen, and Elbridge Durbrow. In designing an Eastern European policy these officials used their commitment to the Atlantic Charter principles as a starting point but soon concluded that although strong public and Presidential support existed for these principles, there was little inclination to risk war with the Soviet Union in Eastern Europe in defense of them. Instead of educating the American public about the difficulties involved in implementing these principles in the face of serious Soviet resistance both Roosevelt and these State Department officials raised "extraordinarily high hopes" about gaining universal acceptance of the Atlantic Charter through the UNO. Second, while American officials never defined any U.S. security interests in Eastern Europe, they still refused to tolerate the creation of a Russian sphere of influence there, because that would have signified the perpetuation of dangerous balance-of-power diplomatic techniques. The ironic result, Davis argued, was that the United States, by its desire to prevent war by ruling out spheres of influence "was brought into conflict with the Soviet Union over the political future of all of Eastern Europe."[101] Third, these State Department officials "invariably linked . . . individual questions in Eastern Europe with other issues. . . ."[102] and "continually expressed the fear that Soviet unilateral diplomacy in Eastern Europe would undermine the whole cause of international collaboration."[103] Moreover, American policy-makers (save Stimson) never questioned the "desirability and feasibility of establishing democratic governments"[104] in Eastern Europe. Rather, they optimistically likened the situation in this region to the conditions which confronted the American Founding Fathers. These officials realized that free elections in Eastern Europe would mean the ouster of Soviet-sponsored regimes, yet they pressed their desire to see representative governments elected. "If the effect was clearly anti-Soviet," Davis observed, "this was not the primary motivation behind the policy."[105]

Finally, she noted that Dunn, Matthews, and the others "became personally committed over time to the implementation of these Atlantic Charter principles and were unreceptive to suggestions for change" which periodically came from advisers like Kennan. Taken together, these five factors, Davis concluded, decisively influenced the American approach to Eastern Europe.

But were they sufficient to trigger the Cold War? According to Davis,

> The origins of Soviet-American conflict over Eastern Europe are not to be found in American misperception of Soviet intentions [i.e., John T. Flynn] or American efforts to ensure economic markets [i.e., Williams] or obstruct the rise of the Left [i.e., Kolko], but rather in the unchanging American commitment to the Atlantic Charter principles.[106]

As it was, the United States pursued the worst possible policy in Eastern Europe, for the pressure it exerted on Moscow was strong enough to irritate Stalin and to escalate tension but too weak to effect any significant change in Soviet behavior. Davis suggested that either of two alternative policies might have been preferable. First, "American officials could have defined clearly for the Soviet Union what they hoped the political future of Eastern Europe would look like and spelled out precisely why they opposed Soviet actions."[107] In order to calm Moscow's fears about a resurgent Germany, the United States could have announced that its military forces would remain in Europe after the war. If Stalin still refused to sanction free elections, the Truman Administration then might have used its economic bargaining leverage to produce a Soviet agreement. But Davis—for unstated reasons—thought such a policy was implausible and proposed a second option. She admitted that "the Soviet Union also had choices to make" but nonetheless noted that it would have been better if the United States had abandoned its opposition to the establishment of minority governments in Eastern Europe. American officials could have

> . . . clearly informed the Soviet Union that the United States did not intend to threaten Soviet security interests in this part of the world. The Soviet Union might then not have felt the need to enforce such complete political control over Eastern Europe, at least not so rapidly. The Soviets might have tolerated Benes-type governments in the other states of Eastern Europe. American

> officials might not have then begun to interpret Soviet actions as indications of aggressive tendencies around the world. Solutions to the differences over Germany, Italy, and Japan might have been made easier if these questions had not become intertwined with the conflict over Eastern Europe.[108]

In other words, the United States *might* have prevented the escalation of tension with the Soviet Union if it had been willing to moderate its liberal ideology and to "decouple" Eastern Europe from other, more important international issues. Davis' advice was certainly compatible with that of the realist revisionists: Be pragmatic, establish priorities, and avoid making symbols out of specific clashes of interest. In chapter eight we will consider Davis' experiences as a policy-maker during the Carter Administration.

* * * * *

Daniel Yergin's SHATTERED PEACE probably had a greater impact on the foreign policy establishment, particularly its younger members, than any Cold War work since ATOMIC DIPLOMACY.[109] It can be described as a post-revisionist interpretation, although Yergin showed more sympathy for Cold War revisionism than Gaddis, Herring, or Davis. A 1968 graduate of Yale Yergin completed the dissertation that would become SHATTERED PEACE at Cambridge University in 1974. His career blossomed quickly, and soon he was regularly contributing foreign policy articles to the NEW YORK TIMES MAGAZINE, the NEW REPUBLIC, and the ATLANTIC MONTHLY. When barely thirty years old Yergin declined two invitations to join the Carter Administration as a member of the State Department's Policy Planning Staff, in part because he had begun to shift his attention increasingly to energy policy.[110]

What helped to make SHATTERED PEACE unusual was Yergin's frank admission of his motivation for writing it:

> I wanted to determine, if I could, the origins of the ideologies, policies, and institutions that played a major role in the U.S. intervention in Indochina. That is, what gave rise to the national security state?[111]

Yergin acknowledged that "it would be simplistic to say that the ideology, policies, and institutions that are the subject of this book in themselves *caused* the Vietnam war,"[112] and he further agreed that the Soviet Union could be likened to a "total security state," yet he suspected that the United States must bear a major responsibility for the long postponment of détente.

Yergin's characterization of Soviet foreign policy was as benign as that of most of the Cold War revisionists. Like them he portrayed the Soviet Union as a cautious, generally reasonable, traditional power guided by geopolitical calculations and possessed of limited aims and interests. But in contrast to those historians Yergin did not obscure the totalitarian and often terroristic nature of its domestic regime. Nevertheless, he criticized those American officials and orthodox historians who presumed that a domestic totalitarianism inevitably translated into a totalitarian foreign policy.

Like the others he emphasized the significance of bureaucratic rivalries, domestic political considerations, and the personalities of individual policy-makers. His incisive sketches of men like James Forrestal, Bernard Baruch, Henry Wallace, James Byrnes, and Dean Acheson concentrated on their individuality and tacitly resisted the revisionist habit of viewing all American leaders as colorless capitalists. Equally important was Yergin's demonstration of how bitter and prolonged interservice squabbling after World War II over the issues of military unification, spending allocations, and control of air power created intense pressures for substantially higher defense budgets even before the preparation of NSC-68.

But surely the most inventive of this book's formulations was the contention that since the interwar period American policy toward the Soviet Union had been recurrently based on one of two guiding images: the "Riga" and the "Yalta" axioms. Originally devised by members of the State Department's "Soviet Service" who had been sent to the Latvian listening-post in the 1920s these axioms ultimately became the foundation of Kennan's Long Telegram and "X" article, the Truman Doctrine, NSC-68, and the strategy of global containment. According to the Riga outlook,

> Doctrine and ideology and a spirit of innate aggressiveness shaped Soviet policy. . . . Thus, the USSR was committed to world revolution and unlimited expansion.[113]
>
> Confronted by such a potential adversary, the United States needed to adopt a stance of wariness and constant vigilance. Great patience and counterassertiveness, an "explicit toughness" were required to cope with the Russian "personality."[114]
>
> The conclusion . . . was that diplomacy with the Soviet Union

> was not merely a questionable venture, but downright dangerous. . . .[115] Germany and Russia were two of a kind; they were totalitarian dictatorships.[116]

Yergin did not hide his evaluation of the Riga axioms:

> . . . the notion that the Soviets worked bv a foreign affairs plan, derived from ideology and with definite objectives, not only gave them more credit than they deserved, but also proved to be a central weakness in the assessments of Soviet policy after the war. For it led U.S. officials to exaggerate the policy coherence of the Kremlin—the role of ideology and conscious intentions. At the same time they understated the role played by accident, confusion, and uncertainty in Russian policy and also mistook mere reaction for planned action.[117]

That the Soviets held similarly distorted views of American intentions and policies further contributed to the shattering of the Grand Alliance by 1946.

The "Riga axioms," however, did not wholly monopolize American strategy toward the Soviet Union, for they were periodically challenged by what Yergin termed the "Yalta axioms." They were "always more tentative than those of Riga, but at their center point, there also lay an image—derived from experience, assessment, and optimism of Soviet Russia."[118] Initially formulated by Roosevelt to describe his outline of the postwar world, they were based on the premise that this peace would have to be grounded in the realities of power:

> This renegade Wilsonian, for that is what he was—mindful of the lessons of the preceding quarter century, a much more subtle and pragmatic politician than the preceding war President, more sensitive to the nuances of personality and of international relations—planned to use spheres of influence and other more traditional tactics from the "old diplomacy" in order to create a new system.[119]

But by the spring of 1943 "public opinion was already forcing Roosevelt to disguise his Great Power consortium in a Wilsonian garb": an international organization.[120] While Americans continued to be "defiantly suspicious of 'big power politics'," Roosevelt had concluded that an executive committee controlled by the Big Four and the Four Policemen could achieve his purposes. In short, "the United Nations itself represented a yoking together of two separate approaches to the postwar order—a Wilsonian peace, reflected in what became the General Assembly, and a Great Power peace, embodied in what became the Security Council."[121] According to Yergin,

> One of Roosevelt's fundamental assumptions was that it was vitally important that the United States have a realistic estimate of Soviet power and the sphere of influence it was carving out, and that it pay close heed to Stalin's "security objectives." Spheres of influence were not a take-it-or-leave-it-matter, but rather a basic datum of international relations.[122]

He hoped that his own behavior could help prevent the Soviet sphere of influence from becoming a sphere of control, and Roosevelt was convinced that his "famous charm" would enable him to "do business" with Stalin. But this very circumstance demonstrated the weakness of the Yalta axioms:

> They were very much the personal possession of Roosevelt and a few powerful independent agents, whose only loyalty was to him. Those axioms had no institutional base in the government; in a sense their very emphasis on high-level personal contacts, outside of bureaucratic channels precluded that. Certainly they were not popular in the State Department.[123]

Secretary of State Byrnes valiantly tried to implement them for a time, but the Riga axioms, which ruled out diplomacy, gradually undermined his efforts. Yergin concluded that

> . . . the year 1946 saw the victory of the Riga axioms in the policy elite, and the interaction of those beliefs with the doctrine of national security to form the distinctive Commanding Ideas of American Cold War policy. The following year, 1947, witnessed two things: the abandonment of diplomacy with its "politics of composition," and the translation of the new outlook into policies of intervention and containment. In 1948 . . . military force became a central concern as policymakers rebuilt an important part of the wartime arsenal, including the establishment of a permanent war economy.[124]

And so, "equipped with the requisite budgets, the national security state grew as an awesome collage of money, institutions, ideology, interests, commitments, capabilities, and firepower."[125] Indeed, the outlook that created it eventually found in Vietnam an area that required American attention:

> The Riga axioms and the doctrine of national security made Indochina appear a crucial arena in what was perceived as a struggle to frustrate the "fundamental design" of communism. The consequences of that intervention have taught us that "fundamental designs" may be illusory and that global implications may be secondary to local issues.[126]

America's defeat in Vietnam, however, had fortuitously encouraged the reemergence of the Yalta axioms as the principles of détente. The weakening of the anticommunist consensus in the wake of Vietnam had helped to make Roosevelt's view of the Soviet Union plausible again:

> Détente is not possible with a world revolutionary state, but it is with a more conventional imperialistic and somewhat cautious nation, interested as much in protecting what it has as in extending its influence. With a country of this sort the United States can uneasily coexist.[127]

Yergin's understanding of the Cold War and Vietnam shared a great deal with that of many officials in the Carter Administration. We will explore these themes in chapters six and seven.

In certain ways SHATTERED PEACE was a revisionist work. Its tendency to exaggerate the coherence of American goals and to underestimate those of Moscow, its habit of presuming that the dialectic of contemporary international life has been American action and Soviet reaction, and its extreme suspiciousness of American military power were sentiments generally shared by the Cold War revisionists. But the consistent rejection of economic explanations coupled with sensitivity to personality, diplomacy, and bureaucratic issues pushed SHATTERED PEACE well beyond the confines of 1960s revisionism. Most significant, however, was the fact that SHATTERED PEACE contained realistic policy implications. Whereas the Cold War revisionists seemed to claim that nothing short of a drastic domestic transformation could improve American foreign policy, Yergin argued that a return to the Yalta axioms could lead to more acceptable U.S.-Soviet relations.

* * * * *

Bruce R. Kuniholm's THE ORIGINS OF THE COLD WAR IN THE NEAR EAST appeared while Kuniholm was a member of the State Department's Policy Planning Staff. We will discuss his year-long service on the PPS more fully in chapter eight, but as we highlight his book here, it should be kept in mind that as liaison for Southwest Asia to the National Security Council staff from August 1979 to July 1980 Kuniholm played an important role in helping to construct a Persian Gulf strategy in the wake of Iran and Afghanistan.

Like Joseph M. Jones' classic THE FIFTEEN WEEKS,[128] but with the aid of new documentation and from a much broader perspective, THE ORIGINS OF THE COLD WAR IN THE NEAR EAST traced the evolution of American policy toward Greece, Turkey, and Iran—the "Northern Tier"—from the end of World War II to the Truman Doctrine. Yet while Jones had focused exclusively on the crisis precipitated in Washington by Britain's inability to defend the eastern Mediterranean by late 1946, Kuniholm placed that crisis in historical perspective and argued that it constituted but a chapter in a centuries-old Great Power rivalry for control of this region.

For our purposes, however, the book's real interest lay in its evaluation of the Truman Doctrine, for, as we will see, Kuniholm's judgments about containment bore a striking resemblance to those of an older generation of realist revisionists:

> The policy of containment in the Near East was a realistic and pragmatic policy. The trouble with it was not its conception. If one were to find fault, it would have to be in its rationalization, and in analogies engendered by the policy's success in the Near East. Subsequent to the Truman Doctrine, the apparent success of American policies in Iran, Turkey, and Greece led the Truman and later administrations to look to those policies as models of how to deal with the Soviet Union and its apparent satellites, not just in Korea, but in Vietnam as well. The public rationalization of American policies in the Near East also created serious impediments to the perceptions of postwar administrations.[129]

In other words, the Truman Doctrine, insofar as it constituted a regional response to Soviet expansionism in an area of vital interest to the United States and Western Europe, could not be faulted. Unfortunately, however, the very success of containment in the Near East created certain "lessons" which soon were misapplied.

For Kuniholm, even the imagery of the Truman Doctrine was reasonable, for it produced the domestic consensus necessary to respond to Soviet threats along the Northern Tier. But while such metaphorical representations were sometimes necessary, Kuniholm warned that they must be constantly and critically evaluated, "so that the imagery a nation employs can be better reconceived relative to new circumstances."[130] This task was not performed, however, and during the 1950s and 1960s "the view of the world presented by the Truman Doctrine hardened into myth."[131]

Why did American policy-makers handle the "lessons" of the Northern Tier so inappropriately? Kuniholm identified two reasons. First, "the Truman Doctrine contributed to a new climate of opinion in which men like Senator Joseph McCarthy could capitalize on the administration's failure to match its rhetoric with concrete policies."[132] In order to placate McCarthyism, he claimed, American policy-makers came to adopt a "simplistic inflexible conception of the world complete . . . with monolithic Communism and . . . falling dominoes."[133] Excessive rhetoric created its own reality, and security interests, which in the 1940s had "dictated the nation's stated international goals," gradually fell prey to increasingly irrelevant abstractions which now determined policy. Second, Kuniholm suggested that because these Near Eastern crises of 1946-1947 represented Truman's first foreign policy victories, they tended to become an important part of the model of "how the United States *should* conduct its relations with the Soviet Union."[134] Later troubles in Berlin and China reinforced the Administration's "perception of Communism as an international, monolithic force" and "gave increased relevance to the lessons suggested by events in the Near East. This process culminated with Korea which Truman referred to as 'the Greece of the Far East.' "[135] But these analogies were not unique to Truman, and Dulles, Johnson, and Adlai Stevenson all saw Asia and Indochina "in the context of implicit analogies associated with the American experience in the Near East."[136] Unlike John Gaddis, who argued that Korea rather than the Truman Doctrine was the primary turning point in the evolution of containment, Kuniholm contended that "the frame of mind which characterized decision-makers during the

Korean War, and in the years that followed, was very much affected by the ordeal that led to the enunciation of the Truman Doctrine."[137] And in contrast to the orthodox account of the Cold War, Kuniholm was plainly critical of the indiscriminate manner in which successive administrations employed the "lessons" of the Truman Doctrine to justify interventions around the globe.

Yet Kuniholm showed little sympathy for the Cold War revisionists. He admitted that "America's competitive superiority meant that countries accepting the principles of the Atlantic Charter, and the principle of equal trading opportunities for all, . . . often found themselves within what was tantamount to an American sphere of influence—a liberal capitalist international order dominated by the United States."[138] But he firmly rejected "the claim that economic interests *dominated* American foreign policy." Rather, "events in the Near East point less to cynicism and strictly economic motives on the part of the United States than they do to an aggressive idealism which, to a considerable degree, derived from a profound belief in the virtues of America's political and economic system."[139] This belief, in turn, "was reinforced by perceived 'lessons' of the past, [drawn mostly from the 1930s] and indirectly although clearly promoted American interests."[140]

Instead of blaming either the United States or the Soviet Union for aggressive behavior in the Near East, Kuniholm preferred "to characterize the conflict along the Northern Tier as another episode in the historical struggle for power in the region, a clash between competing national entities whose interests were ultimately related to the world views or philosophies they espoused."[141] The 1940s' phase of this contest involved a clash between Wilsonianism and Leninism, but Kuniholm "left to the moralist" the task of debating the relative merits of these ideologies. He noted, however, that "the vast majority of people in Greece, Turkey, and Iran preferred alignment with the United States," while these countries' leaders applauded Truman's attempts to maintain the historic balance-of-power along the Northern Tier.[142]

Kuniholm had been motivated to write THE ORIGINS OF THE COLD WAR IN THE NEAR EAST by his doubts that the Truman Doctrine had been conceived by a group of right-wing ideologues,[143] and in preparing the book he concluded that American policy-makers had correctly recognized that a policy of containment was required to uphold an equilibrium of forces in the Near East. At the same time, Kuniholm remained convinced that America should not have extended containment to Southeast Asia. This selective embrace of containment placed him, of course, squarely in the tradition of the realist revisionists.

* * * * *

The publication of these "post-revisionist" interpretations during the 1970s scarcely meant, however, that Cold War revisionism had been fully eclipsed by works more or less indebted to Kennan, Lippmann, and Morgenthau. While it would certainly not be accurate to claim, as William Appleman Williams did, that radical revisionism had become by 1980 "the mainstream of historiography,"[144] neither was it true that the termination of America's involvement in Vietnam spelled the end of Cold War revisionism. In contrast to the sudden and nearly total discrediting of the World War I revisionists after 1941, their Cold War counterparts, notwithstanding the explicit attacks of Maier, Tucker, and Maddox and the more implicit challenges of Gaddis, Herring, Davis, Yergin, and Kuniholm, retained a good deal of academic credibility.

Cold War revisionist books continued to appear, including most prominently Ronald Radosh's PROPHETS ON THE RIGHT: *Conservative Critics of American Globalism,*[145] Blanche W. Cook, THE DECLASSIFIED EISENHOWER,[146] and Robert L. Messer's THE END OF AN ALLIANCE: *James F. Byrnes, Roosevelt, Truman, and the Origins of the Cold War,*[147] but the volume that caused the biggest stir was Martin J. Sherwin's A WORLD DESTROYED: *The Atomic Bomb and the Grand Alliance.*[148]

The atomic bomb issue, as we know, had long constituted one of the bitterest of all Cold War historiographical controversies. Moreover, the constellation of moral, military, strategic, and diplomatic questions that comprised this issue had helped to spur more general academic interest in the origins of the Cold War. Lynn E. Davis' experience was surely not unique: "the simple question of who is right, Herbert Feis or Gar Alperovitz, first provoked my interest in the origins of Soviet-American conflict over Eastern Europe."[149] In short, the pervasive legacy of Hiroshima and Nagasaki, coupled with new indications that American POWs may have been among the victims of these blasts, continued to make the issue divisive.

Sherwin took the Alperovitz thesis and pushed it further by several steps. ATOMIC DIPLOMACY, we will recall, argued that American policy-makers from May to September 1945 used the bomb primarily as a diplomatic weapon designed to wrest concessions from the Soviet Union in Eastern Europe and the Far East. Sherwin agreed that the bomb figured prominently in American political plans for the postwar world and also shared Alperovitz's view that Molotov's refusal to accede to Byrnes' demands at the London Foreign Ministers Conference in September threw Truman's atomic diplomatic strategy "completely off balance" and rendered it "chaotic."[150]

But whereas Alperovitz had contended that this policy had been quickly improvised by anti-Soviet State Department officials shortly after Truman became President, Sherwin charged that Roosevelt and Churchill had been its real authors. He noted that "after more than a quarter-century of experience we understand, as wartime policymakers did not, the bomb's limitations as a diplomatic instrument." The great expectations held for the bomb during the war were "based on the then-unchallenged assumption that its impact on international relations would be decisive." Throughout the war Roosevelt, Churchill, and their advisers "viewed the atomic bomb as a *potential* rather than an actual instrument of diplomatic policy."[151] But "as the war progressed, the diplomatic implications of the weapon's development came steadily to the fore," and "Roosevelt and Stimson became increasingly anxious to convert it into a diplomatic advantage."[152] They were not, however, moved to formulate a concrete plan for carrying out this idea until the bomb was used."[153]

Nevertheless, "the potential diplomatic value of the bomb began to shape [Roosevelt's] . . . atomic energy policies as early as 1943." That is, he "consistently chose policy alternatives that would promote its postwar diplomatic value if the predictions of the scientists proved true."[154] Several of these scientists, including most notably, Niels Bohr, "tried to convince Roosevelt and Churchill to open negotiations with Stalin during the war for the international control of atomic energy," but their proposals were rejected not because FDR and Churchill misunderstood them, but because they "were committed to the course" the physicists opposed.[155] In contrast, "Churchill urged the President to maintain the Anglo-American atomic monopoly as a diplomatic counter against the postwar ambitions of . . . the Soviet Union," and according to Sherwin, in 1943 Roosevelt "began to develop the diplomatic aspects of atomic energy policy in consultation with Churchill alone."[156] Because of this decision, "an opportunity was missed during the war to gauge the extent of Soviet interest in the international control of atomic energy, and the need for a comprehensive postwar policy on atomic energy was ignored." Tragically, "no one thought to consider how the bomb would be used to restructure international relations if the Soviets did not choose to 'cooperate.' "[157]

Sherwin did not dispute that "Roosevelt desired amicable postwar relations with the Soviet Union, or indeed that he worked hard to realize this goal." But he did suggest that FDR's

> . . . confidence in its attainment, perhaps even his commitment to it—and certainly his willingness to risk seeking international control of atomic energy in order to achieve it—have often been exaggerated. His prescriptions for the diplomatic role of the bomb, his most secret and among his most important decisions, reveal a carefully guarded skepticism regarding the Grand Alliance's prospects for surviving the war intact.[158]

Roosevelt's skepticism about the Grand Alliance, however, was not for Sherwin evidence of a healthy pragmatism but, rather, proof of deceit in regard to his real intentions. Even worse, "Truman transformed FDR's concealed skepticism about the likelihood of continued cooperation into the explicit guiding principle of American-Soviet relations."[159]

"Did Truman's policies destroy the possibility of cooperation between the two major allies?" Sherwin admitted that this crucial question could not be "completely resolved without access to Soviet records,"[160] but he did conclude that "as American-Soviet relations deteriorated Hiroshima and Nagasaki rose as symbols of a new American barbarism, and as explanations for the origins of the Cold War."[161] If Roosevelt had sought to involve Stalin in the international control of atomic energy, Sherwin suggested, not only the Cold War but the need to employ the bombs against Japan, might have been avoided.

* * * * *

Two decades after its emergence Cold War revisionism had not been "subdued" by alternative interpretations of American diplomacy. A younger generation of historians trained in the tradition of the "Wisconsin school" continued to produce works that emphasized the aggressive nature of American foreign policy. At the same time, however, it had failed to achieve the academic dominance enjoyed by orthodox historiography during the 1950s. Radical scholars were forced to share the intellectual stage with a growing number of post-revisionist historians variously indebted to both realist and Cold War revisionism. And, as we will discover in chapter seven, the growing interest by the early 1980s in a reevaluation of the Vietnam War served as the occasion for a "neo-conservative" revisionism that bore a close resemblance to the orthodox account of the Cold War.

In the next three chapters we will examine how (and if) recent American foreign policy-makers used historical ideas about the Cold War and Vietnam.

CHAPTER 5: THE REALIST REVISIONISTS AND VIETNAM

The anti-Communist consensus survived the Korean War, for although unpopular with the American public, the war received the nearly unanimous support of the foreign policy establishment. Establishment support for the Vietnam War was almost equally unqualified until the military escalations of 1965 failed to produce a negotiated settlement. Before long disaffected members like J. William Fulbright[1] and Arthur M. Schlesinger, Jr.[2] published books critical of Johnson's Vietnam policy, and soon this trickle of dissent became a flood with the appearance of Ronald Steel's PAX AMERICANA,[3] Edmund Stillman's and William Pfaff's POWER AND IMPOTENCE,[4] George Ball's THE DISCIPLINE OF POWER,[5] Robert W. Tucker's NATION OR EMPIRE?,[6] and several others.

Indeed, by the late sixties many of the internationalists who had led America into Vietnam decided to lead it out, and books like THE ARROGANCE OF POWER attempted to find ways for a still liberal America to chart a course in the post-Vietnam world. Many liberals continued, of course, to defend the intervention, and a few, like Dean Rusk and Walt Rostow, did so to the end, but by 1966 most had come to favor some sort of negotiated withdrawal. It was to the older critics of global containment that these liberal internationalists now turned for guidance.

George Kennan, Hans Morgenthau, and particularly Walter Lippmann emerged as tutors for those who had grown alarmed about the apparent overextension of American power. Yet these anti-war liberals listened selectively to their elders, with some misgivings, and with a trace of embarrassment, for while their teachers had warned of the dangerous implications of the Truman Doctrine for two decades, students like Schlesinger and Fulbright had been mainstays of the

Cold War consensus. They did not, for example, dwell on the alleged historic "insolvency" of American foreign policy but focused instead on its presumably very recent imbalance. That is, they borrowed their new mentors' critique of the the Truman Doctrine and global containment to attack Johnson's Vietnam policy but were careful not to embrace the illiberal spheres-of-influence outlook of Lippmann and the others. Ronald Steel, for instance, who in the 1980s would become Lippmann's biographer, described his defense of the 1965 Dominican intervention as "compelling" and "attractive," but concluded that

> A sphere-of-influence policy is no answer, for it puts the weak too much at the mercy of the strong, whether in Eastern Europe, in Southeast Asia, or in the Caribbean. But it is at least a beginning, for it forces us to recognize that some places are more important than others to the security of the great powers. . . .[7]

George Ball observed that

> We have used the vocabulary and syntax of Wilsonian universalism, while actively practicing the politics of alliances and spheres of influence and balance of power; and it is now time that we stopped confusing ourselves with our political hyperbole. . . .[8]

Yet Ball could not embrace Lippmann, because "no matter how workable Mr. Lippmann's thesis might have been had we consistently applied it since the war, it is hard to see how we could adopt it without substantial breakage."[9] Nor did Ball wish to draw general lessons from the Vietnam War. In contrast to Korea, the conflict in Vietnam, Ball asserted, was "no mere power thrust by Communists lusting to take over the South" but part of a long revolution to unite all of Indochina under Communist control. The "obvious lesson" was that "America must never again commit its power and authority in defense of a country of only marginal strategic interest when that country lacks a broadly based government, or the will to create one."[10] Ball restricted the lessons of Vietnam, because he wished to carve out criteria for future interventions[11]—he certainly did not want to preclude them. His criteria were remarkably similar to those suggested by Lippmann in 1947 and anticipated in some measure the terms of the Nixon Doctrine.

But while Ball could not rule out limited military interventions even in Asia, other critics wished to confine America's international activities to economic ones. For example, Fulbright hoped that

> . . . maybe—just maybe—if we left our neighbors to make their own judgments and their own mistakes, and confined our assistance to matters of economics and technology, instead of philosophy, maybe then they would begin to find the democracy and the dignity that have largely eluded them, and we in turn might begin to find the love and gratitude that we seem to crave.[12]

Thus by the late 1960s many liberal internationalists had grown very skeptical of military solutions, but they refused to walk the last mile with Kennan. That is, while they came to share Kennan's distrust of military power, they implicitly rejected his pessimism about America's ability to use economic aid to bring democracy to the less developed world. Most of these critics remained committed liberal internationalists. While they were eager to lambast the "arrogance" of Wilsonianism as it appeared in the Truman Doctrine and Vietnam, they refused to believe that it could also lurk in apparently benign development assistance programs. Many liberal internationalists moved on from a *Realpolitik* analysis of Vietnam to claim that America's failure in Vietnam proved the *general* disutility of military force and the consequent need to recognize the reality of an interdependent world order.[13] They forsook Lippmann and Morgenthau and distorted Kennan to reintroduce a toothless version of Wilsonianism couched in the new vocabulary of "world order" politics.

* * * * *

If parts of the establishment rediscovered concepts like "insolvency," "overextension," "equilibrium," and "vital" and "peripheral interests" because of Vietnam, what of the arguments of the Cold War revisionists? Did they play a role in the public debate over Vietnam? Unlike the historical revisionism of the interwar period which recommended specific and widely popular actions (e.g,, neutrality legislation) designed to prohibit American participation in another European war, the Cold War revisionists of the 1960s found it difficult to articulate policy proposals which possessed much appeal outside college and university campuses. Charles Beard had testified in support of the Neutrality Acts in the 1930s and Kennan had appeared before the Senate Foreign Relations Committee during its 1966 Vietnam hearings (Fulbright had attempted unsuccessfully to persuade Lippmann to testify),[14] but none of the Cold War revisionists offered testimony to Congress. While this absence was no doubt due in part to the desire of Fulbright and other anti-war Senators and Congressmen to give to their position the fullest possible public legitimacy, other factors were more significant. First, the works of Williams, Kolko, and other radical revisionists were not well known at this time to Congressional critics of Vietnam. Despite the fact that Alperovitz had worked on Capitol Hill in the early 1960s, his ATOMIC DIPLOMACY, while more familiar than other revisionists works to Foreign Relations Committee staffers, did not figure at all in the genesis of Fulbright's THE ARROGANCE OF POWER. It was Vietnam and not historical theories about the Cold War which precipitated the actions of Congressional doves. While it is true that George Kennan's misgivings about Vietnam derived directly from his doubts about the Truman Doctrine (and even earlier events), he was called to testify primarily in his role as critic of Vietnam and not as a Cold War revisionist. Second, the Vietnam writings of the radical revisionists were not publicly compelling. In general, they argued that because of America's structural needs for a liberal capitalist empire, a Vietnam-like situation had long been the inevitable price of expansion.[15] Rejecting liberal contentions that the Vietnam intervention was intellectual error, these historians supported the Johnson Administration's claim that the defense of South Vietnam was a symbolic necessity if America's global credibility was to be maintained. A few contended that the United States was in Vietnam to secure Southeast Asian resources for the growing and restless Japanese economy,[16] but most of them focused on the allegedly irreparable damage which a defeat in Vietnam would ultimately visit upon America's domestic socio-economic institutions. There is no evidence to suggest that their diagnosis was ever accepted by more than a tiny minority of the American public, and its policy implications were bound to give pause to even the most disillusioned members of the foreign policy establishment,[17] for the Cold War revisionists argued that to avoid future overseas disasters, it was first necessary to radically transform the nature of domestic America or at the very least to temporarily entrust the nation's fate to enlightened conservatives. Virtually no one in the establishment was willing to do either of these things.

Nor were many liberal internationalists yet ready to accept Richard J. Barnet's understanding of the Cold War and Vietnam.[18] Despite their misgivings about global containment they could not purge the Cold War of all moral purpose. The Marshall Plan had been for them a wise, moderate, and generous program to rehabilitate Western Europe. Some sort of containment had been required to oppose Soviet expansion. Men like Dean Acheson and others "present at the creation" of these policies had been unfairly characterized by Barnet as amoral national-security managers comparable to the men in the

Kremlin. The Cold War no doubt had been exacerbated by inflamatory rhetoric on both sides of the Iron Curtain, particularly during the 1950s, but these liberals thought that Barnet surely exaggerated the role of psychological misperception in this contest. Furthermore, anti-war members of the establishment could not accept many of the words Barnet used to describe the American effort in Vietnam. To call the war "genocidal," "criminal," imperialistic," and evidence of a "permanent war economy" in the United States was, for them, irresponsible and inaccurate, at least before the election of Richard Nixon. Thus while some of Barnet's specific policy proposals—e.g., a War Powers constitutional amendment, a probe of intelligence agencies, and a decrease in the defense budget—found support in the establishment and on Capitol Hill, they rejected (or ignored) the reasoning about Vietnam that lay behind his recommendations and the more radical structural transformations that he favored.[19]

Fulbright, Steel, and even Ball had concluded that the Cold War was largely over and that American foreign policy needed to adjust itself accordingly. They argued that the Soviet Union had lost its revolutionary zeal; international Communism had become "polycentric"; a plural and interdependent world was threatening to supplant the bipolar reality of the 1950s; and the decolonization process had given birth to fiercely nationalistic regimes determined to resist American and Soviet efforts to control them. Yet these authors were critical of American foreign policy only insofar as it had failed to accommodate itself to these momentous international changes. In other words, the Vietnam intervention represented a form of intellectual error for these liberal internationalists, because it symbolized our continued refusal to acknowledge the new global realities of the 1960s. In a sense, this erroneous judgment of the contemporary world which Steel and the others detected in the outlook of the Johnson Administration could have been interpreted as an unavoidable cost of the pernicious and pervasive "Cold War mentality" identified by Barnet and Horowitz. But this apparent convergence of liberal and radical anti-Vietnam perspectives masked a deeper disagreement about the nature of the Cold War. Horowitz, Barnet, and others who emphasized such psychological factors disputed those who claimed that the bankruptcy of American foreign policy had been precipitated by an inability to adapt to the new international system of the 1960s. Rather, they argued that the measures taken by the United States to wage the Cold War had never reflected real circumstances, and they joined with historians like Williams and Kolko in condemning virtually the entire record of American diplomacy.

In short, the issue of the origins and early development of the Cold War remained separable from that of Vietnam in the minds of most of the anti-war liberal establishment. The fragmentation of the foreign policy consensus in the late 1960s remained less than total insofar as most of the antagonists continued to agree on the historical issue of Cold War origins. To the extent that the foreign policy debate of these years contained an historical dimension, it tended to focus on the course of containment after 1950. The Cold War revisionists apart, very few Americans were willing to question the necessity of containing the Soviet Union after World War II. In contrast to the 1930s, when bitter disagreement about the origins of World War I proved a major impediment to the creation of a foreign policy consensus in the United States (as well as in France and Britain), the fact that the issue of Cold War origins remained outside the parameters of the public (though not the academic) debate over Vietnam meant that a slender symbol of consensus remained to unite the foreign policy establishment. The problem was that agreement about the early history of the Cold War could no longer produce policy agreements about Vietnam.

It would be misleading, however, to suggest that the public debate over Vietnam merely pitted one part of the establishment against the other part. While it is true that the refusal of the "wise men" to support further troop increases in the aftermath of Tet was decisive in Johnson's decision to deescalate and to abandon the 1968 Presidential campaign, many of these senior advisers had, in turn, been impressed by the apparent power of the anti-war movement. The "movement," of course, was more a loose coalition of groups and perspectives than a cohesive, ideologically unified organization, but its favorite slogans—"Stop the War Machine," "Power to the People," and "Smash the American Empire"—were all caricatures of concepts regularly employed by the Cold War revisionists and other Left academics. The civil turmoil produced by confrontation between the anti-war movement and the Johnson and Nixon administrations constituted a significant expression of the public "discourse" over Vietnam. It was in this manner, rather than in its ability to persuade the establishment of the intellectual merits of its arguments, that the Cold War revisionists exerted a public influence during the late '60s and early '70's.

* * * * *

The Johnson Administration, though painfully aware of domestic opposition to the war, was largely unfamiliar with the writings of the Cold War revisionists. According to Arthur M. Schlesinger, Jr.

> I don't think that Cold War revisionism had anywhere near the effect on public policy that post-World War I revisionism had in an earlier day. It is notable, for example, that most influential critics of the Vietnam War—Kennan, Morgenthau, Lippmann, Niebuhr, and Ball—were *not* Cold War revisionists. I never saw any evidence when I was in Washington that senior American officials were affected by (or much aware of) the scholarly debate over the Cold War.[20]

Even the more thoughtful of Johnson's advisers were content to label all dissent as "neo-isolationism." That is, they employed the vocabulary of orthodox historiography.

Senior Nixon foreign policy officials, particularly those with academic backgrounds, were more familiar with the specific arguments of the Cold War revisionists. Two members of Kissinger's National Security Council staff, Robert E. Osgood and Helmut Sonnenfeldt, held broadly representative views within the Administration. Osgood, a highly-respected professor of American foreign policy at the Johns Hopkins School of Advanced International Studies and eminent student of World War I revisionism,[21] had read a good deal of the Cold War revisionist literature before joining the NSC in 1969. Completely unimpressed with Williams, Kolko, and the others, Osgood viewed their writings as "bad history" and was certain that they exerted no influence on the Nixon foreign policy. On the other hand, Osgood believed that the Cold War revisionists' critique of containment shared a great deal with the outlook of McGovernism.[22] Sonnenfeldt, a German-born career Foreign Service Officer and Soviet expert, was particularly close to Kissinger and moved with him from the NSC to the State Department as Counsellor in 1974. Somewhat less familiar with Cold War revisionist writings than Osgood, he had nevertheless read THE TRAGEDY OF AMERICAN DIPLOMACY while teaching part-time at SAIS in the early 1960s, and, a few years later, ATOMIC DIPLOMACY and some essays by Kolko and Barnet. According to Sonnenfeldt, these interpretations were "certainly known" in the White House:

> Kissinger was a historian and certainly familiar with it. Morton Halperin was there. So was Osgood. A lot of people on the NSC staff knew about it. Nixon knew about it, I guess probably was

> very emotionally opposed to it, and saw it as part of the general malaise in the intellectual community, which was part of the whole problem of the Nixon Administration.[23]

Sonnenfeldt also recalled that "there was a lot of talk at the time about the disintegration of the Cold War consensus, and the revisionists were certainly symptomatic of this breakdown."[24] Tracing Cold War revisionism to Henry Wallace's 1948 Presidential campaign, Sonnenfeldt had been aware "for more than thirty years that there were disputes about the origins of the Cold War" and was convinced that while "most of the revisionists asked worthwhile questions, they did so with preconceived conclusions and found evidence to fit those conclusions."[25] Partly because he "had first-hand knowledge of Soviet intransigence during the German occupation," Sonnenfeldt had remained "very skeptical of revisionist accounts that claimed otherwise."[26] Interestingly, however, Sonnenfeldt claimed that both he and Kissinger were Cold War revisionists of sorts:

> I share Kissinger's feeling that mistakes were made in the late '40s, for example, when the United States did not demand something more from the Russians on Germany in exchange for signing the East European peace treaties. The U.S. overestimated Soviet strength in the 1940s, and data gathered by Sovietologists, not diplomatic historians, has been useful in showing that the U.S. had more bargaining leverage than we thought.[27]

This revisionism takes us a good distance from Williams, Alperovitz, and Kolko, but it is a revealing statement from a prime architect of détente. To the extent that the origins of the Cold War became an issue with the Nixon Administration, it did so as a political and a sociological one and not as an historical theme at all.

Can it, then, be claimed that Kissinger's approach to the history of American foreign relations reflected the precepts of the realist revisionists? Did Kissinger's unexpected elevation to National Security Affairs Adviser mean that the maxims of Kennan, Lippmann, and Morgenthau would finally receive unambiguous policy expression? His academic writings of the fifties and early sixties provided no clear answers to these questions. In NUCLEAR WEAPONS AND FOREIGN POLICY, THE NECESSITY FOR CHOICE, and several articles for FOREIGN AFFAIRS[28] his criticisms of the Eisenhower Administration's alleged rigidity, passivity, and hopeless attachment to obsolete strategic concepts were not far removed from those of Walt Rostow. Kissinger's endorsement of notions like limited nuclear war, flexible response, and brushfire wars, plus his enthusiastic support for military intervention in Vietnam brought him to the attention of Kennedy, and he served (albeit uncomfortably) as a White House consultant in 1961 and early 1962. Yet his historical reflections seemingly belied this fascination with military technology and the techniques of counterinsurgency. In A WORLD RESTORED and several essays on nineteenth century European diplomacy, including, most notably, one on Bismarck,[29] Kissinger's consuming interest lay in the nature of conservative statesmanship and what it could do to foster international restraint and equilibrium. Although radical critics like I. F. Stone seized on A WORLD RESTORED as proof of Kissinger's admiration of Metternich (hence one of the sources of his alleged contempt for the poor and the weak), in fact, Kissinger considered the Austrian Foreign Minister to be a timid reactionary increasingly unwilling to risk testing the precarious internal balances of the Hapsburg realm. In contrast, while Castlereagh's understanding of equilibrium was less sophisticated that Metternich's, Kissinger deeply admired his courage in attempting to lead Britain into the European Concert when it would have been politically advantageous to withdraw from involvement until the next threat to the balance-of-power emerged. But Kissinger's real hero was Bismarck, for he combined conservative statesmanship with a subtle appreciation of the European equilibrium. Yet he committed two fatal errors, the first of which was probably avoidable: the annexation of Alsace-Lorraine demonstrated an uncharacteristic lack of restraint which ultimately contributed to the onset of World War I; and the very complexity of Bismarck's alliance system inevitably complicated the task of his successors, for it rested excessively on personal genius. Taken as a whole these historical writings revealed a Kissinger much more concerned with leadership, equilibrium, diplomacy, stability, and restraint than the popular Dr. Strangelove caricature suggested.

But it was in the first volume of his memoirs, WHITE HOUSE YEARS,[30] that Kissinger revealed most directly his understanding of American diplomatic history. His interpretation of that history up to the Korean War, at least, bore an astonishing resemblance to that of Walter Lippmann. Indeed, many of the passages could have fit comfortably on the pages of U.S. FOREIGN POLICY: *Shield of the Republic.* For example, Kissinger, like Lippmann, wrote that

> . . . our Founding Fathers were sophisticated statesmen who understood the European balance of power and manipulated it

> brilliantly, first to bring about America's independence and then to preserve it. The shrewd diplomacy of Franklin and Jefferson engaged Britain's enemies on our side; our negotiating hand thus strengthened, John Jay secured recognition from the British Crown and liquidated the residual problems of our war with England. At that point, however, in the best traditions of the European balance of power, we cut loose from our temporary allies and went our own way. For more than three decades after independence, we lived precariously, like other nations. We went to the brink of war with France and endured the capture of our capital by British forces. But we moved astutely to take advantage of new opportunities. For the hundred years between Waterloo and 1914 we were shielded by our geographical remoteness and British sea power, which maintained global stability.
>
> As the United States grew in strength and European rivalries focused on Europe, Africa, and Asia, Americans came to consider the isolation conferred by two great oceans as the normal pattern of foreign relations. Rather arrogantly we ascribed our security entirely to the superiority of our beliefs rather than to the weight of our power or the fortunate accidents of history and geography.
>
> Thus America entered the twentieth century largely unprepared for the part it would be called upon to play. Forgotten was the skilled statecraft by which the Founding Fathers had secured our independence; distained were the techniques by which all nations must preserve their interests.
>
> Our entry into World War I was the inevitable result of our geopolitical interest in maintaining freedom of the seas and preventing Europe's domination by a hostile power. But true to our tradition, we chose to interpret our participation in legal and idealistic terms.
>
> Later, when totalitarianism was on the rise and the entire international order was being challenged, we clung to our isolation, which had been transformed from a policy preference into a moral conviction. We had virtually abandoned the basic precautions needed for our national security. [T]hen in our absorption with total victory, we spurned the notion that the security of the postwar world might depend on some sort of equilibrium of power.[31]

In Lippmann's terms the United States, which had been without a real foreign policy since the days of John Quincy Adams, needed to achieve a solvency by balancing interests and power.

Yet this apparent congruence between Lippmann and Kissinger is deceptive, for all but the most ardent of Wilsonians could embrace most of this interpretation of pre-1945 American diplomatic history. It was over the issue of containment that the two men began to part company. Kissinger was far from an unqualified admirer of containment, but his criticisms were not the same as Lippmann's. Whereas Lippmann doubted that the United States (even in 1947) possessed the resources required to implement a policy which he thought had unavoidable global implications, Kissinger argued that the fundamental problem with containment was its tacit presumption that power and diplomacy were discrete elements or phases of policy:

> As applied in the diplomacy of Dean Acheson and to some extent John Foster Dulles, we were to mark time until we built the strength to contain Soviet aggression—especially the assault on Central Europe, which preoccupied our strategic thinking. After containment had been achieved, diplomacy would take over.[32]

This approach was unfortunate, because

> It aimed at an ultimate negotiation but supplied no guide to the content of those negotiations. . . . It did not answer the question of how the situation of strength was to be demonstrated in the absence of a direct attack on us or on our allies. Nor did it make clear what would happen after we had achieved a position of strength if our adversary, instead of negotiating, concentrated on eroding it or turning our flank.[33]

As a result, Kissinger concluded, containment suffered from three flaws. First, "its excessively military conception of the balance of power. . . gave the Soviet Union time to consolidate its conquests and to redress the nuclear imbalance."[34] Second, it came to rest inordinately on atomic power and thus forgot that "managing the military balance of power required vigilance on two levels: being strong enough not only strategically with nuclear power but also locally with conventional arms."[35] And third, (Kissinger added this point almost as an afterthought and without elaboration) "containment could never be an adequate response to the modern impact of Communist ideology, which transforms relations between states into conflicts between philosophies and poses challenges to the balance of power through domestic upheavals."[36]

In brief,

> . . . we never fully understood that while our absolute power was growing, our *relative* position was bound to decline as the USSR recovered from World War II. Our military and diplomatic position was never more favorable than at the *very beginning* of the containment policy in the 1940s. That was the time to attempt a serious discussion on the future of Europe. We lost our opportunity.[37]

Put another way, Kissinger, in effect, agreed with the Cold War revisionists' assessment of Soviet and American power in the late 1940s. But whereas the revisionists claimed that containment was an aggressive policy aimed at expanding the American empire, Kissinger suggested that it was not aggressive enough, for it allowed Stalin precious time to recover from the war. This analysis is reminiscent of that of the conservative revisionists of the fifties that we briefly considered in chapter one. In a sense, Kissinger was disappointed that the Cold War revisionists had erred, for if they had been correct, the history of postwar Europe would, from Kissinger's perspective, have been much happier.

Moreover, his dispute with Lippmann was essentially tactical. Like most Americans after the war Lippmann, according to Kissinger, had grossly underestimated the enormity of American resources and hence believed that the United States was incapable of successfully pursuing containment (we leave aside the issue of *moral* resources). Presumably Kissinger would have agreed with Lippmann if, in fact, the American margin had been substantially smaller than it actually was. Containment, then, would have been an appropriate policy if the circumstances had been more like they were to become by, say, the late 1960s. If so, then détente, can be viewed historically as a containment policy designed to account for America's reduced position. Kissinger's quarrel with Acheson (and even Lippmann) was not really about containment but, rather, about its premature adoption in the 1940s.

But what of Kissinger's third objection—that containment constituted an inadequate response to Communist ideology and internal subversion? It is difficult to determine the seriousness with which Kissinger made this charge. The Truman Doctrine, of course, addressed this problem explicitly and Eisenhower's skillful use of the

CIA cast doubt on the alleged incompatibility of containment and counterinsurgency warfare. Nor can Kissinger's criticism refer to Vietnam, for the Johnson Administration contended that the war was essentially one of external aggression, and Kissinger apparently supported that view. Surely détente was not meant to meet Kissinger's objections unless one understands détente to involve a Soviet pledge to practice restraint in the Third World. This may have been one of Kissinger's hopes for détente in 1969, but WHITE HOUSE YEARS appeared a decade later. It is more likely that Kissinger inserted this terse point to defend himself against those who charged that he was insufficiently sensitive to the threat of Communist ideology until rather late in the game. If so, the irony must be appreciated, because during the fifties and sixties Kissinger belonged on the hard side of the domestic consensus and argued, as a geopolitical anti-Communist, that the Soviet Union's revolutionary character prevented the emergence of a legitimate international balance-of-power.

Kissinger's critique of containment bore a marked similarity to the one offered by Walt Rostow twenty years before. But whereas Rostow's analysis indicated that the United States could still seize the initiative squandered by Truman and Eisenhower, Kissinger in 1969 was confronted with a demoralized foreign policy establishment, a shattered domestic consensus, and a relatively weaker American power position. Thus while Rostow's impatience with containment expressed the tone of the New Frontier, Kissinger's pointed in a very different direction. Indeed, the sense of limit and tragedy reflected by him in the following passage forms a telling counterpoint to the enthusiasms of Rostow:

> History knows no resting places and no plateaus. All societies of which history informs us went through periods of decline; most of them eventually collapsed. . . . The statesman's responsibility is to struggle against transitoriness and not to insist that he be paid in the coin of eternity. He may know that history is the foe of permanence; but no leader is entitled to resignation. He owes it to his people to strive,to create, and to resist the decay that besets all human institutions.[38]

Kissinger's self-perceived task was to set priorities, marshall limited resources, attempt to rebuild a domestic consensus, and manage the relative diminishment of American power. In this regard he implicitly invoked Morgenthau: "Moral exuberance had inspired both over-involvement and isolationism. It was my conviction that a concept of our fundamental national interests would provide a ballast of restraint and an assurance of continuity."[39] Stanley Hoffmann correctly observed that "Kissinger's books belong to the same universe of discourse as Morgenthau's and Kennan's. As in their works, one finds a definite disdain for America's behavior in world affairs."[40] Furthermore,

> The critique of American idealism went beyond the standard attacks on legalism and moralism; his was a quest for a *Realpolitik* devoid of moral homilies and of reminiscences of crusades. . . . The model was provided by his analysis of nineteenth century, balance of power diplomacy—not a distinctive point if one compares him to Morgenthau, but an original one nevertheless *if one compares him to the architects of postwar diplomacy.*[41]

Or, Hoffmann might have added, if one compares him to the orthodox interpreters of that diplomacy.

This enthusiasm for the balance heightened, in turn, his anti-Wilsonianism, and like the realist revisionists, Kissinger preferred the intricacies of multipolar diplomacy to the enunciation of universal ideals which supposedly hardened the ideolological stances of the combatants.

Did Kissinger's actions satisfy the precepts of the limitationists? These axioms were not, of course, hard-and-fast rules that predetermined policy, but, rather, tendencies or presumptions which were necessarily responsive to circumstance. Yet, on balance, Kissinger's conduct did evince a sense of limit and modesty which represented a departure from the hubristic exercises of the Kennedy-Johnson years. The gradual development of a Soviet-American "code of conduct," the pragmatic abandonment of Chinese containment, and the restraint apparent in the Nixon Doctrine were all consistent with the advice offered since the 1940s by Lippmann, Kennan, and Morgenthau. Of the misdeeds attributed to Kissinger before 1973—failure to end more quickly the Vietnam War, insensitivity to the Third World, ignorance of international economic problems, an almost pathological secretiveness, an exaggerated concern with Soviet-American relations, and a neglect of Western Europe and Japan—only the last would have been truly upsetting to the older critics of global containment.

But the Administration's reactions to the major events of 1974 and 1975—Watergate and the fall of Saigon—did represent sharp breaks with limitationist concepts. Nixon's attempt to save his scandal-ridden Presidency by making increasingly extravagant claims for détente was ill-advised, because it allowed an unwarranted intrusion of domestic politics into foreign policy, and because the promises made on behalf of détente incorrectly implied that acute competition need not be a feature of Soviet-American relations. Kissinger's efforts to make a stand in Angola—an area of marginal strategic significance—to symbolize American resolve in the wake of Hanoi's victory and his transformation of détente into a strategy of super-containment[42] to meet growing domestic criticism seemingly repeated the errors of Dean Acheson.

On balance, then, Kissinger's performance ultimately disappointed traditional critics of global containment, yet they could find in it much to admire. But it was not according to these criteria that the foreign policy issues of the 1976 Presidential campaign were waged. Human rights, global inequality, arms transfers, Chile, and similar themes were used effectively by Carter and the Democrats. Those anti-war members of the establishment who had invoked Lippmann, Kennan, and Morgenthau in 1966 were ready once again to follow Woodrow Wilson in 1976.

CHAPTER 6: CARTER, THE COLD WAR, AND "WORLD ORDER POLITICS"

All postwar administrations have possessed more or less well-defined notions about how the world should be organized. Academic interpreters of American foreign policy have, as we have seen in the first five chapters, viewed these official understandings of "world order" with drastically differing degrees of enthusiasm. Orthodox historians of the fifties and sixties applauded America's quest for world order as a generous effort to create a peaceful and lawful international environment. For them containment, even in its most exuberant form, represented a healthy willingness to use America's material and moral resources to build a better world. The realist revisionists or limitationists contended that this search for world order had eventually led to an overextension of American power, a preoccupation with military instruments, and an obsessional anti-Communism. They recommended a more classically European approach to order that stressed balance, restraint, multilateral diplomacy, the primacy of the "national interest," and an agnostic attitude toward the internal composition of states. In the last chapter we argued that many of Henry Kissinger's initiatives, at least until détente began to sour, reflected this outlook. The Cold War revisionists claimed that America's brand of world order constituted, in fact, a self-serving ruse designed to spread liberal-capitalist values (and American hegemony) to hostile societies. They urged the replacement of this allegedly exploitative order with a global, socialist commonwealth truly dedicated to peace and equality.

Moreover, we discovered that each of these preferred world orders possessed a distinctive, and often implicit, historical perspective. For example, official American foreign policy and its orthodox defenders placed the Cold War in the context of Munich, American isolationism, and the Western failure to respond decisively to totalitarianism in the 1930s. The realist revisionists, while not unmindful of the experience with Hitler, saw the Cold War primarily as a traditional power struggle that operated according to the axioms of *Realpolitik.* They accordingly tended to invoke historical analogies drawn from eighteenth and nineteenth century Europe and from the Peloponnesian War. Finally, the Cold War revisionists located the roots of the Cold War in America's allegedly hysterical reaction to the Bolshevik Revolution and in the historical development of its capitalist institutions. Unimpressed with European precedents and convinced that American isolationism was a convenient myth, they placed the United States in the middle of their historical universe. In short, those who conducted American foreign policy and those who interpreted it demonstrated a profound interest in "world order."

By the mid-1970s, however, a phenomenon known as "world order politics" had achieved academic stardom, had informed such prestigious undertakings as the Council on Foreign Relations' "1980s Project," and had apparently even been embraced by the Carter Administration. According to Stanley Hoffmann, the Harvard professor who functioned as the unofficial philosopher of Carter's foreign policy, "world order politics" was "obviously 'in'," [1] and a brief review of the speeches of the President and his advisers reveals an abundant use of "world order politics" terms and phrases like "complexity," "chaos," "change," "interdependence," "global management," and "just world order."

So alarmed were "neo-conservative" critics of the Carter Administration by the alleged dangers of "world order politics" that they claimed that its practitioners constituted a new foreign policy establishment committed to the repudiation of postwar American diplomacy. For example, Carl Gershman argued that in its total rejection of containment this cabal "broke unequivocally with thirty years of historical experience" and had "rejected everything that had gone before." He further suggested that

> . . . it was the new establishment that devalued the importance of national-security concerns . . . , saturating American foreign policy with defeatism masquerading as optimism and "maturity" and "restraint," cravenly following international political fashion even if this meant denigrating the interests and values of one's own country, and worrying less about American security than about Soviet insecurity, in the nature of which virtually any Soviet action could be condoned or blamed on the United States.[2]

Composed mostly of members of the Cold War foreign policy establishment who had lost their nerve in the wake of Vietnam; radical intellectuals who prized equality more than liberty even if the price was totalitarianism; and neo-Wilsonian academics and foreign policy analysts who wished to breathe new purpose into America staggered by Vietnam and Watergate, this elite, according to Gershman, formed the core of a "liberal-populist" governing coalition "wherein a Southern President who campaigned as a populist staffed his foreign-policy bureaucracy with members of . . . the *new* foreign policy establishment."[3]

Ostensibly wracked by guilt and paralyzed by tendencies which bordered on isolationism and appeasement, at the heart of this group's outlook lay the conviction that military force was no longer a suitable foreign policy instrument for America to employ. Rejecting the bases of thirty years of American foreign policy—the containment of Communism and the "lessons of Munich"—this new elite embraced the "lessons of Vietnam" as the foundation of a new American diplomacy. And from the primary Vietnam lesson—that containment was counterproductive, unfeasible, and unnecessary—this establishment, Gershman claimed, drew several corollaries. First, "world order" must replace "national security" as the organizing concept of American diplomacy. Second, the United States should adopt an attitude of "equanimity" toward changes in the world which previously would have been considered injurious to its interests. Third, because the Soviet Union was essentially a *status quo* power, American foreign policy ought not to be preoccupied with relations with Moscow. Fourth, to avoid isolation in a world filled with revolutionary change, America had to learn to become more flexible and less ideological in its dealings with the Third World. Finally, our moral strength, rather than a primary reliance on military power, should be used to help alleviate such "global problems" as hunger, racial hatred, and the arms race. Gershman's claims, as we shall see, represented a caricature of the Administration's actual outlook.

Conversely, other observers saw little new in the Administration's foreign policy team despite its apparent preoccupation with "world order politics." To Roger Morris, a former NSC staffer and Foreign Service Officer who had resigned in angry protest over the Cambodian "incursion" in 1970, these appointments were disappointingly predictable. Writing as "Suetonius" in *The New Republic* in early 1977 the rather jaded Morris suggested that

> . . . it is almost inevitably, a group with little diversity. Corporate clients, law office and foundation politics, past government

> service, homogenized articles, it is a world not of the innovator, the reflective, or even the politician occasionallv in touch with the grass roots, but rather of the Washington hanger-on. Anthony Lake, who left Kissinger's NSC staff at the invasion of Cambodia, is the *only* man in the group with a record of resignation on principle.
>
> So in foreign affairs it will be mostly a goverment of patrons and protegés, and in too large a measure it will be dull, in more than one sense of that word. With few exceptions, they are not the best and the brightest any more than their predecessors were in the 1960's. They are simply the most available.[4]

According to this view the Administration was comprised of little more than unimaginative sycophants as eager to serve Carter as Johnson or Nixon and certainly not about to abandon thirty years of American foreign policy.

* * * * *

Viewed historically the Carter Administration assumed office at a particularly interesting moment. Of America's two chief international experiences since 1945—one, the Vietnam War, had ended, and the second, the Cold War, appeared comatose. Furthermore, the Administration was staffed, at all but its most senior levels, by people who had no adult memory of either Munich or World War II. For those many officials who had attended college in the 1960s the memory of Tet and My Lai was bound to be more compelling than for the Cold War generation which had been permanently seared by very different events.

This foreign policy "generation gap" had been frequently noted and constituted another expression of the fragmentation of the old Cold War consensus, but Graham Allison's portrayal best captured its essence and long-term implications. Writing in the first issue of FOREIGN POLICY, a journal that would nurture many future Carter lieutenants during the Nixon-Ford years, Allison predicted that

> . . . the attitudes of young Americans today are a harbinger of the future. More than half our population is under age thirty, and many of these young men and women will soon be assuming positions of influence in the government and the society. By the end of this decade, their attitudes will have a significant impact on our foreign policy.[5]

He probed about one hundred "25-34 year-old elite Americans"' for their "deeper foreign policy axioms"[6] and uncovered a substantial generational gap separating their foreign policy opinions from those of the older Cold War consensus. In their attitudes toward Communism, nationalism, the Soviet Union, American power, military budgets, the utility of military force, and the relative importance of foreign policy, these future potential leaders differed markedly from the outlook of those who had directed American foreign policy since 1945. Not surprisingly, Allison identified the Vietnam experience as the primary source of this generational disparity. What had Vietnam taught these young people? First, to disbelieve the axioms of the containment generation; second, to doubt the reliability of the American government as a source of information; third, to question the alleged moral superiority of the United States; and fourth, to realize that America was not invincible in foreign ventures.[7] The longer-term implications were inescapable:

> What lies beneath their surface insistence on "No More Vietnams" is a deep-seated doubt about why U.S. troops should in any circumstances be engaged in military operations in any other part of the world. What will soon be known as the "lessons of involvement" will . . . be no less rooted in the consciousness of young Americans today than were the "lessons of isolationism" in the previous generation.[8]

Did these convictions about Vietnam produce a wholesale revision of views towards modern American diplomacy? By the late 1970s these people would be old enough to assume responsible foreign policy positions. What would their outlook be then? What sort of policies would be produced by a generation disillusioned by Vietnam and schooled in (or at least exposed to) Cold War revisionism?

How, then, did the Carter Administration define itself historically? Did it perceive itself as the heir, repudiator, or modifier of the foreign policies of the six previous postwar Presidents? Or was it largely oblivious to these sorts of questions? What did it mean by "world order," and how did it differ from its predecessors' understandings? Did the Carter Administration's apparent embrace of "world order politics" signal its adoption of a certain kind of historical revisionism? Did members of the "Vietnam generation" who served Carter share an outlook at all indebted to that of the Cold War revisionists? What were the policy implications of that outlook? Did Carter officials employ historical analogies that were informed by either realist or

Cold War revisionist interpretations? We will consider these questions in the remainder of this chapter and in part of the next.

* * * * *

Since neither official policy statements nor journalistic accounts of Carter's foreign policy addressed these sorts of questions, we relied heavily on personal interviews to gain an understanding of the Administration's historical sense of itself and the manner in which it used historical analogies. In the spring of 1981 we conducted about two dozen interviews with officials who had served on the National Security Council and the Policy Planning Staff during the Carter years. These were supplemented with additional interviews during the late winter of 1982. We decided to focus on the NSC and the PPS for several reasons. First, in contrast to the regional and country desks of the State Department which are almost exclusively preoccupied with daily international events, the National Security Council and the Policy Planning Staff possess, in addition to their "fire-fighting" and crisis management functions, a broader planning capacity. Consequently, since their creation in the late 1940s, both have tended to be disproportionately staffed with professional academics and by Foreign Service Officers noted for "taking the longer view."[9] Second, these agencies played central roles in the formulation and articulation of the Carter Administration's foreign policy. Despite his public misgivings about the preeminence of Kissinger's NSC, Brzezinski fought hard to make his agency the centerpiece of the Carter foreign policy apparatus, and especially after Vance's resignation in April 1980, largely succeeded in this aim. The Policy Planning Staff, except for a golden moment of significant influence during the early days of Kennan's directorship, had never realized its potential even within the State Department. But during the Carter Administration the PPS, despite frequent personnel changes, reemerged as a relatively central planning, coordinating, and speechwriting unit. Secretary Vance, in contrast to many of his predecessors, took it seriously and maintained close relations with W. Anthony Lake, its director for the entire span of the Carter Presidency. Furthermore, the Policy Planning Staff frequently representsd the interests of the State Department in the nearly continuous jousts between Vance and Brzezinski. Finally, the staffs of both bodies contained large numbers of young, academically-oriented members of Graham Allison's "Vietnam generation" who as students had been serious critics of American foreign policy. We expected these officials to be especially sensitive to broad questions about the meaning of the Cold War, the legacy of Vietnam, and the role of historical ideas in policy-making. But before considering their responses, we need to examine the unifying themes of the Administration's foreign policy.

* * * * *

Previous administrations had, of course, sought to distance themselves from their immediate predecessors by ostensibly substituting diplomatic creativity, energy, and new priorities for inflexibility, indecisiveness, and immobility. Eisenhower's "new look," Kennedy's New Frontier, and Nixon's "new structure of peace" all claimed, at least rhetorically, to rescue and revitalize American foreign policy without renouncing the interests, commitments, and principles of the nation. Yet this rhetoric should not be allowed to obscure the shared, compelling experience of the Cold War and the interpretation placed on this conflict by the foreign policy establishment and its academic supporters which intensified an underlying sense of historical continuity. But, as we have seen, Vietnam and the Cold War revisionists shattered the establishment consensus and the academic consensus respectively, and both remained fragmented throughout the 1970s.

During the first two years of his administration Jimmy Carter explicitly sought to dissociate himself from important parts of the postwar American foreign policy record while simultaneously embracing what he considered to be the truly enduring dimensions of the national heritage. First, as the only President to criticize directly American policy *aims* in Vietnam (he claimed they suffered from "moral and intellectual poverty"), Carter maintained an ambivalent attitude toward the strategy that had ultimately sanctioned American intervention there: containment. Although never wholly repudiating America's Cold War efforts his refusal to defend so central an episode as the Vietnam War was unprecedented in American postwar history. Not since Franklin D. Roosevelt briefly (and rather obliquely) accepted the conclusions of the World War I revisionists had a President committed a comparable act, and, in fact, Carter went much farther than Roosevelt in denouncing a past American intervention. Second, Carter and his advisers were convinced that the Cold War had ended. Détente, though allegedly mismanaged by Kissinger, had created conditions which had finally liberated the United States from an "inordinate" concern with the Soviet menace. More attention could now be given to "world order" problems like nuclear proliferation, new international economic arrangements, overpopulation, malnutrition, the law of the sea, and human rights—problems which ostensibly possessed few relevant historical precedents. In view of these circumstances, the continued salience of the "lessons" of the Cold War were necessarily questioned by the Administration. Finally, Henry Kissinger cast a powerful if uncertain shadow over the Carter Administration. Virtually every aspect of Kissinger's record had been attacked by candidate Carter in 1976—his "cozy" relations with dictators, his "neglect" of traditional allies, his "insensivity" to the "just" demands of the developing nations, his "amoral" arms transfer policy, his "shocking" disregard of human rights issues, his "neo-Bismarckian" diplomatic manipulations and secrecies—yet he was paid a certain homage by the very self-consciousness with which the Administration tried to fashion a non-Kissingerian foreign policy. Indeed, our interviews revealed that many Carter officials were privately awed by his performance even as they publicly disparaged it.[10] Given the historical discontinuities which apparently separated to an unparalleled degree the Carter Presidency from its predecessors, it is significant and somewhat surprising that ex-President Carter nevertheless attempted to make himself an heir of Harry Truman and other postwar Presidents:

> I don't think anyone who has not served there can adequately appreciate the continuity of problems and challenges and decisions. The things that Jerry Ford decided when he was in office. affected me daily. Even things that Harry Truman decided thirty years before I went into office affected me daily.
>
> You can make modifications of a previous president's policies, but there is a stream of decisions and ideals and goals and hopes and dreams and problems and disappointments that transcends the identity of the president in the Oval Office. They come from the American people themselves. We share that.[11]

No doubt this statement was in part politically inspired, coming as it did less than a year after his massive 1980 electoral defeat, but it also expressed Carter's perception of himself and his understanding of American foreign policy. At bottom this was the testimony of a neo-Wilsonian populist who saw American diplomacy not primarily in terms of geopolitical interests but as the external reflection of popular "ideals and goals and hopes." Administrations change but these aspirations persist. Policies can be modified, but they must respect both previous decisions and democratic values. To the extent that Carter challenged the American foreign policy record he did so because it had allegedly strayed too far from "the people." Carter's self-proclaimed legacy, therefore, was to reconnect American diplomacy with its popular base. In this sense, Carter saw himself not so much as the inheritor of a diplomatic tradition, but as the restorer of timeless American (and universal) values.

Above all Jimmy Carter wanted to construct a "just world order" in an "interdependent world" delivered from the Cold War and Vietnam. The fullest elaboration of this vision appeared in Stanley Hoffmann's PRIMACY OR WORLD ORDER. Suggestively subtitled *American Foreign Policy Since the Cold War,* this book accurately anticipated (with a few exceptions) the priorities of the new administration and was simultaneously a critique of Kissinger and a handbook on "world order politics." Although the messages were radically different, it did for Carter what Rostow's THE UNITED STATES IN THE WORLD ARENA had done for the Kennedy Administration almost two decades earlier.

Hoffmann recommended an American "world order policy" based on "moderation plus" to manage the problems of global interdependence. Such a policy was aimed at an international environment that Hoffmann found full of "ambiguity" and "complexity." He argued that American leaders had since at least 1947 felt primarily responsible for the achievement of world order, yet their version involved mainly the erection of a dam against Communism.[13] Containment was directed with an unfortunate blend of paranoia and moral arrogance, yet, for Hoffmann, its "objective" accomplishments were undeniably "impressive."[14] The debit side of the record "consisted largely, not of communist successes, which were few, but of mere manifestations of America's incapacity to roll Communism back: in North Korea, in Eastern Europe, at the Bay of Pigs."[15] Yet despite the long string of successes—the integration of the former Axis powers into the "American world system," Israel's power, Berlin, the Congo, the Cuban Missile Crisis, and decolonization—by the late 1960s Americans felt "a sense of failure."[16] While this malaise could be in part attributed to the failure of containment to provide anything more exalting than the indefinite pursuit of more containment, Hoffmann argued that Vietnam had been the real cause:

> The misapplication of containment to that country seemed to have petrified and paralyzed American policy throughout the world. It now appeared as the extreme but logical, absurd but unavoidable end of the policy of confrontation. Thus it put into question the policy itself. . . . It would not have seemed to spell

> defeat for the whole strategy of containment, had the means involved not been so huge, and had the inflation of these means not led officials to inflate the stakes as well (as had happened in the First World War).[17]

At the root of America's failure in Vietnam lay the same "neglect of local circumstances" that had doomed its effort in China.[18]

Nevertheless, Kissinger attempted to preserve American "primacy" by mapping a neo-Bismarckian course ostensibly characterized by "moderation." He believed that

> primacy would be assured at less cost, in two ways. One was a modicum of disengagement from areas whose importance to the national interest could now be acknowledged as secondary. This was the meaning of the so called Nixon doctrine. . . .
>
> A second way of reducing costs was a change in the instruments of primacy. There would be fewer overt military interventions, more covert action . . . , less food aid and assistance, more food and arms sales . . .[19]

Furthermore, Kissinger sought to move beyond containment to a "stable structure" of peace grounded in the Sino-Soviet-American "triangular relationship" and preserved by a judicious admixture of "carrot and stick" diplomacy.

Hoffmann concluded, however, that Kissinger failed to realize his vision of world order, and by 1976 American foreign policy had again lost its way:

> Whereas Metternich's foreign policy was dictated by his concern for Austria's internal vulnerability, Kissinger was a practitioner of the primacy of foreign policy. But one can say of him what he said of Castlereagh: his own country defeated him. His policy turned out to be simultaneously too complex in execution for the domestic forces whose support he needed, and too simple in design for the present-day world, despite its being far more subtle than the earlier simplicities of containment.[20]

Its execution was too complex to retain domestic support because the "web of dependencies" in which Kissinger tried to enmesh the Soviet Union had actually created a host of domestic American interest groups, some of whose well-being rested on "carrots" and others who demanded "sticks." In the absence of a new foreign policy consensus Kissinger discovered that he could not garner sufficient support for a

Soviet policy which required a subtle blending of carrots and sticks. His legacy was to leave America at least as internally divided as he had found it with "gloomy, grumpy, flamboyant"[21] neo-conservative anti-Communists accusing him of appeasement; neo-Wilsonian 'radicals" clamoring for the United States to "purge itself of all the evil forces" that had led to its "corruption" by proclaiming "a wholly new moral and political order"[22]; and "moderate activists, without hegemonic pretenses, eager to draw on the reservoir of American moralism on behalf of international cooperation,"[23] by enthusiastically supporting Jimmy Carter.

Hoffmann contended that Kissinger's world design was "too simple for today's world," because it allegedly rested on obsolete notions of world politics. That is, his vision mistakenly presumed that the "diplomatic-strategic chessboard" still contained the only significant international "game," whereas Hoffmann argued that a series of recent and momentous changes had transformed the nature of the global environment. Now the classical chessboard shared the spotlight with several new games, and while these newcomers had not yet destroyed the ultimate decisiveness of the older contest, they had created an exceedingly ambigious international system. No longer could the United States define world order in terms of American hegemony, either overtly as in the Truman Doctrine or covertly as in the Nixon Doctrine, but, rather, it had to adjust to the post-Vietnam reality of "complex interdependence":

> We have moved from the age of supremacy based on one nation's enlightened interest to the age of compulsory bargaining and compromise. This does not mean abdication: the final deal will certainly have to reflect in part the assets of relative preponderance. But the preponderant power must make concessions.[24]

But, Hoffmann warned, in its search for a world order policy, American leaders could not rely on traditional intellectual roadmaps, for this new world was so unique that classical political and historical theories and prescriptions had only the barest relevance.[25] In short, the past as described by Thucydides, Rousseau, Wilson, and even Dean Acheson was dead.

How had the world been transformed? First, there had been a "change in the number and nature of actors."[26] In addition to a tremendous increase in the number of states, non-state actors of many types who behaved "*as if* they had . . . autonomy[27] had lately emerged. Furthermore, the nature of states' objectives had altered so that foreign policy was now "the external dimension of the universally dominant concern for economic development and social welfare."[28] Whereas "control" had historically been the primary end of foreign policy, actors now sought "milieu goals" through the achievement of "influence."[29] While it is true that Hoffmann had noted the same phenomena almost a decade earlier in GULLIVER'S TROUBLES,[30] what had earlier been identified as a tendency had now become a compelling reality. Second, through its "diffusion," because of the growth in the number of actors and foreign policy issues, and in its "diversification"—"the kinds of supplies needed to exert influence" were "so varied that the old quasi identification with military might" had "become absurd"—the nature of power had undergone "radical change." Moreover, the use of power supplies had grown in complexity, and the existence of new restraints on that use now affected "the old logic of interaction." To express the significance of this extraordinary transformation Hoffmann offered a homely metaphor:

> . . . in the traditional usage of power states were like boiled eggs. War, the minute of truth would reveal whether they (or which ones) were hard or soft. Interdependence breaks eggs into a vast omelet. It does not mean the end of conflict: I may want *my* egg to contribute a larger part of the omelet's size and flavor than *your* egg—or I may want you to break yours into it first, etc. . . . But we all end in the same omelet.[31]

Third, the international hierarchy, which had formerly been based exclusively on military or geo-military power, now had fragmented into "separate functional hierarchies, and in each one the meaning of being 'top dog' " was "far from simple."[32] In contrast to the past when supremacy carried with it unambiguous benefits, the new international system had become "a trying world for top dogs, because of the general difficulty (the interference of other actors and one's own domestic accidents) of using one's might to achieve desired results, because of the difficulty of making might in one area affect outcomes in another (linkage), and because of the handicaps proper to each area."[33] Fourth, not only had the traditional "diplomatic-strategic chessboard" lost its previous monopoly over international life, but its nature had been transformed as well. The nuclear revolution had produced a "fear of force" which made the " 'minute of truth' more hypothetical" but had also privileged "other kinds of power."[34] This presumably universal fear had changed the "rules of the 'game of power' " by producing a "strange blend of arms race and restraints," by subverting the bipolar hierarchy of states through the proliferation of non-nuclear forms of violence, and by worsening strains among allies. Finally, the allegedly unprecedented political significance of economic interdependence had spawned "extraordinarily complex" games in which the "use of force" was very "unlikely."[36] For Hoffmann, "this interdependence, the possibility or obligation to weave one's power into the web," was "both an opportunity for and a restraint on the actor." But, as it turned out, interdependence had disproportionately crippled giants and empowered pygmies:

> The games of interdependence obviously favor the United States; its economic capabilities are huge, its threads are all over the tapestry. . . . And yet, serious inhibitions on the use of America's power limit its capacity to obtain outcomes proportional to its capabilities (and provoke dismay in a public that is not used to vulnerabilities, dependencies and forced restraints). . . . Thus the capacity of the strong to exploit fully the favorable asymmetries of interdependence is limited. The United States may be at the top of almost every hierarchy of economic power, but here, as in the strategic realm, it is a Gulliver tied, not a master with free hands.[37]

In short, interdependence had so altered the conditions of interaction that "rules prescribing states what to do and what not to do," such as Bretton Woods, were "no longer enough." They needed replacement by "international organizations with considerable powers either of administration or even of policy making."[38] Needless to say, the United States would find it impossible to control these new institutions.

Momentous as these changes were, however, they had not yet caused the demise of the nation-state as the world's primary political unit. The concept of the national interest may have splintered into "many alternatives," but Hoffmann advised "prudence" and concluded that "the present scene" was a "triumph of ambiguity."[39] Despite these enormous changes the state retained surprising resilience; it had been "neither superseded nor tamed"; and individuals still turned to it for "protection, welfare, and justice."[40]

How, then, should the United States respond to this ambiguously transformed world? On the one hand, Hoffmann rejected the advice of the Cold War revisionists:

> [their critique] all too often avoids discussing the "relationship of major tension"; or it assumes that it has settled the problem by pointing out that the Cold War is not a zero-sum game and that not every U.S. retreat means a Soviet advance, or by exorcising the "war system" rhetorically one more time. But one cannot wish away problems that are written into the very essence of world affairs and into the very nature of one's chief rival.[41]

But if America ought not listen to Richard Barnet and Gabriel Kolko, neither should it imitate the conduct of previous administrations.

> . . . world order today requires not merely a broad, long-range view of the national interest, as in the late 1940s and throughout the 1950s, but compromises between competing interests, genuine concessions to interests opposed to those of the United States. Instead of a choice between two ways of calculating American benefits—a long-range and a short-term definition—we will be faced with a choice between such compromises and the risks of chaos.[42]

Rather, it should pursue a "world order policy" of "moderation plus," a policy which would, in effect, graft the new complexities (and constraints) of interdependence onto the moderation of the realist revisionists. But the task will not be easy, because "the passion for control, so deeply rooted in American history, the universal moralism, so deeply expressive of America's civil religion, must now yield to an external policy of extreme delicacy."[43] Patience, compromise, co-operation, sensitivity, and nuance were required. Yet

> . . . the experience of the recent past—eight years of [Kissinger's] "amorality" tacked onto the long immorality of Vietnam—will make the curbing [of aggressive idealism] difficult. If historical activism is strong, historical memory is weak. The instinctive desire to save the former creates the legend that Vietnam was merely a product of cynicism and elitism, rather than a catastrophe resulting from misplaced idealism.[44]

Hoffmann warned that a world order policy must not become the excuse for a new wave of neo-Wilsonian crusading but must serve as the basis of a policy that reflected the complexity, ambiguity, and intractibility of the real world.

To a remarkable degree the Carter Administration shared not only Hoffmann's view of the contemporary international situation but also accepted his historical interpretation of postwar American foreign policy. Three qualifications, however, need to be made. First, Hoffmann evinced much more skepticism about making "human rights" the linchpin of a "world order policy" than did many members of the Administration:

> The old Kantian or Wilsonian question remains valid and disturbing. Can one expect a moderate world order unless the domestic regimes are themselves founded on the principle of consent and the rule of law? But all the tyrannies and all the regimes of social injustice simply cannot be suddenly wisked off the face of the earth. To make their elimination an explicit *goal* of world order would be slightly suicidal; any attempt at world order must initially try to enlist them. Their elimination can be a desired effect, not an open objective.[45]

Surely Hoffmann would have been alarmed at this statement of Colonel Leslie G. Denend of the National Security Council staff:

> . . . I think that the U.S. really has an appealing story to tell. It has an appealing system of government, ideology, basic notion of the individual, and we ought to go on the offensive in telling that story rather than react to the initiatives of others. If you, in an ideological sense, go on the offensive, and if you have a story that indeed is sympathetic, and if you find a sympathetic audience, then you ought to do that.[46]

For Hoffmann, such an "ideological offensive" would have threatened the very kind of world order that the United States should have been building. In short, he feared that the Administration's evident desire to find a world audience for its understanding of human rights could all too easily degenerate into a moralistic quest for "primacy" that would represent the antithesis of a true "world order policy." Second, the Carter Administration was victimized by a variety of internal disputes—bureaucratic, tactical, strategic, sometimes even philosophical—and not everyone embraced Hoffmann's analysis and recommendations with an equal degree of enthusiasm. These fissures became increasingly obvious when Brzezinski, in order to design and rationalize a Persian Gulf strategy, came to rely heavily on Cold War "lessons" rather than those of Vietnam. Finally, as will we see, the

Administration significantly altered its course during its last two years of life, so that PRIMACY OR WORLD ORDER served as a much more reliable intellectual guide for the initiatives of 1977 and 1978 than for the adjustments of 1979 and 1980. Nevertheless, Hoffmann's "moderation plus" formulation better captured the essence of the Administration's outlook than any comparable academic statement.

* * * * *

Jimmy Carter brought to the White House the most ambitious foreign policy agenda of any President since John F. Kennedy. Freed at last from Vietnam American diplomacy, the Administration argued, could now address a wide variety of problems neglected for too long by Johnson, Nixon, and Ford. The termination of the war thus provided the United States with an opportunity to construct a "complex" foreign policy responsive of the several ongoing world revolutions which were delivering "rapid change" to the entire planet. The President outlined his "global agenda" at the United Nations in March 1977 and at Notre Dame two months later, but the most comprehensive early articulation was offered in June 1977 by Policy Planning Staff Director Lake in Boston.[47] He announced that six themes and ten sub-themes would comprise the major foci of the Carter "foreign policies." Ranging from détente and arms control to energy, overpopulation, pollution, human rights, and the North-South dialogue, all were apparently to be given roughly equal attention, and together they defined a "complex" approach to a "pluralistic" world. Echoing Hoffmann Lake argued that the significant growth in political and economic interdependence and the dispersion of international power in the wake of decolonization and the emergence of the "non-aligned movement" had helped to inaugurate a newly diverse world.[48] It was America's task to participate "in the construction of a pluralistic world order in which all states, of necessity, must join."[49] In addition to supporting its security alliances, upon which world peace would continue to rest, the United States was obliged to assist in the construction of new "global coalitions,"

> . . . which will be in constant motion, coming together on one issue, but moving apart on another. Any state will belong to many different coalitions, with loyalties and interests that cut across traditional lines.[50]

Fortunately, this post-Vietnam role was neatly tailored to America's domestic strengths:

> No other people has so well learned the workings of a pluralist world and the political skills needed to keep it working. No other nation is composed of such diverse groups and shifting coalitions as the United States. Our domestic tradition is now our greatest international asset.[51]

In effect, Lake pledged the Carter Administration to an enormously ambitious program underwritten by America's unique domestic attributes.

Yet if the size of the agenda was impressively large, the number of foreign policy instruments which the United States might employ to achieve these goals was more limited than at any time since World War II. Indeed, in its apparent unwillingness to use or threaten military force, the Carter Administration shared more with Herbert Hoover than with the New Frontier, although after mid-1978 Zbigniew Brzezinski and most of the National Security Council staff became notably more enthusiastic about the utility of military power than their State Department colleagues.

Carter's "world order policy" was given coherence by the concepts of "complexity" and "change." Time and again Administration spokesmen articulated these notions and applied them to the entire fabric of American diplomacy. In East-West relations "complexity" implied a multi-dimensional approach geared to both competition and cooperation with Moscow. In a North-South context it emphasized the wide range of "global issues" which needed to become part of a "negotiating agenda." Brzezinski, Vance, and other senior officials continually reminded us that we were living in a world of unprecedented change, and that our central task was to become "constructively relevant" to this new reality. Such a policy ostensibly required great sensitivity to deeper historical trends and forces lest the chaotic nature of daily events overwhelm us. Brzezinski, for example, in 1979 asked,

> What is the true nature of our times? What is the real significance of the problems we face? Are the seemingly random and unrelated changes we see around us part of an intellectually coherent pattern? Unless we regularly take time to pose questions like these, we risk losing our sense of direction. We risk finding ourselves merely buffeted by the forces of history—but unable to guide those forces.[52]

In its quest to make the United States relevant to a pluralistic world characterized by "inexorable political, economic, and social change,"[53] did the Carter Administration "repudiate thirty years of American foreign policy" and offer a radically new definition of America's role in the world? What was its understanding of the Cold War? Which of this conflict's "historical lessons" did it find relevant? Did the Cold War revisionists play a role in defining those lessons for the administration? Did the axioms of the realist revisionists exert any influence?

* * * * *

We turn now to our interviews with members of the National Security Council and the Policy Planning Staff. Almost all of them were reasonably familiar with the academic debate over Cold War origins, and at least two younger officials, Robert A. Pastor of the NSC and Samuel R. (Sandy) Berger, a deputy director of the Policy Planning Staff, had been strongly drawn to the radical revisionist critique. Pastor, who was only 29 years old when he joined Brzezinski's staff in early 1977, felt "very much a product of the Vietnam generation."[54] Having spent his junior year in college as a student in Britain where he helped to organize anti-war demonstrations, Pastor returned to the United States determined to discover the historical roots of our Vietnam involvement. This study soon forced him to examine the origins of the Cold War, and he spent two years doing little else but reviewing this literature. Though he read "virtually everything on the subject," Pastor noted that David Horowitz's *From Yalta to Vietnam*[55] had "had a dramatic impact" on him and had helped to explain how the United States had gotten into Vietnam. Furthermore, it had propelled him through a large number of books to determine if Horowitz's Cold War thesis had any validity. Pastor concluded that Horowitz's psychological critique of America's "Cold War mentality" was much more persuasive than his examination of economic motives for Vietnam. Unlike several of his colleagues on the NSC and counterparts on the PPS, he had never been very impressed by "limitationists" like Kennan, Lippmann, and Morgenthau. Finding their accounts of both the early Cold War and the American intervention in Vietnam "ambiguous," Pastor argued that while Kennan, for example, claimed that our strategic interests did not extend to Vietnam, he "begged the question about *how* you define those interests."[56] In retrospect, Pastor recognized that both revisionist and orthodox explanations of the Cold War "suffered from the same sort of *hubris*" by attaching blame to one side or the other, and that, in general, Americans in the 1960s were "too eager to fix blame rather than understand"[57] public issues.

Four years of service on the NSC significantly altered his outlook. Pastor, who served as coordinator of Caribbean and Latin American policy, suggested that, in contrast to his views in 1976 or even 1977, he came to realize that Cuban objectives and actions made it much more difficult for the United States to pursue its legitimate interests. While asserting that his earlier attitude toward Cuba was never really "favorable," Pastor admitted that "as part of the revisionist critique" he had "tried to find some things, particularly internally, that the Cubans did which were not bad."[58] By 1981, however, Pastor had concluded that "there is a natural disagreement, which at times can become conflictual, between Cuba and the United States," and in that conflict "we're right and they're wrong."[59] Indeed, "the group in the United States today that argues that Cuba is benign or should be emulated is obviously much smaller than in the 1960s," and "those who continue to so perceive Cuba are more committed and ideological than many of those in the late '60s." Yet "having passed through this phase intellectually" Pastor believed himself more able to "dialogue" with Cuban sympathizers than his NSC predecessors would have been. On balance, Pastor acknowledged that whereas his former colleagues at Harvard had remained very sympathetic to Cold War revisionism or at least to Yergin's version of post-revisionism, his own experience in Washington had led him to reevaluate these critiques.

Sandy Berger underwent a comparable metamorphosis. Berger graduated from Cornell in 1967 where he majored in government, and although he took a diplomatic history course from Walter LaFeber, he had been much more taken with George Kahin's course on Vietnam during the 1964-65 academic year. Remembering Kahin's impact as "profound" Berger shortly thereafter became involved in the anti-war movement, "primarily taking part in marches, writing letters, and things like that."[60] He had been aware of the Cold War revisionists, especially Williams, and at the time "was fairly enamored of that perspective." Berger expressed its attractiveness in this way:

> I think that for my generation—we came to political adolescence in the '50s during a period of anti-Communist hysteria and a period in which every problem was cast in East-West terms—the Soviets were behind every rock, and I think that we developed instinctively some reaction to that oversell. We also then became

> preoccupied with the fundamental problems that beset this society, for example, the civil rights movement. Along comes the Vietnam war, which confirms the culpability of the United States for the problems of the world—again pulls our direction inward—and . . . we, perhaps, did not focus sufficiently on the Soviet Union, and the nature of that society, and its foreign policy.[61]

Even in 1981 Berger could find "some validity" in the revisionist critique, although not nearly as much as he once did.

After graduation from Harvard Law School in 1971 Berger went to work for Senator Harold Hughes of Iowa who was mounting an anti-war campaign for the Democratic Presidential nomination. When Hughes' bid collapsed, Berger went through a succession of candidates, including John Lindsay, before joining George McGovern in March 1972, first as deputy campaign manager for the California primary and finally as one of McGovern's three top speechwriters. The following year he became a member of the prestigious Washington law firm of Hogan and Hartson. With this admittedly "rather modest background in foreign policy" Berger joined the Policy Planning Staff in the summer of 1977. He soon became a deputy director functioning primarily as a speechwriter for Vance and Muskie. After the Soviet invasion of Afghanistan Berger began to think seriously again about the origins and development of the Cold War:

> I was outraged by Afghanistan. I read the intelligence reports, and that is a brutal war where the Soviets have placed land mines disguised as children's toys on the Afghan-Pakistani border:[62]

Berger concluded that the Cold War revisionists had grossly underestimated the ambitiousness of the Soviet Union, but he resisted the temptation to fly "to the other extreme":

> You have to separate out the arms race, because the U.S. holds enormous responsibility for its dynamic and the way in which the arms race has developed, but I think that there was in that writing too great a leap from that proposition to a view that did not analyze very carefully internal Soviet politics and Soviet foreign policy. We need to restore that balance.[63]

Yet it is undeniable that, like Robert Pastor, Sandy Berger's perceptions of the Cold War had been significantly altered as a result of service in the Carter Administration. Two further examples underline this point. He had been at one time largely prepared to locate the roots of the Cold War in the socio-economic structures of the United States and the Soviet Union. In 1981 he was much less sure:

> I still think obviously that there is a dimension to American foreign policy that relates to America's economic interests, and that does to some extent drive our foreign policy, but I guess I don't think it's as simple as I thought it was.[64]

Similarly, Berger's view of the Soviet Union became more traditional after Afghanistan:

> . . . I was at the University of Wisconsin speaking on behalf of SALT before a group of clergy and laity much like those I had worked with in the '60s and had felt very comfortable with. I said that I found it to be anomalous that we were incapable of summoning the same kind of moral indignation and outrage against the abusive use of Soviet power. That, combined with what we've learned over the past five or six years about the treatment of dissidents and refusniks, the kind of intimidation now being used against Poland, really ought to lead us to restore some balance in the other direction. But that doesn't lead you to become a knee-jerk Cold Warrior. But there's a fundamental difference between recognizing that the Soviet Union is a society that is antithetical to our objectives—to our way of dealing with the individual—and of translating that into a touchstone for our policy. But in political terms I think that liberals have badly hurt themselves over the last five or ten years because they have been unwilling to use the rhetoric of a Daniel Moynihan.. . .[65]

To a significant degree Robert Pastor and Sandy Berger had as college students in the 1960s embraced the foreign policy axioms of Graham Allison's Vietnam generation. Bright, articulate, highly educated, and vociferous opponents of the war, both clearly belonged, in outlook at least, to that group of "elite young Americans" portrayed by Allison in 1970. Moreover, each of them, for somewhat different reasons, had found the Cold War revisionists to be very persuasive in exposing the alleged roots of the Vietnam intervention. Pastor had been attracted to the psychological explanations of David Horowitz, while Berger had been impressed with the economic arguments of William Appleman Williams. If Cold War revisionism was to gain an analytical foothold in the Carter Administration, surely it would have done so with the help of apostles like Pastor and Berger. Yet, as we have seen, neither official sustained his initial outlook when confronted with evidence that seemingly contradicted the arguments and assurances of the Cold War revisionists. For Pastor "Cuban adventurism" in Africa, the Caribbean, and Central America cast serious doubts on the critiques of Horowitz and even Yergin, while for Berger the spectre of Soviet brutality in Afghanistan convinced him that the warnings of Daniel Patrick Moynihan should be carefully heeded.

As far as we could determine about one half of the members of the Policy Planning Staff and approximately one third of the *original* NSC staffers broadly shared the early inclinations of Pastor and Berger. Beginning in 1978, however, the views of the NSC began to change, partly because incumbent members like Pastor adjusted their outlooks, but chiefly because newer appointees tended to hold much more "hard-line" attitudes toward the Soviet Union and its allies than had their predecessors. According to one NSC staffer who resigned in frustration in 1979, for the first year or so of the Administration Brzezinski had scrupulously attempted to implement the "world order" views of the President. But as the Russians and the Cubans began to threaten the Horn of Africa in 1978, "Zbig's instincts," which were allegedly of primarily of an East-West nature, dramatically resurfaced, and he started to restructure his staff to reflect this circumstance. In the words of one adviser who joined the NSC that year, "the balance of power, the head count on the staff, really wasn't terribly important. The key question is, 'Where were things trending? What were Brzezinski's preoccupations?' " And the preoccupations clearly focused on Soviet "adventurism," Moscow's arms build-up, the Persian Gulf strategy, and the appropriate use of American military power. One staffer laughingly claimed that "We [i.e., the newer NSC members] formed the 'hard' side of Brzezinski's staff. We called ourselves the Leninist core of the Central Committee." On balance, those who joined the staff in 1978 and 1979 were older, more traditionally oriented than their predecessors, and skeptical of "world order politics." In the words of one of them,

> At that point Brzezinski was staffing up some people that he knew and trusted, whereas he was kind of given a staff when he came in in '77. It had really been built by others with a couple of exceptions.[66]

Among the more prominent latecomers were F. Stephen (Steve) Larrabee, Madeleine Albright, and Fritz Ermarth.

Larrabee graduated from Amherst in 1966 and during his senior year took a course on Vietnam which he, like Berger, remembered as the most important of his college career. He spent the next year in Greece where he was "very affected" by the Colonels' coup and by America's seeming acquiescence in it. Returning to the United States in 1967 he enrolled as a graduate student in political science at Columbia. By then Larrabee had become deeply worried about Johnson's Vietnam policy and its disastrous domestic consequences. Skeptical of Dean Rusk's assertion that Chinese Communism needed to be contained in Southeast Asia, unlike Pastor, Larrabee found the Vietnam critiques of Kennan, Lippmann, and Morgenthau very pragmatic and persuasive. By 1969 he had decided that Vietnam could not be understood apart from the Cold War and, along with a handful of other graduate students, asked Brzezinski to conduct a seminar on its origins. Brzezinski agreed, even though his teaching load was already full, and the group proceeded to meet over lunch to discuss orthodox and revisionist accounts of the Cold War. No one, including Brzezinski, had been previously exposed to radical revisionism, and the seminar intensively studied Williams, Kolko, Alperovitz, Horowitz, Gardner, and the others. Larrabee, however, was unimpressed with their arguments:

> I believed that the mentality and attitudes [of the Cold War] very much conditioned our getting in there [i.e., Vietnam]. To stabilize France we gave them a lot of aid for Indochina. It was a Eurocentric policy at the beginning. Being Eurocentric myself I felt very definitely that we were neglecting important interests elsewhere which in the long run were far more important. We were spending an inordinate amount of resources there for something that was, by all rational criteria, unwinnable. It was having an across-the-board detrimental effect—alienating a whole generation.

Opposed to the war on limitationist grounds and repulsed by what he saw as the excesses of many leftist students at Columbia, Larrabee was haunted by a "feeling of despair that this country was being torn apart, the center could not hold. . . . It was a Spenglerian scenario if ever I've seen one—a decline of civilization."[68] A week after his Ph.D. exams in 1970 he left for Europe and spent the better part of the next seven years there. Looking back on this period from the perspective of 1981, Larrabee felt sure that he had

> . . . never agreed with the revisionists that we were the bad guys. I felt that we had made mistakes, but they had to do with overeaction, lack of understanding of the internal situation in the Soviet Union, a certain amount of inevitable mistakes made by any major power that had to do with a lack of historical experience in world affairs. . . , but this had very little to do with conscious efforts to expand American influence.[69]

Rather, much like the George Kennan of the Policy Planning Staff, Larrabee considered the Soviet Union to be a victim of a "defensive paranoia—a paranoid sense of insecurity—which oftentimes led it to do the very opposite thing and thus increase the insecurity of the other side."[70]

When he joined the NSC midway in the Administration, Larrabee found himself at odds with the "moralism" of some of Carter's policies. Describing himself as "much closer to a kind of Kissinger approach, with more of an emphasis on Europe," he was "much more sympathetic to the positions adopted at the end, after [Carter] . . . began to turn around,"[71] in 1978.

Madeleine Albright had also been a student of Brzezinski's at Columbia in the 1960s. The daughter of Joseph Korbel, a Czech diplomat who had been ambassador to Yugoslavia at the time of the 1948 coup, Albright came to the United States as a child, graduated from Wellesley in 1959, and began graduate school three years later. Captivated by Brzezinski's course on diversity in the Communist world, Albright soon became very interested in the origins of the Cold War. She had first studied the Soviet takeover of Eastern Europe at Wellesley where she wrote an honors thesis on the role of Zdenek Fierlinger, the Czech socialist leader in the 1948 Communist coup, but in the mid-'60s she began to read Cold War revisionism. After looking at this literature Albright concluded that

> . . . the United States was, in effect, reacting to a whole series of actions that the Soviets had undertaken in a very consistent way. I had obviously been influenced by my father who had been a victim. I watched the Communists in Yugoslavia so I had a very personal experience. . . . So there was never any doubt in my mind about how the Cold War began, and I did feel that these revisionists were, in effect, responding more to the tenor to their own time rather than to what had actually happened.[72]

Terming much of this writing "present-minded" Albright believed that

> A lot of it was a reaction to Vietnam and the desire to see the United States in a bad light. I came from a background in which the United States was seen as the savior—a country where Woodrow Wilson had the answer to everything. I didn't think the United States could be an evil or imperialistic force.[73]

Yet her admiration for post-war American foreign policy was not unbounded:

> Now, in later years, as I have studied things myself, I can see serious problems with Yalta and with some of the ways the United States developed an active policy as, for example, the Dulles Doctrine vis-à-vis Eastern Europe. But as far as the *origins* of the Cold War go I would place the blame in the Soviet Camp.[74]

Albright worked as a fundraiser for Muskie and Mondale in the 1972 Presidential campaign but not for McGovern. Beginning in 1975 she served on Muskie's Senate staff as a senior legislative assistant with primary responsibility for foreign policy and defense issues. In March 1978 Brzezinski, with whom she had remained very close, asked her to become the NSC's Congressional liasion. Albright felt frequently frustrated in this post because of those members of Congress who, still gripped by the "lessons" of Vietnam, "seriously distrusted the projection of American power abroad."

Albright had been a solid supporter of the Vietnam War until the shock of Tet convinced her that the costs of pursuing it had come to exceed its stakes. Yet she believed that the "legacy of Vietnam" had taken an even higher toll than the war itself:

> The terrible part of Vietnam is more the effect that it's had in the United States. Obviously the people of Vietnam have suffered desperately and the image of the United States suffered desperately, but I think the kind of internal ageny that two or three generations of people have gone through and the way it had affected American foreign policy is the great crime of Vietnam.[75]

Fritz Ermarth, a Sovietologist and strategic expert, joined the NSC in 1978. A "Henry Jackson–Max Ascoli Democrat," and "the product of a Cold War upbringing" when he entered college in 1957, he was, nevertheless, impressed with Khrushchev's de-Stalinization campaign and "eager to give the Russians the benefit of the doubt."[76] This attitude gradually evaporated, however, as Ermarth began an intensive study of Russian history and Soviet affairs at Harvard. There he studied primarily with Merle Fainsod, Adam Ulam, and Henry Kissinger in the early 1960s, when "things in the Soviet Union were their most relaxed."[77] Ermarth noted that

> When you study those things, nine times out of ten you come out a hawk. People who study China learn to love the Chinese people. People who study the Soviet Union learn to admire and even like the Russians, but they learn to hate the Soviet Union.[78]

Although generally aware of Cold War revisionism, he had never been persuaded by it nor had he believed it to be particularly important as an intellectual current:

> Even when the Vietnam problem reached a peak between '68 and '72 when I was at RAND, it [i.e., Cold War revisionism] really didn't interact with a revisionist view of the Soviet Union. In fact, among those who had focused on the Soviet Union, the revisionist period had really occurred in the mid-1950s. They remembered certain hopes and looked back on them as illusions about what was going to happen to the Soviet system. But by the late '60s [the USSR] was an aspirant super-power, a revolutionary actor in the sense that Bismarck was a revolutionary actor, and a challenge to our fundamental moral values as well as to our security. The [Cold War] revisionist literature was generally regarded with suspicion, a certain amount of contempt, and an inclination by some to see [its authors] basically as fellow-travelers.[79]

According to Ermarth,

> My own orientation is a function of my educational background. By '73 or '74 I was uncompromisingly of the view that the bear was coming out of his cage and was going to cause us no end of trouble. The United States was hourly falling behind this challenge. My job was to cry alarm and mobilize resources, and that's what Brzezinski had me on the staff doing. There was no question about that.[80]

All of the NSC and PPS members that we interviewed expressed attitudes about the Cold War which fell along this spectrum. Brzezinski's orientation most closely resembled Albright's. Finding the scholarship of the radical revisionists often shoddy, he interpreted this literature "more as a social phenomenon than as a serious effort to understand what really transpired."[81] Far from repudiating the Truman Doctrine as a useful historical analogy, Brzezinski "drew President Carter's attention to it" and "made some parallels between it and what subsequently came to be called the Carter doctrine (regarding the Persian Gulf)."[82]

Anthony Lake had discovered Cold War revisionism while a graduate student at Princeton in the late 1960s. Unlike Brzezinski he did not view these writings as social phenomena, yet still found them largely unpersuasive, particularly their economic arguments about American foreign policy. On the other hand, Lake was equally critical of Herbert Feis and the other orthodox historians of the 1950s and likened his own interpretation of the Cold War to that of Daniel Yergin's SHATTERED PEACE.[83] He placed "somewhat more blame" for the Cold War on the Soviet Union than America but was sensitive to the conflict's psychological dynamic—an "action-reaction process" in which tensions spiralled and expanded. Reluctant to "ascribe a single set of motives to any country, including the Soviet Union," Lake compared his understanding of Russia with that of the early George Kennan, though not the Kennan of the "Riga axioms."

In sum, our interviews uncovered no unreconstructed Cold War revisionists. None suggested that the United States had been primarily responsible for the onset of the Cold War, nor did anyone assert that America's economic institutions were responsible for the creation of an Open Door Empire. We found no one who thought that the Soviet Union was essentially a force for good in the world, nor anybody who claimed that America was chiefly a force for ill.

On the other hand, we failed to find any officials who embraced wholly the "Riga outlook." That is, nobody claimed to see the Soviet Union solely, or even predominantly, as a revolutionary state enslaved by ideology and dedicated to limitless expansion. Even those political scientists and strategists who comprised the NSC's "Leninist core" professed much more concern about Soviet military capabilities than about the regime's ideological compulsions. They tended to see the Soviet Union not so much as the reincarnation of Hitler's Reich than as the descendant of Wilhelmine Germany. Yet if the Yalta axioms nevertheless remained alien to most on the NSC, members of the Policy Planning Staff looked rather favorably on them. These officials emphasized the transitory nature of Soviet gains, the frequently improvised character of its foreign policy, and the hope that détente would become possible again once Reagan's approach proved counterproductive. If Yergin's contention that American foreign policy had generally been based on the Riga axioms ever since their formulation in the 1920s was correct, then Carter's State Department can be termed "revisionist" insofar as it rejected this outlook. And while the NSC, especially by 1980, was "orthodox" in relation to State, it was not orthodox by the older standards of the Cold War.

If any single historical work captured the attitudes of the Carter Administration, particularly its first two years, it was surely SHATTERED PEACE. In its bare toleration of American military power, its contention that the arms race had been severely exacerbated, if not caused, by the United States, and its conviction that the Yalta axioms could form the foundation of Soviet-American relations,this book reflected the outlook of many officials. Furthermore, Yergin's dislike of "ideology," his faith in diplomacy, and his misgivings about the "national security state" were largely shared by an Administration outraged by Watergate and haunted by Vietnam.

At the same time, most of those interviewed believed that the history of the Cold War, however interpreted, had only very limited relevance for them as policy-makers. No doubt this conviction resulted in part from their tendency to perceive themselves primarily as problem-solvers regardless of academic background. Roger C. Molander, an arms control expert who served on the National Security Council staff from 1974 to 1981, put it this way:

> There was a lot of talk about the origins of the arms race, but not of the Cold War as such. It was more like "let's solve this problem" rather than "let's figure out how we got in this mess," even though certainly I would understand if somebody said, "Now look, it's easier to solve problems sometimes if you try and figure out how you got there," but that [i.e., the late 1940s] was so far back, and since we were dealing with a problem which is in a very different political and technical-military landscape, it never got anywhere close to being prominent. I suppose that if one of the individuals who had more of a diplomatic history-political science background had said, "Look, Roger, before you go any further, you'd better read the following Kennan piece," I would have done so, but nobody ever said that to me.[84]

Similarly Robert Gallucci, a former political science professor and author of a book about Vietnam,[85] who handled proliferation issues for the Policy Planning Staff, confirmed that the Administration's historical memory was rather limited:

> The thing that was on everybody's mind was how would Kissinger do it. If you were talking about how you respond to a country's nuclear test, for example, we had a case where we had Kissinger's idea of how to respond to the Indian test.[86]

In short, the alleged newness of the issues meant that the past had little to teach contemporary policy-makers, particularly those who concentrated on "world order" issues. Even Gallucci, who had studied the Cold War as a graduate student at Brandeis and taught it as a member of the Swarthmore College faculty, contended that the experiences of previous administrations—Nixon-Ford excepted—were not of much interest to most Carter officials. Rather, they agreed with Stanley Hoffmann that the "management of complex interdependence" required a "world order policy" liberated from the dreary legacy of the Cold War.[87]

* * * *

"Amnesia," of course, constitutes a particular kind of historical revisionism, but notwithstanding the testimony of Molander and Gallucci and the ostensible requirements of "world order", the Carter Administration frequently behaved as if the Cold War still contained relevant "lessons" for contemporary American foreign policy. We will investigate the degree to which these lessons were "revisionist" by focusing on three specific Administration policies: the Persian Gulf, China, and Nicaragua.

Brzezinski's historical understanding of the Truman Doctrine figured prominently in the Carter Administration's response to the fall of the Shah and the Soviet invasion of Afghanistan. The NSC took the bureaucratic lead in designing Persian Gulf policy. As one NSC staff member involved in this planning recalled,

> . . . no one else took the initiative: the Defense Department took no initiative, the State Department took no initiative. It was like pulling teeth. . . . And ideology has very little to do with this. It's just sloth. You could take all those guys, put them a bag, and drop them in a river. And it's still that way.[88]

Significantly, Brzezinski and his staff did not look to the Eisenhower Doctrine for historical guidance, because despite its geographical relevance, it had allegedly led America ultimately to Teheran via Bagdad.[89] The "lessons" of Vietnam (as the next chapter will try to show) likewise counselled against an inordinate reliance on unstable clients. It was, rather, the Truman Doctrine which provided the NSC with a compelling historical analogy for its Persian Gulf strategy, and it did so for at least four reasons. First, Brzezinski continually equated the Soviet threat to the Persian Gulf with that posed to Greece, Turkey, and Western Europe in 1947.[90] Indeed, Brzezinski, in a manner very reminiscent of Truman's treatment of Greece, infused the fate of the Persian Gulf with broader significance:

> . . . in the course of the last thirty years there emerged three central strategic zones in the independence and well-being of which the United States has a vital interest.[91]

Noting that these three areas were Western Europe, the Far East, and the Middle East-Persian Gulf, Brzezinski claimed that

> The fates of these three zones are interdependent and a threat to the security and independence of one is a threat to the other two, for self-evident political and economic reasons.[92]

In other words, while Brzezinski could not pretend that the new Soviet threat was directly aimed at "free peoples" attempting to resist subjugation by armed minorities, as Truman had argued, the economies and political systems of the West and Japan would be jeopardized by Russian "adventurism" in Southwest Asia.

And if the threats were related, so were the appropriate American responses. Despite long-standing criticism of the Truman Doctrine by some commentators (including Yergin) on the grounds that its extravagant rhetoric and imperial definition of American security had involved the United States in an avalanche of commitments culminating in Vietnam, Brzezinski and his aides looked back with fondness on the 1947 speech. For example, Madeleine Albright remembered it as

> . . . one of the best pieces of American policy, and I think that certain members of the Carter Administration tried to emulate it in terms of extending such a commitment to the Persian Gulf. I think it played a very important part in setting down a marker as to what U.S. interests and moral obligations were.[93]

Robert E. Hunter, the NSC staffer who actually penned the Carter Doctrine, rejected the revisionist assertion that the Truman Doctrine had "universalized" containment and suggested that Truman's language had merely reflected the political realities of his day.[94]

Obviously, Brzezinski was too sophisticated to mechanically equate the Persian Gulf of 1979 to the Europe of the late 1940s. He recognized that the situation in the former region was

> much more nuanced and complex than even the Western European area or the Far East. We have to be sensitive to the desires for independence and distinctive identity of some of the countries concerned—and also to the significant ideological differences among the countries.[95]

Nevertheless, Brzezinski was "prepared, recognizing these nuances, to work to create a cooperative security framework for the region."[96]

But the Truman Doctrine had more than strategic appeal for the Carter Administration: it also contained at least two political lessons. That American foreign policy since the late 1960s had been without the support of a firm domestic consensus had become a truism, and one clearly recognized by many in the Carter Administration. As John Holum, a long-time McGovern aide who joined the Policy Planning Staff in early 1979, put it:

> . . . the Carter Administration was trying, maybe imperfectly, but valiantly, to devise a new consensus. . . . [W]hat the Carter Administration was trying to do at a minimum was to say, "Look, the world had changed dramatically, they are over a hundred new countries, there's economic interdependence, there's a whole series of problems that urgently need our attention . . . and our foreign policy has to be about a lot more things than it has been in the past.[97]

This new domestic consensus was to be constructed on a "complex" foundation which included a "sensitivity" to change, especially in the Third World, a renewed concern for human rights, and arms control with the Soviet Union. But Holum admitted that no such new consensus ever emerged: "It was a tragedy that those new directions in foreign policy were so precariously based—they didn't have a popular foundation yet—that the whole thing could come unraveled over something like Iran."[98]

The acute realization by Administration officials that a new foreign policy consensus was essential, the growing recognition by 1979 that the Administration had thus far failed to successfully cultivate that consensus, and the increasing unpopularity of the Carter Presidency, combined to convince Brzezinski that the Persian Gulf crisis could be used to help save the Administration from electoral defeat in 1980.[99] Not unmindful of Truman's remarkable 1948 comeback, Brzezinski used the Carter Doctrine to give a pronounced anti-Soviet cast to the Administration's foreign policy. In an attempt to recapture the political center from the Republicans, Brzezinski began to attack "McGovernite" elements in the Democratic Party as Truman had done with Henry Wallace in 1948. In short, the Persian Gulf crisis provided both the opportunity to fashion a "new" domestic foreign policy consensus based on principles which had worked for twenty years and the possibility of retrieving an otherwise lost Presidency.

Opponents of Brzezinski's strategy within the Carter Administration did not directly dispute his appeal to the Truman Doctrine analogy but, rather, asserted that the "lessons of Vietnam" should have been decisive in devising a Persian Gulf strategy. Implicitly, of course, these officials presumed that the Truman Doctrine and Vietnam were linked, but this historical argument was rarely, if ever, made. In other words, Vietnam, and not a revisionist understanding of the early Cold War, served as the relevant explicit historical model for Brzezinski's State Department critics, though their perceptions of Vietnam were, in turn, colored by a less than orthodox view of the Cold War.

* * * * *

The Carter Administration's China policy was clearly informed by an historical sensitivity to Sino-American relations, but in contrast to the Persian Gulf, it was not to the early Cold War that it turned for analogies. Orthodox historians and the foreign policy establishment had until the late 1960s unanimously seen the late 1940s as the golden age of American diplomacy toward the Soviet Union. The realist revisionists had, of course, applauded the European focus of these initiatives. Only the Cold War revisionists had condemned programs like the Marshall Plan for their allegedly exploitational intentions. But no such unanimous academic or establishment approval had ever been given for America's China policy. There were several reasons for this difference. First, unlike many Sovietologists who saw Mao as the puppet of Moscow (a "Riga" corollary), many of the "China Hands" believed that a posture of vigorous support for Chiang, non-recognition of the PRC, and unremitting hostility toward "Red China" constituted geopolitical absurdity. These Sinologists had already produced revisionist histories of Chinese-American relations when they were purged from the State Department by John Foster Dulles. Second, the bipartisan Cold War consensus never fully embraced the China issue. "Who lost China?" remained a Republican question asked of Democrats, and a satisfactory answer was never given. Third, the lack of a firm consensus was to some degree reflected in the writings of American diplomatic historians. Those orthodox historians like Herbert Feis who had so vividly chronicled the march of "Red Imperialism" across Europe could not quite achieve the same fervency when they turned their attention to China. For some, of course, like Samuel Flagg Bemis, the rape of China and the abandonment of Chiang could easily be compared to the rape of Czechoslovakia and the abandonment of Benes. But, in general, the American decision to isolate Mao received less academic support than the decision to contain Stalin.

Primarily because of the Vietnam War a radical revisionism eventually did grow up around Asian-American relations, and not surprisingly, America's China policy was one of its chief targets. Whereas the revisionism of Williams and Kolko had flourished at a time when the Cold War with the Soviet Union was apparently ending, this Asian radical revisionism emerged during the Cultural Revolution's xenophobic excesses and President Johnson's policy of Chinese containment. Many of these historians belonged to the Committee of Concerned Asian Scholars, an anti-war academic group, and it was this organization which indirectly gave birth to one of their most influential books, AMERICA'S ASIA,[100] which appeared in 1969. An anthology comprised of essays by a dozen radical young historians, this volume indicted the United States for a wide range of misdeeds, including its Japanese occupation policy, its alleged goading of North Korea and China into war in 1950, its supposed destruction of Laotian neutrality, and its adamant refusal to recognize the positive contributions of Mao. It was not enough to normalize relations with the mainland regime. Indeed, such attempts would fail, these scholars warned, so long as the United States treated Asia as a colonial dominion. Until Americans became willing to respect and learn from the Chinese revolution, relations with the PRC would remain hostile. The book's editors concluded that,

> In the era of America's Asia, until we know America we cannot understand Asia, and until fundamental changes are forthcoming

> in American policy, only Asian revolutions can make Asian autonomy and independent development other than hypocritical official myths. Challenging perceptions of ourselves and the world is a vital first step toward a more human foreign policy and a more humane society.[101]

For these historians the "geopolitical" errors of America's China policy identified in the '40s and '50s by Kennan, Morgenthau, and the China Hands implied a diplomacy that was little better than the *status quo.* It was not to John K. Fairbank that these young radicals looked for inspiration, but to Mao.

Yet, the "China card" that Nixon and Kissinger played was most definitely based on geopolitical calculations related to détente and Vietnam. Indeed, so strategic did Kissinger's Chinese diplomacy become, especially after Soviet-American relations grew more tense in 1975, that Mao's successors were eager for the Carter Administration to design a policy less exclusively wedded to "triangular principles."These desires were partially thwarted by the Sino-Vietnamese war and the Soviet invasion of Afghanistan, but between these two events, in August 1979, Vice President Mondale made a speech at Peking University,[102] which could have been written by John Stewart Service and the other "old hands." Compare, for example, these passages:

> China is only superficially a meeting point between the United States and the Soviet Union. Fundamentally it is a society alien to both Russia and America, which is developing according to its own traditions and circumstances. The greatest error that Americans can make is to look at China but think only of Russian expansion.

> And despite the sometimes profound differences between our two systems, we are committed to joining with you to advance our many parallel strategic and bilateral interests. Thus any nation which seeks to isolate or weaken you in world affairs assumes a stance counter to American interests.

The first quotation appeared in the opening paragraph of Fairbank's classic 1948 work, THE UNITED STATES AND CHINA,[103] book which for years had been roundly condemned by American supporters of the Kuomintang, while the second came from Mondale's Peking University speech and was written by Michel Oksenberg, an NSC staffer on leave from the University of Michigan. The United States, of course had for two decades done more than any other state to "isolate and weaken" China "in world affairs," so it was not without irony that Mondale, with Fairbank in the audience, embraced the framework of his 1948 analysis but focused it now on the Soviet Union. Yet this speech, even in its irony, implicitly repudiated America's China policy from the time of Korea to that of Vietnam and thus constituted an indirect acceptance of the old assertions of the China Hands. In 1977 Oksenberg had written these words,

> In retrospect, it appears that those closest to the situation, foreign service officers—particularly John Stewart Service, John Carter Vincent, and John Paton Davies—had the clearest perceptions. . . . But their voices were lost, and later they were sharply attacked.
>
> Chilled by this inheritance, the China policy of the 1950s became frozen around the Korea, Taiwan, and offshore islands issues.[104]

Although he had consistently rejected the arguments of the Cold War revisionists since learning of them at Columbia in the late 1960s, and although he had never joined the Committee of Concerned Asian Scholars (indeed, he had been rather critical of some of its publications), Oksenberg fell within the revisionist tradition in Sino-American diplomatic history pioneered by Fairbank and the China Hands in the '40s and '50s.[105] It was this sense of historical consciousness which Oksenberg brought to Mondale's speech, and more generally, to his post as chief NSC Sinologist. Even in his daily functions Oksenberg defined himself as a "revisionist" insofar as he was aware of sitting in the same office as men who had made "disastrous China policy" in the past.[106]

There have been few more blatant examples in post-World War II American foreign policy of an official sanctioning of a previously suspect historical revisionism (a process begun, of course, by Nixon). Three circumstances help to explain this turnabout. First, the inability of the bipartisan Cold War consensus to fully encompass China had damaged the strength and legitimacy of America's Far Eastern policy, and the Republican normalization initiatives in the early 1970s, consolidated by Democratic actions a few years later, gave to this new China policy a firm bipartisan foundation which the old (and now discredited) one had never enjoyed. Second, the existence of a long-standing revisionist literature, produced by scholars and observers who had been victimized by McCarthyism, influenced and supported American policy-makers who wished to transform China policy. This situation was quite unlike that of the Cold War revisionists whose public credibility was seriously hurt by their (real or imagined) identification with the New Left. Finally, and most crucially, the adoption of a Sino-American historical revisionism did nothing to threaten a more or less conventional understanding of Soviet-American relations.[107] In this sense it was a derivative revisionism. As we noted above, Fairbank's early warning that the United States ought not to isolate or weaken China was used by Mondale in the service of Soviet containment thirty years later, and Brzezinski's eagerness to accelerate normalization with Peking fit nicely with his Persian Gulf strategy. At the same time, it was also acceptable to the State Department for somewhat different reasons. All of which merely states the obvious: Fairbank's brand of revisionism would have remained outcast if the PRC and the USSR had remained close Communist allies.

* * * * *

The realist revisionists had never shown particular interest in Latin America, primarily because of the overwhelming power enjoyed by the United States in most of the region. There was, to be sure, a revisionist literature dating back to the Progressive Era which had maligned America for "dollar diplomacy," "the Big Stick," and its support of reactionary military regimes, but, in general, this writing did not challenge the right nor question the ability of the United States to exercise influence in Latin America. For the Cold War revisionists, however, the major issue was not "power" or "liberal democracy," but "American imperialism," and they sought to demonstrate how the United States had used the Cold War to perpetuate and expand its neo-colonialist links with Latin America. William Appleman Williams, for example, charged that Washington's treatment of Castro had inevitably driven him into Soviet arms and merely constituted the latest chapter in an unhappy story of American exploitation, interventionism, and hypocrisy in Cuba.[108] A few years later Richard Barnet thoroughly condemned the 1954 overthrow of Arbenz and the 1965 Dominican intervention.[109] These were but two of many radical revisionist attacks on virtually every aspect of America's Latin policy from the OAS through the Alliance for Progress to the toppling of Allende. And in Latin America a growing number of radical economists, sometimes called "dependency theorists," asserted that the "structure" of U.S. relations with Latin

America worsened poverty, encouraged economic stagnation, and retarded industrialization.[110]

The Carter Administration boldly pledged to inaugurate a new era in U.S.-Latin American relations, and much of its early diplomatic energies were invested in the completion and ratification of the Panama Canal Treaties. Furthermore, it launched frequent and public attacks on the human rights policies of countries like Chile, Nicaragua, Argentina, and Uruguay. Indeed, some critics argued that these reprimands "destabilized" the regime of Anastasio Somoza Debaye by bolstering the waning morale of the Sandanista rebels. Whatever the validity of that charge it is true that by September 1978 the United States was for the first time in twenty years confronted with the prospect of the overthrow of a Latin American government by left-wing guerrillas.

In searching for a response to the Nicaraguan revolution four courses of action were in principle open to the Administration: (1) the rapid abandonment of Somoza, the quick recognition of the Sandanistas (while still belligerents), and the adoption of a generous economic and military aid program for the rebels; (2) a posture of genuine disinterest on the grounds that the outcome of the Nicaraguan civil war did not threaten the vital interests of the United States; (3) a policy of staunch support (including military assistance) for Somoza to help ensure the defeat or moderation of the Sandanistas; and (4) an attempt to steer a "middle course" between Samoza and the Sandanistas by identifying and encouraging popular and pliant moderates. The evidence shows, however, that the Carter Administration considered seriously only the last two policy options. Its ultimate adoption of the "search for moderates" alternative indicated a willingness to follow a quite traditional American policy of "liberal interventionism," a policy that was unusual only in the clumsiness of its implementation. A few NSC staffers would have apparently preferred a more conservative course entailing substantial aid and strong moral support for Somoza in a manner reminiscent of the Eisenhower Administration's treatment of the Armas regime in Guatemala, but in light of Carter's censure of Somoza's human rights record, such actions would, if nothing else, have raised even more questions about the Administration's consistency. Furthermore, many advisers firmly believed with Stanley Hoffmann that the United States "had to get on the right side of change," and, if it was hard to embrace the Sandanistas, so too was it difficult to cradle Somoza. Many officials, especially in the State Department, had been outraged by Nixon's support of Pinochet in Chile and were determined to avoid a replication of that situation. What ensued, therefore, was a halting, unsteady, and increasingly unrealistic search for a "moderate" alternative to the Left and the Right. When this search failed, Secretary Vance embarked on a futile last-ditch, Dominican-like effort to send an OAS "peacekeeping" force to Nicaragua.

It was not until after the fall of Somoza that members of the Administration became concerned to avoid "another Cuba." As one senior State Department official put it in an unattributable remark,

> There was quite a lot of likening of this situation to Cuba in 1959. The lessons that liberals have learned from Cuba is that you don't force them into the hands of the Soviets, although even some liberals in government would say that Castro probably had this this up his sleeve the whole time. . . . I think that people were conscious of not letting this be a second Cuba.[111]

Not that the Sandanistas were greeted with enthusiasm even by State:

> Nobody was pleased. It was clearly a defeat for U.S. policy. But there was probably a sense that . . . we were acting . . . in a mature way by ultimately accepting the *fait accompli.* There were some younger FSOs in the Latin American Bureau who did look on the Sandanistas maybe not so bad, but none was in a policy position.[112]

It was this decision to "get on the right side of change," if only after the fact,that distinguished the Carter Administration's policy during the post-revolutionary phase. Far from reflecting a "revisionist" understanding of U.S.-Latin American relations, this approach to Nicaragua was "profoundly interventionist,"[113] very sensitive to East-West ramifications, favorably impressed (at least in June 1979) by the "lessons" of the Dominican episode, and only belatedly aware of the Cuban analogy. Nevertheless, to Jeane Kirkpatrick, soon to become President Reagan's Ambassador to the United Nations, Carter's misplaced desire to "avoid a second Cuba" constituted "a posture of continuous self-abasement and apology vis-à-vis the Third World" which was "neither morally necessary, nor politically appropriate."[114] Instead of vigorously supporting Somoza, admittedly an autocrat but also a firm American friend, the Carter Administration allegedly adopted "an oddly uncompromising posture" in dealing with him, "even though the State Department knew that the top Sandanista leaders had close personal ties and were in continuing contact with

Havana."[115] Kirkpatrick claimed that the Administration had forsaken a traditional understanding of the national interest in order to impose on Nicaragua a "deterministic and apolitical" theory of modernization that justified (indeed demanded) American passivity in the face of "complicated, inexorable, impersonal processes."[116]

The Carter Administration's Nicaraguan policy was, in fact, far from passive. In its long and unsuccessful search for a "democratic" alternative it became deeply enmeshed in Nicaraguan politics. If, in the end, it rushed to be on the "right side of change," this dash was largely an exercise in damage control and hardly signified a new definition of the national interest despite Hoffmann's claim that the old one had become obsolete. Guided in its course by doubts about Eisenhower's handling of Castro, admiration for Johnson's decisive Dominican intervention, and a determination to prevent transforming Somoza into another Pinochet, the Carter Administration pursued a rather traditional, if liberal, policy that was unusual only insofar as it never seriously contemplated the use of military force to achieve a solution.[117] The refusal to consider military intervention had more to do with Vietnam , however, than with Nicargua and will be a focus of the next chapter.

* * * * *

We return to the questions with which we began this chapter. Did the Carter Administration repudiate postwar American foreign policy? Did it accept the historical arguments of either the Cold War or realist revisionists? What was the relationship between "world order politics" and historical revisionism? Was the Administration's outlook informed by any compelling historical "lessons?"

From our analysis of Stanley Hoffmann's preferred world order policy, our interviews with National Security Council and Policy Planning Staff officials, and our summary of the Administration's Persian Gulf, China, and Nicaragua policies, it should be clear that these questions yield no simple answers. Carter and his advisers entered office convinced, like Hoffmann, that the world had changed dramatically. These were sincere convictions and not merely campaign hyperbole. These new global conditions, expressed most generally by the concept of "pluralism" and involving notions like "interdependence," "complexity," and the "growing disutility of military force," led not so much to the explicit repudiation of postwar American diplomacy as it made parts of that record apparently irrelevant. The Administration did, to be sure, renounce "anti-

Communist" containment, but so had Nixon and Kissinger. If nothing else, the Nixon Doctrine and the opening to China had signified the rejection of NSC-68 and the simultaneous acceptance of limitationist axioms.

But did Carter go further and abandon as well the containment of the Soviet Union? Did he, in other words, adopt the policy implications (if not the assumptions) of the Cold War revisionists? Ultimately, the Administration accepted the necessity of containing Soviet power, but, unlike its predecessors, it did so in a grudging and unenthusiastic way. According to Hoffmann and the precepts of "world order politics," the United States historically had expended far too much energy combatting Communism and the Soviet Union. This preoccupation was partly justifiable in the immediate aftermath of World War II when the contest was bipolar and polycentrism not yet a reality. But with the growth of "interdependent games" which Moscow did not play; with the relative decline in the significance of the "diplomatic-strategic chessboard"; and with the emergence of unprecedentedly complicated "global issues" America could not afford to devote as much attention to the Soviet Union. Indeed, it need not devote as much attention. It was all a matter of priorities, and new ones beckoned. The Carter Administration, even in 1977 and 1978, and despite its efforts to "decouple" SALT and the Third World from Soviet-American relations, did not pretend that the Soviet Union was no longer a "competitor." Rather, in its enthusiasm for "world order issues" the Administration more or less tacitly renounced an "obsessive" interest in Soviet activities in "marginal" areas. When in 1979 and 1980 Carter concluded that Russian "adventurism" had become intolerable, Brzezinski sought to construct a Persian Gulf strategy with a Presidential doctrine self-consciously fashioned to the *regional* lessons of the Truman Doctrine. In short, "world order politics" now had to be subordinated to the containment of Soviet power in the Persian Gulf, for without oil the Western (and Southern) "games of interdependence" would have lost their stakes (and most of their players). Similarly, when confronted with the prospect of a Sandanist victory in Nicaragua, the Administration retreated to a timeworn strategy framed by the East-West conflict.

The policy recommendations of the World War I revisionists had been specific, concrete, and achievable within the framework of the American political system: neutrality laws designed to keep the United States out of future foreign wars. The Cold War revisionists, conversely, advocated policies which, according to their own admissions, could not succeed in the absence of radical domestic change.

Williams, it is true, thought that American expansionism might be arrested by a conservative governing class dedicated to a Hoover-like national interest, but this solution was strictly temporary and could not hope to create the necessary conditions for a real socialist community. Similarly, Kolko's claims that the United States could do nothing to stem the inexorable tide of peasant revolutionary movements did not translate easily into firm policy advice. Of all the Cold War revisionists Barnet came closest to playing the role that Beard had filled in the 1930s. His condemnation of the "war game," his suggestion that the United States could initiate disarmament without necessarily abandoning capitalism, and his demand that Congress reassert its foreign policy prerogatives against an imperial Presidency were hardly cries in the political wilderness but, rather, expressed an outlook certainly shared by many in the Democratic Party during the 1970s. Yet notwithstanding his undeniable appeal for the "Vietnam generation" and his comparatively realistic recommendations, younger Carter officials who otherwise found Barnet's message convincing had difficulty fitting it into a policy context. Several of those we interviewed agreed with PPS member Richard Feinberg's appraisal:

> I think I've always found Barnet's writings pretty persuasive. He lays things out in a pretty clear way. Where I would fault him as well as a lot of others who write in that vein . . . is that they don't tell you what to do if you're in government. They don't tell a policy-maker very much.[118]

Furthermore, bureaucratic "facts of life" conspired to diminish Barnet's attractiveness to otherwise sympathetic Carter officials. The Cold War revisionists wished to decentralize radically American political and economic institutions. Failing that, at least in the short term, they wanted to reduce the power of the Presidency in order to make future Vietnams less likely. Some, of course, like Kolko evidently hoped for many Vietnams to expose the alleged bankruptcy of the American system. John Holum, whose outlook owed a good deal to Barnet, had tirelessly worked for the passage of the War Powers Act and other Congressional initiatives designed to discourage "presidential wars." Nevertheless, after joining the Policy Planning Staff in early 1979, one of his top priorities was to gain the repeal of the War Powers Act![119] As Robert Gallucci put it: "Anybody who's worked in government for any period of time and still doubts that 'where you stand depends on where you sit' hasn't been working in this government."[120] In short, any radical critique, regardless of the personal appeal it may hold, must confront the realities of bureaucratic life, and any radical *historical* critique must face the additional barrier of a bureaucracy submerged in daily routine and standard operating procedures.

"World order politics," although primarily a description of the present international system and a prescription for the future, did rely on an historical interpretation of the Cold War that bore a resemblance to that of the Cold War revisionists. Like Williams, Kolko, and Barnet, world order advocates contended that traditional interpreters (both orthodox and realist) had grossly understated the significance of economic issues and had seriously overrated the centrality of the Soviet-American contest. Moreover, whereas the Cold War revisionists argued that the modern nation-state had been largely eclipsed by the emergence of egalitarian revolutionary movements, Hoffmann contended that its primacy was under challenge by a variety of non-state actors committed to a "just world order." He did not, of course, accept their economic determinism nor did he share their enthusiasm for revolutionary upheaval, but in his assurances that "complex interdependence" had created a world quite unlike the one defined by the Cold War Hoffmann implicitly embraced the radical revisionist claim that American supremacy had been irreversibly destroyed.

Indeed, "world order politics" constituted an historical revisionisn that had considerable appeal for would-be Cold War revisionists who, as policy-makers, were frustrated by the unworkability of the radicals' policy recommendations. For world order supporters America's Cold War conduct had been characterized by arrogance, paranoia, and an aggressive idealism that, in its exaggerated reliance on military solutions, had led to Vietnam. But while America obsessively pursued the Cold War, world conditions were changing dramatically. These changes, world order advocates suggested, did signify the end of the American Century but also presented the United States with an unprecedented opportunity to help manage this new and complex world. In other words, the requirements of interdependence had (or should have) liberated America from the legacy of the Cold War.

But if the Cold War was no longer to be mined for historical "lessons," where was a "world order" Administration like Carter's to turn for such guidance? Our interviews revealed that it was Vietnam and not the Cold War that served to orient the Carter Administration historically. Earlier Presidents had used the Cold War to interpret and justify Vietnam. That is, they had viewed Vietnam in the global context of Soviet-American relations. Carter and his advisers reversed this procedure and interpreted the Cold War against the backdrop of Vietnam. This implicit rejection of the "Munich model" meant that this Administration divided postwar American foreign policy into two fundamentally different phases: before and after Vietnam. Vietnam had changed the world and America's role in it so drastically that earlier "lessons" had become largely irrelevant. In this restricted sense, the Carter Administration was "revisionist."

But, as we have seen, it proved unable to sustain this "world order" outlook against the shocks of 1978 and 1979. The Horn, Iran, Nicaragua, and Afghanistan represented crises that led the NSC to claim that the lessons of Vietnam had been "overlearned." Not surprisingly, it was to the Cold War that Brzezinski turned for compelling historical analogies.

CHAPTER 7:
CARTER, REAGAN, AND THE VIETNAM REVISIONISTS

As we saw in chapter one the Truman and Eisenhower administrations, with the enthusiastic participation of the American academic community, fashioned an historical interpretation of the Cold War which constituted an important feature of the anti-Communist foreign policy consensus. This "orthodoxy," although challenged almost immediately by the realist revisionists and much later by the Cold War revisionists, retained overwhelming public and academic support until the mid-1960s. But as we found in chapter five, many of the same liberal internationalists who had used this interpretation to defend American intervention in Vietnam now borrowed selectively from the realist revisionists in order to condemn the war. The Ball-Schlesinger-Fulbright-Steel critique of Vietnam (and global containment), which thus had originated as a revisionist position, rapidly acquired tremendous "establishment" support and served as the basis in the 1970s for a new Vietnam orthodoxy. This orthodoxy had received elaboration in the pages of FOREIGN POLICY by many future Carter officials and enthusiasts and provided, in turn, the immediate intellectual context for "world order politics." And, as we argued in the last chapter, the "moderation plus" formulation of Hoffmann represented, in some respects, a blending of Cold War and realist revisionist positions.

What was the nature of the new Vietnam orthodoxy? According to the Ball-Schlesinger-Fulbright-Steel critique of global containment, the Vietnam intervention had been motivated by good intentions, but the costs required to deny Southeast Asia to the Communists had come to outweigh any possible benefits and had resulted in over-extended power, an unbalanced diplomacy, and crippling domestic dissent. The Johnson Administration had argued that the critics' narrow cost/benefit accounting techniques were unacceptable, because Vietnam symbolized America's resolve, credibility, and dedication to a peaceful and lawful world order ("peace is indivisible"), and because it believed that American means were inexhaustible.

In meeting Johnson's claims liberal critics of the war might simply have asserted that it was time to return to a traditional world based on balance-of-power calculations, and, indeed, as we saw in chapter five, a portion of Kissinger's diplomacy implicitly acknowledged this advice. But those who were to construct the new Vietnam orthodoxy were so impressed with the pluralistic and disorderly, yet increasingly interdependent character of the world that they wished to chart a wholly new course. For them Vietnam had not only been infeasible (i.e., too costly) but ultimately unnecessary as well, because the old bases of global containment had disappeared. Eschewing the counsel of limitationists like Kennan and Morgenthau, who would have followed a policy of selective containment in the name of reduced American interests, these analysts expanded the number and nature of these interests while assuring themselves that military power would probably not be needed to pursue them. "Pluralism" had ostensibly reduced both the utility and the necessity for military force, but it was pluralism's alleged requirements that would, if properly understood, prevent America from sinking into a post-Vietnam isolation. The diffusion of economic and political power, the proliferation of competing ideologies, the explosion of social and ecological problems such as inequality, overpopulation, the demand for human rights, and pollution were all expressions of that pluralism. An unresponsive America would risk irrelevancy, but if it could draw the correct lessons from Vietnam, the end of the war would inaugurate a new era of opportunity for America in the world.

This rather sanguine analysis, though elevated to the status of official orthodoxy by the Carter Administration, never obtained the nearly unanimous support enjoyed by Cold War orthodoxy during the fifties and early sixties. The new Vietnam orthodoxy quickly suffered attack from several quarters, but most prominently from a vigorous "neo-conservative" movement active in Norman Podhoretz's COMMENTARY. From the beginning, then,the Carter Administration's interpretation of Vietnam represented a very tenuous sort of "orthodoxy"—an unsurprising circumstance in view of the absence of a coherent foreign policy consensus—and if it reflected the general public feeling that Vietnam had been a "mistake," that the defense budget needed reducing, and that the United States had to rediscover its moral compass after Nixon and Kissinger, it nevertheless failed to lay the groundwork for a new consensus.

Not everyone in the Carter Administration embraced this explanation of Vietnam with equal abandon. Some advisers, especially Brzezinski and the majority of the NSC staff, gradually concluded that the "lessons of Vietnam" had been learned too well, and that the threat or use of military power could no longer be proscribed. Leslie H. Gelb, director of the State Department's Bureau of Politico-Military Affairs, wrote a book, THE IRONY OF VIETNAM,[1] which challenged parts of the new orthodoxy, while other officials, sometimes led by Carter himself, offered an account of Vietnam that acknowledged the war's immorality. Yet notwithstanding these amendations which, except for Brzezinski's, were, as we will see, relatively insignificant, the orthodox interpretation of Vietnam exerted a powerful influence on the Administration. Indeed, by providing Carter and his advisers with a compelling historical analogy, this account, in conjunction with the axioms of "world order politics" to which it was closely related, gave to the Administration much of its intellectual distinctiveness.

* * * * *

The "lessons of Vietnam" hovered like a mist around the Carter Administration. Though rarely invoked explicitly, they informed many of its most important foreign policy statements. For example, on May 1, 1979 Secretary of State Vance delivered a speech in Chicago which, according to key aides, expressed his philosophy in an especially cogent manner. These officials further recalled that the wording of the following passage became the subject of a long and rather contentious discussion within the Policy Planning Staff. In the speech Vance asked:

> In seeking to help others meet the legitimate needs of their peoples, what are the best instruments at hand? Let me state first that the use of military force is not, and should not be a desirable American policy response to the internal politics of other nations.[2]

In the words of one PPS member who participated in this debate:

> That word "desirable" was a compromise position between those who wanted to simply say that the use of military force is not an appropriate instrument, and those who felt that we could not rule that out in *every* circumstance. The great example that was given was . . . Saudi Arabia. The debate took place between

> the poles. And there was a lot of playing out of Vietnam in the course of that discussion both explicitly and implicitly.[3]

Vance, himself, apparently had difficulty in deciding the issue, and his indecisiveness highlighted a nagging problem for the Administration: What had Vietnam "taught" America about military interventions? From the time of the Truman Doctrine's enunciation until the emergence of significant domestic opposition to Vietnam, presidents had reserved the right to intervene anywhere to "help free peoples" remain free. In essence, this meant that while the United States would abstain from military action in Eastern Europe (notwithstanding the rhetoric of rollback), it refused to rule out armed assistance for others, whether threatened from without or within. But, although the Truman Doctrine had given equal priority to combatting external aggression and internal subversion, in practice, presidents invariably discovered evidence of outside support (usually Soviet) whenever they contemplated military intervention. Vietnam was no exception, and while the Johnson Administration justified its policy in abstract, universalist terms, it consistently claimed the the war also represented an external (and illegal) aggression by "Hanoi."

Vance sought to amend the Truman Doctrine by explicitly reducing America's perceived stakes in *some* purely domestic upheavals. Military force would no longer be a "desirable response to the internal politics of other nations," even, evidently, if "free peoples" were threatened by subversion. But if, for example, Islamic fundamentalists or Marxist revolutionaries toppled the Saudi monarchy and withheld petroleum, the United States, according to Vance's formulation *might* nevertheless be required to intervene—not to uphold some imperial principle of world order—but to ensure the economic survival of the West. American security had not been at stake in Vietnam—a domestic revolution—so, as President Carter observed,

> . . . the unfortunate experience that we had in Vietnam has impressed on the American people deeply, and I hope permanently, the danger of our country resorting to military means in a distant place on Earth where our security is not being threatened. . . .[4]

But what if Western economic survival was not directly endangered by either domestic subversion or external aggression? Until Vietnam presidents had assumed that all external aggressions threatened American security, but Vance's formulation seemed to alter the old equation. How would the Carter Administration view, for example, a pro-Soviet coup in a Third World nation? PPS Deputy Director Paul Kreisberg described the State Department attitude in the following way:

> I think that the notion that the Soviets were making a gain and that we had to draw lines and say "here, and no further" was really, from the State Department's point of view, alien to our basic thinking about the world. It implied that specific places around the world were turning points, and that if the Soviets gained influence in, for example, Ethiopia or South Yemen, or in any other given place, that this (a) was irreversible and (b) would transform fundamentally the strategic balance. [Our] approach was basically to say that the world is a place that is in constant flux, things are never totally black or white, and, on balance, Soviet influence has been diminishing in recent years in a whole series of countries that seemed to be firmly in the Soviet camp.[5]

Like several of those interviewed Kreisberg admitted that this approach was not without its difficulties:

> The trouble . . . is that it's a very subtle policy, and subtlety is a characteristic that is hard to sell politically. It's hard to make a speech about change, . . . a speech which says there are fourteen major problems in the world, and we have to deal with them all . . . [People] kept asking, "Where are the priorities?", and the argument that the priority was the East-West struggle began to appear . . . more attractive [to the Administration] by the end of 1978. . . .[6]

Pluralism would render Soviet gains temporary and reversible in certain instances, but pluralism frequently required time to work, and in the meantime a policy of patience and restraint was susceptible to domestic American pressures for action.

Brzezinski was acutely aware of this problem and was more impressed than his State Department counterparts with an additional danger: the psychological impact that the "loss" of a marginally important country might have on nations of vital significance. This worry had plagued American policy-makers in the days before global containment was embraced, and it lay at the heart of the Acheson-Kennan dispute in the late 1940s. Acheson agreed with Kennan that a Sino-Soviet split was inevitable but argued that the United States could not afford to wait for it to develop. The dilemma had, in principle, been transcended with the adoption of NSC-68, for this document, by identifying international Communism as the enemy, prohibited the United States from "picking and choosing" where it ought to intervene, but the Carter Administration's implicit renunciation of global containment rekindled the old dilemma.

By late 1978 Brzezinski and the NSC had begun to move closer to Acheson's position (i.e., psychology counts, but the *Soviet Union* is the threat). But for Brzezinski to admit, in effect, that a pluralistic world might nevertheless require American military intervention in areas of questionable strategic significance, he first had to depart from the orthodox interpretation of Vietnam. In short, Brzezinski searched for a way to justify such interventions without recourse to a new doctrine of global containment. He gradually reached the conclusion that many in the Administration, plus "McGovernites" in the Democratic Party, had "overlearned" the lessons of Vietnam by ruling out the use of force in all circumstances.[7] Brzezinski believed, rather, that the rapid and judicious use of force in places like South Yemen or Somalia could be justified in order to deny them to the Soviets or to bolster the morale of regional friends. In the words of a very close aide,

> I think that's one of the legacies of Vietnam—we are afraid to use power. The tragedy of Vietnam is that there are a series of people that were in the government who felt that the use of power was something alien to America, because it had been misused. I think that what we needed to do was to get at the selective use of that power instead of saying, "we can't do that."[8]

Not surprisingly, Brzezinski's desire to use American power selectively in response to "disorderly change" satisfied neither the Left nor the Right. To "McGovernites" it proved that the United States had forgotten Vietnam and would now embark on a new interventionist course, while to "Reaganites" it further demonstrated the Administration's repudiation of anti-Communist containment. Yet despite Brzezinski's desire to avoid "overlearning" the lessons of Vietnam his revisionism attacked the orthodox interpretation's analysis of the war's *consequences* rather than its judgment of the war itself. He had no quarrel with the view that America had been sucked into a "quagmire" because of a combination of inadvertence, bad information, and intellectual error. What he did come to question was orthodoxy's assurances that an emerging pluralistic world order would make future American military interventions both unnecessary and infeasible.

* * * * *

Leslie H. Gelb directly challenged the "quagmire thesis." First in a widely-read article in FOREIGN POLICY and then in THE IRONY OF VIETNAM, Gelb argued that its political-bureaucratic decision-making system had served the United States rather well during the Vietnam War:

> The system worked. Presidents and most of those who influenced their decisions did not stumble into Vietnam unaware of the quagmire. U.S. involvement did not stem from a failure to foresee that the war would be a long and bitter struggle. Very few persons, to be sure, envisioned what the Vietnam situation would be like by 1968. Most realized, however, that the light at the end of the tunnel was very far away, if not unreachable. Nevertheless, the presidents persevered. Given the international compulsions to "keep our word" and "save face," domestic prohibitions against losing, and high personal stakes, U.S. leaders did "what was necessary," did it about the way they wanted to, were prepared to pay the costs each administration could foresee for itself, and plowed on with a mixture of hope and doom.[9]

The "system," in short, had produced a Vietnam policy that embodied the precepts and values of the Cold War domestic consensus. On the whole this policy was neither deceitful nor aberrational (in the context of the Cold War) but, rather, implemented the terms of the Truman Doctrine. Yet Gelb's analysis hardly constituted a ringing endorsement of America's involvement in Vietnam. The system may have worked, but the system was in the service of bad policy and a defective vision. Gelb argued that the presumed need for a broad domestic consensus to lend legitimacy to American foreign policy had led historically to Presidential doctrines which were "public relations exercises designed to limit rational and critical discussion of policy."[10] "Doctrines demand too much consistency," and "an overall policy consensus generates political paranoia and intellectual rigidity."[11] "Facts are forced to fit the theory, . . . all the facts begin to look alike, . . . discrimination, which is the essence of sound policy is lost, and policy choices are reduced to a single unchanging response—stop communism."[12] To avoid future Vietnams, Gelb concluded in a short essay commissioned by his close friend Anthony Lake, "a significant change in attitudes and some minor institutional reforms"[13] were required. In brief, these changes entailed (1) the substitution of consensus on particular policy questions for a broad consensus conferring a blanket legitimacy on all policies; (2) the refusal by presidents to articulate doctrines which manipulate symbols in order to build a general consensus; (3) a media less critical of delay in the government's reactions to foreign events and more critical of doctrinal pronouncements by Presidents; (4) the institutionalization instead of the domestication of dissent in the executive branch; and (5) a Congress determined to question the goals of the Administration.[14] The doctrine of global containment had trapped successive administrations in Vietnam. The system could be faulted only to the extent that it had failed to challenge the doctrine. Gelb's reforms were designed to guarantee dissent from the conventional wisdom.

The policy implications of Gelb's revisionism differed significantly from Brzezinski's. While it would be overly clever to claim that the apparent policy inconsistencies that plagued the Carter Administration signified a tacit acceptance of Gelb's advice to eschew doctrine and consensus, the President's decision in January 1980 to issue a general warning about the Persian Gulf did represent a clear rejection of Gelb's Vietnam "lessons." Calling the Carter Doctrine "dangerous and unworkable,"[15] Gelb, by then an analyst with the Carnegie Endowment, likened it to the Truman Doctrine but suggested that it was even more ambitious: "There was nothing in the Truman speech . . . to compare to the amazing list of Carter responses to the Russians."[16] Because it called upon us to stop the Russian thrust almost everywhere it crops up," Gelb asserted, Carter's new policy "would seem to tie us to regimes that do not have the internal legitimacy and strength to survive."[17] In short, Pakistan could become another Vietnam, but now, "if the Russians are as strong as Carter and the right say they are,"[18] the Persian Gulf might prove even more dangerous to defend than Southeast Asia in the 1960s. In an interview we conducted with Gelb he described his own approach as very close to what Kennan's had been insofar as they both shared a distrust of blanket commitments, symbolic doctrines, and a primary reliance on military solutions.[19] Moreover, he implied that by 1980 the NSC had become populated with the intellectual heirs of Acheson and Nitze. What Gelb failed to mention, however, was that he, in contrast to the early Kennan who was a balance-of-power nationalist, accepted the main outlines of the pluralist argument. That is, Gelb's Vietnam revisionism did not quarrel with the orthodox account's treatment of the war's consequences—i.e., the emergence of a pluralistic world order in need of non-military American management—but only with the explanation of its roots. In order to avoid future Vietnams, it was not enough to be "prudent," as the orthodox interpretation suggested, for so long as administrations relied on sweeping doctrines designed to cultivate domestic consensus and curry the favor of Third World clients, a prudential foreign policy could not be maintained. Institutional reforms and attitudinal changes were necessaary to underwrite prudence. Gelb's revisionist analysis of Vietnam, in effect, took the orthodox explanation one step further, and it clearly captured much of the Carter Administration's early mood. Bureaucratically it was manifested in PPS and NSC staffs of almost unprecedented diversity wherein dissent was actively encouraged by both Lake and Brzezinski;[20] rhetorically it was exemplified by the President's call at Notre Dame to abandon an "inordinate fear of Communism"; and substantively it appeared in policies like the rejection of the "internal settlement" in Zimbabwe and the initial efforts to normalize relations with Hanoi and Havana. But the NSC's shrinking political spectrum after 1978, the President's famous post-Afghanistan admission of error in his perception of the Soviet Union, and, most significantly, the articulation of the Carter Doctrine demonstrated the Administration's growing disenchantment with Gelb's brand of Vietnam revisionism and its simultaneous embrace of Brzezinski's rather Achesonian analysis.

* * * * *

Most anti-war members of the foreign policy establishment had concluded that the American intervention in Vietnam had been imprudent, strategically mistaken, and, perhaps, arrogant, but unlike segments of the anti-war movement few challenged U.S. policy on primarily moral grounds. Nor did the orthodox explanation of Vietnam which grew out of this 1960s' critique condemn American aims as criminal, immoral, or obscene, but it nevertheless maintained an ambivalent attitude toward those purposes. For example, several senior members of the Carter Administration apparently did experience guilt to one degree or another for their roles in framing and implementing Johnson's and Nixon's Vietnam policies. According to one NSC staffer,

> . . . I don't think that I shared what I think I saw in some of the other people in the State Department, in particular, and I don't want to overdraw this, but let's say [Richard] Holbrooke and [Anthony] Lake and some of these people who were very much influenced by . . . their own involvement in policy-making in

> Vietnam . . . now tended to be very skeptical about the use of American power, almost guilty about it.[21]

On the other hand, a member of the Policy Planning Staff put it quite differently:

> Tony [Lake] . . . went through a rough period with Kissinger and Cambodia, but those of us who knew Tony only by reputation, we all remarked, after being on the staff for six or eight months, that if you're going to paint dove's feathers on people, Tony would not be the first person you'd go up to with a brush. His orientation to issues was liberal and consistent with Carter Administration foreign policy, but he's a very hard-nosed political thinker. There was no one among us who would come out in favor of the use of milltary force easily. We had a great sense for the difficulty of pulling back from something like that, and that undoubtedly was a feeling that was impressed on us by Vietnam.[22]

Stanley Hoffmann, surely a chief architect of what became the othodox interpretation of Vietnam, argued that

> Others still believe that whatever else may be said, our effort [in Vietnam] was not immoral because our intentions were good. But the ethics of political action is not an ethics of motives, it is an ethics of consequences. Ends that cannot be reached at a price commensurate with the importance of the stakes, and means disproportionate to the stakes yet ineffective and destructive of the very values one pretends to save, are components of an ethical catastrophe.[23]

In this somewhat restricted sense many in the Carter Administration did believe that the war had been immoral, and some of those officials like Lake and Holbrooke, who had been deeply involved in the intervention, felt a certain "consequential guilt." Their policy advice had allegedly helped to produce disastrous consequences—profound domestic divisiveness, the apparent destruction of the country they wished to save, the encouragement of a Watergate mentality at home, a radical skewing of foreign policy priorities, and the postponement of Soviet-American détente—but they had resulted not from willful malfeasance but from intellectual error.

But some Carter officials evidently went farther and condemned the *intentions* of the involvement as well. For instance, in May 1977 the President suggested that

> For too many years we have been willing to adopt the flawed and erroneous principles and tactics of our adversaries, sometimes abandoning our own values for theirs. We have fought fire with fire, never thinking that force is better quenched with water. This approach failed, with Vietnam the best example of its intellectual and moral poverty.[24]

Thus the decision to intervene in Vietnam had been intellectually impoverished insofar as it rested on the precepts of global containment which demanded "fire" to uphold its notion of world order. Here Carter merely restated the orthodox position; but in what sense had the policy been *morally* defective as well? According to the President, America's "inordinate fear of Communism" had too frequently compelled it to embrace regimes which were contemptuous of democratic values. American support for repressive governments like the one in Saigon was morally indefensible, for in trying to save leaders like Diem, Ky, and Thieu, the United States had inevitably renounced its traditional principles and purposes. The Vietnam War had not been immoral in the Left's sense that it had exemplified imperialism, exploitation, racism, and aggression, but rather, because it had signified the abandonment of American principles at home and abroad. In the future, President Carter promised, America would employ the cooling "water" of a vigorous human rights policy to make other nations immune to the "fire" of Communist intimidation. No doubt many in the Administration more or less shared this attitude, though it is clear that the human rights theme did create additional tensions between the NSC and the State Department and even within these bureaucracies. But in indicting the Vietnam War for moral as well as intellectual poverty and in proposing the cleansing bath of a universalist human rights program President Carter followed a road walked most prominently by Woodrow Wilson and Cordell Hull. Vietnam orthodoxy did not demand that this course be taken, yet in its moral ambivalence about the war, it could certainly be invoked to sanction a Wilsonian path as well as a world order policy of "moderation plus."

Two explanations of Vietnam received no hearing by the Carter Administration. The first, an economic interpretation, had, of course, been offered by some of the Cold War revisionists. This thesis argued that America had been forced to intervene in Vietnam to preserve its vision of a liberal-capitalist international order and, ultimately, to protect the integrity of its domestic socio-economic institutions and those of its allies. Unless the United States radically transformed these institutions, writers like Gabriel Kolko had warned, it would be faced with a future full of Vietnams. No one with any policy responsibility in the Carter Administration had much sympathy for this view. Several officials who in the 1960s had opposed the war partly on economic grounds now thought that this explanation was unpersuasive, while others like PPS member John Holum felt "embarrassed" by Kolko's claims and reiterated that "one of the things that from the outset made the war most appalling was that we had no interests in Vietnam."[25]

More surprising was the fact that the second view, the so-called non-interventionist critique, did not find more support within the Administration, particularly among those who believed that military force had become largely unusable. This perspective, which was most dramatically articulated by Earl Ravenal in NEVER AGAIN: *Learning From America's Foreign Policy Failures,*[26] but which had been anticipated by Robert W. Tucker's A NEW ISOLATIONISM?[27] some years before, contended that neither Vietnam orthodoxy nor Gelb's revision of it could in principle be used to rule out future and necessarily disastrous American military interventions. Neither a careful cost/benefit analysis nor the mere renunciation of "doctrine" in favor of a case-by-case approach was sufficient to ensure against future Vietnams, Ravenal warned. Rather, the United States must learn from the war that the nature of the contemporary world and the character of its domestic society precluded the success of *any* American military intervention. Thus both the Carter Administration's ambitious "global agenda" of 1977, though packed with attractive equity programs, and Brzezinski's Persian Gulf strategy of 1979-80, though the beneficiary of the alleged "lessons" of Vietnam, had nevertheless laid the groundwork for future disasters.

But Ravenal's counsel was considered either defective or impractical by the Administration. For example, PPS Caribbean coordinator Richard Feinberg stressed its unworkability in this way:

> A problem with the Vietnam generation's approach is its negativism, that basically there isn't very much good that the United States can do. What we really ought to do is just practice non-intervention. But there're problems with that: (1) the U.S. has so much influence, particularly in the Caribbean Basin, that there's really no such thing as non-intervention; doing nothing

> isn't doing nothing, because it actually favors certain internal forces over others; and (2) the weight of the bureaucracy is toward action, toward choosing sides, and toward intervention.[28]

On the other hand, the NSC staffer who rolled his eyes and muttered, "Oh, that isolationist," upon hearing Ravenal's name, typified a widespread Administration view that found his recommendations wholly misbegotten.[29]

"World order politics" enthusiasts also found Ravanel's advice dangerous. Hoffmann, for example, contended that

> He is right in stressing domestic and external constraints on America's ability to control the world. But, like earlier isolationists, . . . Ravenal forgets that no great power defines its interests in terms of strategic control or physical security alone. Influence is the name of the game. . . .
>
> . . . only by an effort at creating world order will America be able to reduce vulnerabilities—if not without pain or risk, at least with less damage than the retrenchers would provoke. For only within a framework that receives wide assent and provides for some "devolution" will the United States be able to trim its sails without sinking. Some retrenchment might be a goal. Some world order is the condition.[30]

In short, Vietnam orthodoxy (and "world order politics") did not counsel isolation despite its profound misgivings about the utility of military power. The Carter Administration had "learned" from Vietnam that the United States needed to redirect its energies toward the achievement of "milieu goals" like "influence" without reducing its commitment to world order. But in the wake of Vietnam such order would now be pursued with vastly different instruments. As a result of this redirection the Carter Administration defined "world order" in less hegemonic terms than any of its postwar predecessors.

* * * * *

But, as we suggested earlier, "neo-conservative" critics of the Carter Administration soon offered a direct challenge to its interpretation of Vietnam. In contrast to the Cold War revisionists of the 1960s, whose reinterpretations rested to some extent on the discovery of new documentation, the neo-conservatives showed no inclination for archival research. Even the most elaborate of their efforts—

Norman Podhoretz's WHY WE WERE IN VIETNAM[31]—relied entirely on well-known sources published years before.[32] This circumstance was partly the result of the inaccessiblity of documents, for in the absence of further unauthorized leaks by other Ellsbergs, little new Vietnam material can be expected in the near-term. But the primary reason for the neo-conservatives' seeming unconcern with such matters lay in their frankly political motives: They wished to rehabilitate the memory of Vietnam as a first step toward the global reassertion of American power in the 1980s.

Such motives were not, of course, unique to the Vietnam revisionists. As we have seen all scholarly investigations of American diplomatic history have been affected by the prevailing "climate of opinion." The Cold War revisionists claimed that "semi-official" orthodox historians like Herbert Feis had acted as apologists for an allegedly imperialistic American foreign policy. Conversely, Robert James Maddox argued that the Cold War revisionists had conspired to defend their New Left political positions by distorting and fabricating historical evidence. While both charges were somewhat exaggerated, they certainly contained a grain of truth. The neo-conservatives were likewise moved by partisan considerations to revise the orthodox explanation of Vietnam.

COMMENTARY served as the midwife of this revisionism. Skillfully guided by the literary critic Norman Podhoretz, COMMENTARY had at one time been a vehicle for the New Left and prominently featured such countercultural heros as Norman O. Brown and Paul Goodman. But Podhoretz grew disenchanted with the alleged hypocrisy and totalitarian proclivities of this radicalism, and, after a period of agonizing introspection, he reemerged in the early 1970s as an "anti-Communist liberal,"[33] determined to point COMMENTARY against the "neo-isolationism, Malthusianism, and redistributionist egalitarianism"[34] of McGovernism and its friends. Surrounding himself with an assortment of ex-radicals, defense intellectuals, Straussian political philosophers, and conservative foreign policy analysts, Podhoretz launched a broad attack against what he saw as the growing radicalization of American liberalism. The media, the "adversary culture," the "new class" and other symbols and symptoms of cultural and political decadence were regularly drawn and quartered in COMMENTARY. Nor was American foreign policy immune to such criticism, and by the mid-1970s COMMENTARY had become a leading opponent of the Nixon-Kissinger Grand Design.

In view of these circumstances it was, perhaps, inevitable that the pages of COMMENTARY would spawn a comprehensive Vietnam revisionism. It received its first full airing in a July 1975 symposium tellingly entitled "America Now: A Failure of Nerve?". There writers like Peter Berger, Michael Novak, and Irving Kristol—dispargingly dubbed "neo-conservatives" by Michael Harrington—commenced a reconsideration of Vietnam and its "lessons."

These revisionists initially focused on the alleged reasons for America's defeat in Vietnam. The orthodox explanation had claimed that any successful defense of the corrupt and repressive Saigon regime against such a dedicated national revolutionary movement would have required enormous and unacceptable costs to the United States. The revisionists attacked this argument (and its premises) from several angles. First, they asked why, if the Thieu government had been so villainous, had hordes of refugees fled *toward* Saigon in April 1975 instead of remaining to welcome their revolutionary liberators?[35] Second, it was not true, as Vietnam orthodoxy claimed, that the enemy had constituted some vast, inexorable national movement, but, rather, the North Vietnamese regular army backed by the Soviet Union and China that had simply overrun the South in a very unrevolutionary manner. Far from a popular uprising the Spring 1975 offensive had been a traditional military invasion.[36] And finally, contrary to the prevailing view, Saigon could have successfully resisted this final assault had Congress not sabotaged the Nixon-Ford Administration's program by drastically reducing military and economic assistance to South Vietnam in 1974.[37]

The revisionists proposed instead an alternative explanation for America's failure in Vietnam. The United States, they claimed, had ultimately been defeated, not by the allegedly unstoppable forces of revolution, but by itself, or, more accurately, by particular domestic groups. The media, the anti-war movement, Congress, and parts of the foreign policy establishment had snatched defeat from the jaws of victory. "Upwardly mobile foreign correspondents of American newsweeklies and television, and commentators," who transparently viewed themselves as "smarter and morally superior to the generals, ambassadors, and foreign officials" they interviewed, supposedly harbored a "theology of *ressentiment,*" because they were "doomed by their profession to be reflectors of the deeds of others." Michael Novak argued that "their shortest road to superiority" was cynicism with respect to the reputations, aspirations, and accepted wisdom of others." Furthermore, these journalists had an "almost childlike expectation that the world should be better, more rational, more dedicated than it is." This sense of moral outrage allowed them "to serve the role in the conscience of the foreign policy elite the liberal clergy once provided." The establishment, for its part, was acutely susceptible to this sort of brow-beating and during the Vietnam War "became morally suspect even to itself."[38] This failure of nerve, loss of confidence, and growth of guilt and self-doubt by those who had traditionally conducted American foreign policy had subverted the will to perservere in Vietnam.

The Vietnam revisionists also blamed the anti-war movement for America's defeat. While it may originally have served as a "constituency of conscience" opposed to the inhumanity of the war, Peter Berger suggested, the movement was soon captured by anti-American elements in the thrall of revolutionary illusions.[39] Not only did these protesters give sustenance to Hanoi, but their domestic political influence (grossly exaggerated by the media) undermined Johnson's war strategy, pressured Kissinger into accepting less favorable peace terms than otherwise obtainable, and persuaded Congress to reduce drastically American aid to Saigon. Congress, in addition to virtually cutting off funds for South Vietnam, had further damaged the war effort by legislatively crippling the ability of the President to pursue it. In short, the war could have been won, and with only modest additional cost, but for the unseemly attitudes and activities of these groups.

The revisionists also addressed the charge that American conduct of the war had been immoral and illegal. This assertion, as we earlier noted, had never formed an integral part of the orthodox account, although many who had opposed the war did so primarily on those grounds. The most comprehensive attempt to deal with this issue was Guenther Lewy's AMERICA IN VIETNAM[40] which, while not uncritical of U.S. conduct, rejected the claims of Daniel Ellsberg,[41] Richard Falk,[42] and others that American actions had been systematically genocidal and illegal.

By the end of the 1970s, however, the focus of the revisionists' attention had shifted to the war's consequences. According to Charles Horner,

> . . . Vietnam was unique in producing the general belief that failure there would have few adverse consequences. This, at least, was the dominant view when South Vietnam crumbled before the last North Vietnamese offensive of 1975. A war which had failed in part because there was no coherent theory of victory ended in a debacle for which no theory of defeat was deemed necessary.[43]

Thus Vietnam orthodoxy had been incredibly naive about the war's anticipated effects, but instead of the pluralistic and complex world it had so confidently predicted, a much simpler, bleaker, and more traditional reality had emerged. Despite the undeniable growth of interdependence in the West and polycentrism in the East, the world remained essentially bipolar with one crucial difference: now the Soviet Union exercised strategic superiority, while the United States seemed unwilling and increasingly unable to use its military power. Moreover, the domestic attitudes produced by the war—an anti-defense outlook, a "hypermorality" that inevitably judged America and its leaders by a double standard, and an apparently unshakeable psychological malaise—had underwritten a shocking decline in American military capabilities.[44]

The revisionists identified other "dominoes" as well. All of Southeast Asia had succumbed to an unspeakably barbaric form of Communism: South Vietnam was transformed into a Gulag, Cambodia became a vast Auschwitz, and Vietnamese imperialism threatened to engulf Thailand.[45] Faced with this peril and unable to call on a paralyzed America for help, the remaining free states of the region might be forced to come to terms with Hanoi. Other parts of the world also felt the crush of the totalitarian boot: Angola, South Yemen, Ethiopia, Afghanistan, and Nicaragua now possessed unsavory regimes who owed their power, directly or indirectly, to America's defeat in Vietnam.

Yet despite this disastrous series of setbacks the Carter Administration continued to fear the consequences of *American* power and believed that its emasculation would prevent future Vietnams.[46] As Horner put it,

> Such a militant misunderstanding of the Vietnam war and the consequences of our defeat there hovers over everything else. When was there a government so determined to think the worst of the military power of its own country, but equally prepared to put the most innocent construction on the armed forces of others?
>
> The [Carter] administration view of our experience in Vietnam is the single greatest restraint on our capacity to deal with the world, and that capacity will not much increase unless the view behind it is changed, thoroughly and profoundly.[47]

Thus, like most revisionists, the neo-conservatives wished to do more than simply set the historical record straight. The orthodox understanding of the war had supposedly justified defeatist attitudes and appeasing policies. Before a reassertion of American power could take place, the "lessons of Vietnam" would have to be drastically changed.

Their pugnacious rhetoric notwithstanding, the Vietnam revisionists' contention that the war had produced disastrous consequences did not differ substantially from Brzezinski's claim that the orthodox lessons of Vietnam had been "overlearned." Podhoretz and his allies were contemptuous of his conceptual baggage, but they could scarcely have opposed Brzezinski's assaults on "McGovernites" and "do-gooders" or to his apparent determination to defend the Persian Gulf with American military power. Yet the neo-conservatives steadfastly linked him with the most "planetary" of the Carter "humanists."[48] This was, no doubt, in part a political tactic, for by 1980 many of the revisionists had become staunch Reagan supporters and some would even join his administration, but they also maintained intellectual reservations about Brzezinski's brand of containment.

Podhoretz had grown increasingly optimistic that "the culture of appeasement," allegedly sustained by the orthodox interpretation of Vietnam, could soon be swept away by a "new nationalism." In April 1980 Kristol contended that

> . . . what we are witnessing is a powerful nationalist revival in this nation, a revival that coincides with the twitching death-throes of an American foreign policy that has always regarded American nationalism more as a problem than as an ally.[49]

Nevertheless, Podhoretz feared that despite several promising signs the new nationalism did not yet possess a moral core, for America's grass-roots responses to outrages like Iran and Afghanistan had been muted by selfish economic considerations. Before a real policy of containment could be inaugurated, "Communism" had to be readmitted to the American political vocabulary. Only then, Podhoretz warned, would Americans recognize that the conflict with the Soviet Union was "a struggle for freedom and against Communism."[50]

But he did detect in the public mood the first stirrings of a "repressed strain of internationalist idealism" which could launch the nation on a new Wilsonian crusade to make the 1980s safe for democracy.[51] The neo-conservatives, however, professed not to be mere populists. Kristol, for example, observed that "precisely because it lacked intellectual guidance and articulation, popular sentiment on foreign affairs has frequently degenerated into crude chauvinism, isolation, or even downright paranoia.[52] To avoid these "democratic excesses" America allegedly needed a new foreign policy establishment, dedicated not to a "world order" ideology that shunned the use of force, but rather, committed to a nationalist perspective intent on reasserting American global leadership.

Reagan's landslide victory demonstrated to Podhoretz the existence of a new and powerful consensus that demanded actions significantly more assertive than Brzezinski's and that could serve as the intellectual basis for a new foreign policy establishment.[53] Vietnam, according to Podhoretz, had actually proven that public support was "impossible to maintain in the absence of a convincing moral rationale for our effort there."[54] Having intervened in Vietnam

> . . . for idealistic reasons (in the strict sense that there was no vital geopolitical or material interest at stake, and that what we were actually trying to do was save the South Vietnamese from the horrors of Communist rule that have now befallen them), we tried to justify our involvement in the language of *Realpolitik.* But no good case could be made in that language for American military intervention; and even if it could, it would not in the long run have convinced the American people.[55]

Likewise,

> . . . the Nixon, Ford, and Carter administrations robbed the Soviet-American conflict of the moral and political dimension for the sake of which sacrifices could be intelligibly demanded by the government and willingly made by the people.[56]

Thus,

> a strategy of containment centered on considerations of *Realpolitik* would be unable to count indefinitely on popular support. Sooner or later (probably sooner rather than later) it would succumb to a resurgence of isolationism, leaving a free field for the expansion of Soviet power.[57]

What was required, therefore, was "a strategy aimed at containing the expansion of Communism,"[58] or, though he shunned the term, global containment. Only such a policy could satisfy the new consensus and slow the growth of Soviet power.

All of this, of course, bore a close resemblance to the Johnson-Rusk-Rostow outlook of the 1960s. The Vietnam revisionists were not wholly uncritical of their conduct of the war. In addition to their failure to develop a "coherent theory of victory" and to sufficiently emphasize the war's moral dimension, Johnson and his advisers were also allegedly guilty of "academic Machiavellianism": "Wrong were all those who had ingenious, computerized strategies derived from game theory which encouraged us to believe that a graduated escalation of hostilities would, at some point, achieve a disequilibrium of costs and benefits to the enemy that would cause him to accept a cease-fire."[59] Yet if the strategy used to fight the war had been flawed, the intention to deny South Vietnam to the Communists was not. The message of the Vietnam revisionists was quite simple: The war had been moral insofar as its aim was to halt the spread of Communism in Asia; the doctrine which Johnson had invoked to justify the intervention was correct, because it perceived the world as a battleground between freedom and totalitarianism; and the consequences of an American defeat in Vietnam had been exactly what Johnson and Rusk had predicted—U.S. demoralization, international doubt about the credibility of the United States, a psychological windfall for the Communists, and the continued advance of Vietnamese imperialism throughout Southeast Asia. These results had been immeasurably worse than those which would have flowed from a refusal to withdraw from Vietnam. The United States could have prevented a Communist victory in Vietnam—and thus prevented the disasters of the 1970s—but for the unholy influence of Congressional and establishment Cassandras. Furthermore, those who had defended the war had exhibited infinitely more moral character than either America's Asian enemies or our domestic dissenters.[60]

But wouldn't a new strategy of anti-Communist containment run the risk of future Vietnams? Podhoretz admitted the possibility but thought it remote for three reasons. First, to reject such a policy for its alleged indiscriminate interventionism was a bit like the "Pope in Latin America warning people who have only just begun to afford wearing shoes about the dangers of consumerism and rampant materialism."[61] A country suffering from a decade-long paralysis need not yet worry about more Vietnams. Second, the "rule of prudence," while not able to guarantee absolutely against future Vietnams, would offer a good deal of protection against rash U.S. behavior. Eisenhower, for instance, had eschewed intervention in Indochina in 1954 while remaining faithful to global containment. Thus, Podhoretz's version of anti-Communist containment, in direct contrast to the Johnson-Rusk formulation, would apparently allow American presidents "to pick and choose" where and where not to intervene. What such exercises in *Realpolitik* would do to the moral core of his preferred strategy or to public support for it remained unclear. After all, could Johnson have refused to intervene in Vietnam and still preserved the Cold War consensus that had legitimated anti-Communist containment? And hadn't Eisenhower's "prudent" decision of 1954 merely laid the entire problem in Kennedy's lap? Furthermore, Podhoretz's rule of prudence bore an ironic resemblance to orthodoxy's chief lesson of Vietnam: It seemed to accept Hoffmann's conclusion that America had tragically neglected local circumstances in Vietnam. In short, the intervention in Vietnam had been imprudent. Third, and this point was only implied by Podhoretz, perhaps another massive, anti-Communist intervention would not be an unalloyed disaster. The United States, after all, might have staved off defeat in Vietnam if not for self-imposed restraints. A new war strategy supported by a new and increasingly powerful domestic consensus and led by a determined and popular President might silence dissent the next time.[62]

In any case, the neo-conservatives correctly realized that the legacy of Vietnam required revision before a revitalized policy of anti-Communist containment could be adopted. So long as substantial numbers of Americans continued to believe that interventions inevitably produced Vietnams, it would be difficult to significantly reassert American power. Only by convincingly altering the "lessons of Vietnam" could a new Administration hope to gain domestic support for global containment. Just as the legacy of World War I had temporarily helped to foil Roosevelt's rearmament efforts in the 1930s, so would the memory of Vietnam, the neo-conservatives feared, undermine Reagan's plans to revitalize American military power in the 1980s.

* * * * *

Ronald Reagan entered the Presidency with an electoral mandate to reverse the domestic and international decline of the United States. A stagflationary economy had combined with setbacks in Iran, Afghanistan, and Central America to defeat Jimmy Carter. Since the mid-1970s public opinion polls had shown with increasing clarity that the tide of anti-defense sentiment that had helped Carter in 1976 had ebbed significantly. In 1979 the Chicago Council on Foreign Relations released the results of a comprehensive survey that had been completed before the Shah's overthrow and the Soviet invasion of Afghanistan. Nevertheless, the data indicated the growth of a mood that rejected the introspective guilt of the post-Vietnam period without, however, fully reembracing the liberal internationalism of the Cold War consensus. This disposition could, perhaps, best be described as "conservative nationalism," for it was informed by several defense-oriented, yet anti-interventionist tendencies. Higher defense budgets, more military (but not economic) aid, a willingness to protect NATO allies and Japan (but not Taiwan), and more support for CIA covert activities were responses that appeared with higher frequency than in the Chicago Council's 1974 survey. No clear national consensus had emerged, but the trends pointed to

> . . . a mood of increasing insecurity in the American public. . . . [It] shows an increasing attraction toward such "conservative" symbols as military power and anti-Communism, but not toward extending our commitments abroad or renewing the tradition of Cold War interventionism. It is this defensive and self-interested quality that distinguishes the current mood from that of the Cold War.[63]

The sense of vulnerability, the desire for security, the preoccupation with Soviet military power, the disinclination for a global crusade, and the somewhat contradictory dual wishes for American world leadership with reduced and restrained foreign commitments characterized the *tendencies* in public attitudes about foreign policy shortly before the 1980 election.

In these circumstances Carter's conversion to anti-Soviet, if not anti-Communist, containment "only reinforced the politically fatal image of an indecisive, somewhat schizoid President presiding over an erratic, incoherent policy."[64] Reagan capitalized on this mood by promising to modernize America's defenses and to conduct an assertive, if largely unspecified, foreign policy. Yet in view of the public's apparent desire for primacy without intervention, it was far from clear how Reagan would revitalize containment. Beyond that, would the Administration, in its efforts to implement its electoral mandate, embrace the historical arguments and policy recommendations of the Vietnam revisionists?

After somewhat more than two years in office these questions still did not command clear answers. Some of the Administration's actions apparently reflected a desire to embark on a new strategy of global containment, yet Reagan's failure to confront and systematically defend the intervention in Vietnam raised doubts about its real intentions.

Notwithstanding the President's persistent refusal to deliver a grand foreign policy address the Reagan Administration took several steps that pointed in the direction of anti-Communist containment. First, proposals for a $1.6 trillion, five-year defense program—by far the largest in American history and undertaken in tandem with domestic budget cuts—were designed to make feasible, at least, a global strategy. That is, this ambitious goal was announced in the absence of the usual comprehensive strategic review undertaken by new administrations and depended primarily on equally ambitious domestic recovery forecasts. According to one sympathetic observer, "The scattershot approach to defense spending, along with Secretary of Defense Caspar Weinberger's decentralization of the management of programs and resources into the hands of the separate armed services, meant that defense expenditures would be undisciplined by strategic guidance until budgetary and other constraints compelled choices among priorities."[65] Nevertheless, the groundwork was laid for a significant reassertion of American power. Second, Weinberger's articulation of a "three-war" strategy aimed at fighting protracted, non-nuclear wars in several theaters simultaneously around the Soviet periphery represented the most ambitious operational concept since, perhaps, NSC-68. At the very least, it envisioned the containment of the Soviets at the conventional level and in regions other than Europe, the Persian Gulf, Japan, and Central America.[66] Third, Secretary of the Navy John F. Lehman, Jr.'s announcement (and Weinberger's endorsement) of plans to achieve "unquestioned maritime superiority" based on a six hundred-ship fleet with fifteen battle groups built around large aircraft carriers, surface ships armed with cruise missiles, and improved amphibious capabilities, further indicated movement toward a global strategy. According to Lehman, "We have a whole new geopolitical situation. What's new is a consensus within the administration that the Soviet threat is global. It's not just central Europe."[67] As Osgood put it, "If nothing else, these intimations of all-purpose strategic goals indicated the Administration's firm intention to change what a number of its officials had criticized as America's Euro-centered strategy and to prepare the armed forces, for once, to support the nation's global commitments with truly flexible, global capabilities."[68] Fourth, the Reagan Administration did or said nothing to suggest that it contemplated any diminution in the number or extent of American interests and commitments. Far from embracing an outlook that justified a strategy of selective or limited containment, as some of Reagan's academic supporters had urged,[69] the Administration showed no inclination to rope off or stand aloof from any Soviet or Soviet-supported geopolitical or ideological initiative, and since it identified Moscow as the "source" of virtually all global instability, this attitude effectively placed every issue in an East-West context. Finally, in one of the President's major foreign policy speeches to date, the Caribbean Basin aid program of February 1982, he described the Soviet threat in very traditional Cold War terms: "A new kind of colonialism stalks the world today and threatens our independence. It is brutal and totalitarian. It is not of our hemisphere but it threatens our hemisphere. . . ." Moreover, his portrait of Central America recalled Truman's 1947 picture of the world:

> The positive opportunity is illustrated by the two-thirds of the nations in the area which have democratic governments. The dark future is foreshadowed by the poverty and repression of Castro's Cuba, the tightening grip of the totalitarian left in Grenada and Nicaragua, and the expansion of Soviet-backed, Cuban-managed support for violent revolution in Central America.[70]

What did the Cubans and the Russians hope to accomplish in Central America?

> Very simply, guerrillas armed and supported by and through Cuba are attempting to impose a Marxist-Leninist dictatorship on the people of El Salvador as part of a larger imperialistic plan.
>
> If we do not act promptly and decisively in defense of freedom, new Cubas will arise from the ruins of today's conflicts.
>
> We will face more totalitarian regimes, more regimes tied militarily to the Soviet Union, more regimes exporting revolution. . . .

But if sufficient U.S. economic and military assistance helped to check the totalitarian threat to Central America, Reagan predicted a happy future:

> I have always believed that this hemisphere was a special place with a special destiny. I believe we are destined to be the beacon of hope for all mankind.
>
> With God's help we can make it so; we can create a peaceful, free, and prospering hemisphere based on shared ideals and

> reaching from pole to pole of what we proudly call the New World.[71]

Much of America's postwar, pre-Vietnam foreign policy had been routinely explained and defended in terms eerily similar to those invoked by President Reagan.

At his Senate confirmation hearing in January 1981 Secretary of State-Designate Alexander Haig had argued that

> Imaginative remedies might have prevented the current danger. Unfortunately, . . . over the last decade, America's confidence in itself was shaken, and American leadership faltered. The United States seemed unable or unwilling to act when our strategic interests were threatened. We earned a reputation for "strategic passivity," and that reputation still weighs heavily upon us and cannot be wished away by rhetoric. What we once took for granted abroad—confidence in the United States—must be reestablished through a steady accumulation of prudent and successful actions.[72]

What would "a steady accumulation of prudent and successful actions" entail? Haig did not, of course, specify concrete examples at the time, but, his early steps against Nicaragua, the Salvadoran guerrillas, international terrorism, and Libya revealed a desire to avoid a direct challenge to Moscow until American military forces were gradually modernized. While Haig proved as reluctant as Reagan to unveil a grand design on which to hang this new assertiveness, he did intimate on several occasions that the Administration's foreign policy rested on what might be termed "grand inclinations": the so-called "four pillars" of peace. They consisted of (1) the restoration of American economic health and military strength; (2) the renewal of traditional alliances and the development of new friendships; (3) the promotion of peaceful progress in developing nations; and (4) the achievement of a relationship with the Soviet Union based on restraint and reciprocity.[73]

The fourth of these pillars particularly stirred the ire of the neo-conservatives. According to Podhoretz, although Reagan had "shown every sign of fidelity to the new consensus, both in spirit and substance," there were disturbing indications that the Administration, and especially Secretary Haig, had failed to embrace a strategy of anti-Communist containment.[74] His stand on El Salvador, while "very strong," was based on "the need to hold back Soviet expansionism and not on the wish to prevent the establishment of a Communist regime there."[75] Worse still, in speaking of

> establishing "norms of international behavior" to govern the conduct of both the Soviet Union and the United States, he even seem[ed] to be invoking the 1972 Basic Principles of Détente as the objective toward which a new strategy of containment should aspire. Yet as he must surely know, experience suggests that no such arrangement is possible.[76]

Podhoretz complained that in El Salvador, Afghanistan, and Poland "we . . . have not yet begun saying . . . much for liberty,"[77] and he warned that

> a strategy of containment which defines the problem of Soviet expansionism alone will be unable to sustain the requisite political support and will therefore lead almost as surely as the retrenchments of the Carter era to a Soviet-dominated world . . . by the end of the 1980s.[78]

Only a strategy of anti-Communist containment, he concluded, held out "the hope of a breakup of the Soviet empire," and the ushering in of a new world "in which the free institutions and the prosperity we in the West have enjoyed would have a much better chance of spreading and finding local nourishment."[79]

Other Administration actions could hardly have soothed the Vietnam revisionists. Reagan's adamant opposition to the reinstitution of a military draft; his termination of the Soviet grain embargo (plus his rather confused response to martial law in Poland); and Haig's promise of offensive weapons for China coupled with the Administration's refusal to sell Taiwan the aircraft it preferred all doubtless disappointed Podhoretz's hopes for a righteous anti-Communism and led one observer to see in this diplomacy a "selfish materialism."[80] In short, after more than two years in office the depth and clarity of the Administration's commitment to a moral anti-Communism remained a puzzlement, and Haig's successor, the enigmatic George Shultz, failed to diminish this ambiguity.

Even Reagan's evident wish to reassert American power was tempered by economic and international constraints. Much of his program, of course, depended on a dramaticrecovery of the American economy, but as the recession persisted Congress began to eye the defense budget as a way to reduce the stupendous anticipated federal deficits. Moreover, a variety of international events, led most prominently by the European peace movement and soon followed by a nuclear freeze movement at home, made it difficult for the Administration to "modernize" American strategic forces without political costs. But, for our purposes, Reagan's strange reluctance to confront Vietnam constituted the most interesting aspect of his foreign policy.

To reiterate, the neo-conservative revisionists had correctly claimed that the orthodox understanding of Vietnam had to be overturned before a revitalized strategy of anti-Communist containment could be effectively justified. A revised memory of Vietnam was a first step along the road to a truly resurgent American foreign policy. The Reagan Administration, however, did virtually nothing to alter the public's perception of Vietnam or to educate it about the war's "real" lessons. True, candidate Reagan had claimed that it was "time we recognized that ours was, in truth, a noble cause. We dishonored the memory of 50,000 young Americans when we gave way to feelings of guilt as if we were doing something shameful."[81] Reagan left little doubt that the cause had been "noble" because its aim had been to defeat Communism in South Vietnam. Then in May 1981 the President announced the death of the "Vietnam syndrome" and the birth of a new American spirit: "The people of America have recovered from what can only be called a temporary aberration. There is a spiritual revival going on in this country, a hunger on the part of the people to once again be proud of America, all it is and all that it can be."[82] Moreover, Jeane Kirkpatrick, the Administration's most prominent neo-conservative academic, focused on a favorite revisionist theme when she told the American Legion the following February that "I don't think that we were driven out of Vietnam—I think we left. I think that's an important distinction and one we should not lose sight of" when raising the issue of El Salvador. "By the way, I don't think the French were driven out of Vietnam either. They left too."[83] Yet these rather off-handed remarks scarcely represented a systematic program to defend explicitly the American intervention in Vietnam. Nor did the Administration suggest that a reasservative America could conceivably ask its citizens to sacrifice their lives in future conflicts. Quite the contrary. Rather, through its rhetoric and its actions the Reagan Administration attempted to ignore Vietnam by invoking historical analogies that had not been seriously raised since the 1960s except for a brief flirtation by Kissinger in 1975. Reagan, Haig, and Shultz disinterred the domino theory, warned of piecemeal aggression, and attempted to place Central America in the context of the Cuban precedent. Furthermore, the Administration's embrace of a "three-war" strategy seemed to accept the risk of future interventions in areas "on the periphery."

How can we explain this almost total silence about Vietnam? Why did the Administration undertake efforts to revitalize (some sort of) containment in the absence of any concerted attempt to resuscitate the memory of Vietnam? American political leaders, as we have seen, rarely speak of specific historical events, particularly controversial ones. They prefer to present themselves as faithful followers of timeless American (and universal) values largely oblivious to the tides of history. It is true that Carter referred to Vietnam on several occasions, but he did so in order to assure his audience that he meant to return America to its eternal path—a path that had been tragically cut by Vietnam. Reagan no doubt felt that a public that evidently supported a significantly enlarged defense budget did not need to be told about Vietnam. Yet this circumstance notwithstanding, as soon as the Administration took specific military steps in Central America the Vietnam analogy hit it like an avalanche.

As we suggested earlier, Secretary Haig apparently envisioned a "two-track" foreign policy whereby an accumulation of low-risk victories in places of America's choosing would rebuild confidence in the United States at the same time that large defense increases would more slowly rebuild its tangible military power. And, after a period of several years, these tracks could be unified as more ambitious goals became supportable with increased power. Haig's early and well-publicized Salvadoran initiative seemed designed to win a quick victory upon which others (e.g., against Libya) could then be piled. In short, Haig thought that El Salvador would provide an opportunity for a modest and immediate reassertion of American power in circumstances ostensibly very different from Vietnam. The Johnson Administration, we recall, defended its Vietnam policy primarily on psychological and moral grounds by stressing America's credibility with its allies, its obligation to create and sustain a stable international order, the need to contain the expansionistic dimensions of the Chinese Revolution, and the right of South Vietnam to determine its future free from aggression. Haig, on the other hand, attempted to justify the dispatch of military aid and advisers to El Salvador by more restrictive arguments. He emphasized, for example, the relatively small size and geographical proximity of El Salvador, and while he, like Johnson and Rusk, underlined the allegedly crucial outside support received by the insurrectionaries, Haig also identified the specific security interests ostensibly at stake in Central America: the

Panama Canal and Mexican and Venezuelan oil. Finally, both Haig and Reagan relied on historical arguments about the unique virtuousness of the Western Hemisphere that originated in the nineteenth century. Though the Johnson Administration tried to provide an additional rationale for Vietnam by invoking the "sacred obligations" of SEATO, this pact clearly lacked the powerful symbolism implicit in Reagan's claims about a Hemispheric "community." In sum, the Reagan Administration refused to justify its involvement in El Salvador in purely Cold War terms, but, rather, attempted to draw nice distinctions between Central America and Southeast Asia. Yet these arguments wilted before the powerful public resurgence of the so-called Vietnam analogy.

Even the outcry raised against the sending of a few dozen American military advisers in February 1981 had been sufficient to prompt the White House to silence Haig for fear of diverting attention and enthusiasm from Reagan's domestic budget and tax cuts. During the summer of 1981 the State Department apparently undertook negotiations with Cuba and Nicaragua in order to dry up the alleged "source" of Salvadoran rebel support. But by the autumn these talks had broken down, and Haig again rang alarm bells in Central America. What began as an opportunity for a quick victory now threatened to engulf the Administration in a Vietnam-type domestic and international controversy.

Public opinion polls taken in February and March 1982 reflected Reagan's dilemma. More than anything else, they indicated the continued attractiveness of at least part of the orthodox explanation of Vietnam, and it was significant that the Administration did little to try and alter the public's perception of that war. An astonishing 89% of those polled by Gallup in mid-February opposed sending any American troops to El Salvador, and 74% believed that U.S. involvement there was very or fairly likely to turn into a Vietnam-like quagmire demanding more and more American resources.[84] At the same time, a NEW YORK TIMES-CBS NEWS poll indicated that while 57% thought that El Salvador and Central America were "very important to U.S. defense interests," 63% urged the Administration to send no aid at all.[85] Finally, a WASHINGTON POST-ABC NEWS survey revealed that although a solid majority of those polled believed that a Communist victory in El Salvador would endanger U.S. security, and although 81% predicted that the loss of that country would probably trigger a domino effect throughout Latin America, fully 51% said that they would support U.S. draftees who refused to fight in El Salvador.[86] The results of these polls, of course, stood in direct contrast to those conducted as late as 1966 when public support for Johnson's escalation in Vietnam ran at 3 to 1.

Public hostility was matched by Congressional skepticism and Allied criticism. In early March 1982 Senate Minority Leader Robert C. Byrd introduced an amendment to the War Powers Act to require prior Congressional concurrence before combat troops could be sent to El Salvador.[87] Several Senators and Congressmen toured El Salvador and returned with warnings against U.S. support for the ruling junta, and Congressional reaction to the Caribbean Basin plan was subdued at best. International enthusiasm was similarly muted; West European Christian Democrats generally applauded President Duartes's reform efforts, but Social Democrats urged negotiations with the left; France recognized the belligerent status of the guerrillas in August 1981; and only a handful of nations agreed to send observers to supervise the March 1982 Constituent Assembly elections. Finally, the region's most powerful members, Mexico and Venezuela, offered to moderate the dispute between Washington and Havana.

In the face of these circumstances, the Reagan Administration could no longer ignore the legacy of Vietnam, but it steadfastly refused to defend its conduct in El Salvador by attempting to rehabilitate Vietnam. Rather, it went to great lengths to distinguish between the two cases and to argue that Cuba constituted the real historical analogy. That is, the Administration, when confronted with the concrete reality of a possible military intervention, shied away from Vietnam revisionism. For example, Haig tried to deal with the Vietnam analogy by claiming that while there had always been an ambiguity whether Southsast Asia constituted "a vital challenge to fundamental American interests, in El Salvador, by contrast, "we're talking about the strategic vulnerability of the Canal. . . . We are, in effect, at the very core of United States hemispheric interests."[88] On the other hand, some former Vietnam planners advised Reagan to openly equate Vietnam with El Salvador. Walt Rostow suggested that " 'It's the same bunch' of 'left-intellectuals' and journalists who undermined the Vietnam war effort who are at work now undermining our effort to help Salvador. 'I fear for my country.' "[89] But the Administration showed no signs of adopting Rostow's strategy. Although leaks about a $19 million covert operations program to "destabilize" Nicaragua reminded some observers of Dulles' campaign against Arbenz's Guatemala, by early March 1982 the Reagan Administration had evidently ruled out the use of American troops in El Salvador.[90] Furthermore, in December Congress ordered the

Administration to cease its destabilization efforts against the Sandanistas.

But if Reagan seemed to embrace some of orthodoxy's Vietnam "lessons"—e.g., that direct military intervention in support of undemocratic right-wing regimes will prove counterproductive and that the dispatch of U.S. combat troops risks creating a "quagmire" that will suck in more and more blood and treasure—he did so less out of a deep conviction about orthodoxy's wisdom than from the political need to come to terms with a public that apparently still accepted the orthodox account of Vietnam. Given the priority Reagan clearly attached to the reconstruction of the American economy, he was not about to chance the defeat of his domestic program by trying to educate the public about the "true"—i.e., revisionist—lessons of Vietnam. At the same time, however, the Administration certainly rejected orthodoxy's more sanguine predictions: that the American withdrawal from Vietnam would permit long overdue attention to the "global agenda"; that the forces of pluralism could be largely entrusted to manage an interdependent world; and that the East-West conflict would no longer require obsessive U.S. attention. But, of course, by 1979 the Carter Administration had also concluded that these predictions could not be fulfilled.

Indeed, after two years in office the Reagan team, notwithstanding its ideological inclination to resurrect global containment to fight Communism, found it difficult to successfully defend even its more restrictive Central American policy. It faced a public that was apparently willing to underwrite the largest military buildup in American peacetime history, that took the Soviet threat seriously again, and that believed vital United States interests to be at stake in El Salvador, but that was almost unanimously opposed to sending American combat troops to Central America. The mood of "conservative nationalism" detected in the Chicago Council's 1979 survey—and seized on by the Vietnam revisionists as the forerunner of a new groundswell of "international idealism"—seemed by 1983 to have moved instead toward a new "conservative isolationism." The Reagan Administration confronted a public that wished to spend vast sums for a military capability that would apparently only be used to deter a direct Soviet attack on the American mainland! The neoconservatives were not thrilled by the prospect of a reincarnated Fortress America.[91]

CHAPTER 8: REVISIONIST HISTORY AND AMERICAN FOREIGN POLICY

We will now try to tie some of these themes together by (1) briefly reviewing the historiographical controversies surrounding the Cold War and Vietnam; (2) indicating the influence that realist, Cold War, and Vietnam revisionism may have exerted on American opinion and policy; and (3) speculating about how U.S. officials might make better use of diplomatic history in the future.

The orthodox historical account of the Cold War, like the foreign policy that it applauded, argued that Soviet-American tension had been caused by Moscow and that Western values could best be preserved by the patient pursuit of containment. These simple and easily grasped convictions formed the heart of the Cold War consensus, a consensus that supported and helped to legitimate American foreign policy from the late 1940s to the late 1960s. The orthodox historiography of Feis and his colleagues reinforced United States policy in several ways. First, the nearly unanimous allegiance of the American historical community to the premises and contents of containment stood in stark contrast to the divisiveness of the interwar years. Although the Cold War consensus might have survived a hostile or deeply divided academic community, the fact that so many historians and political scientists enlisted in the cause of liberal internationalism after World War II should not be lightly dismissed. The orthodox account of the history of the Cold War flowed logically into a defense of current American policy. The United States, according to this view, had done everything reasonably possible to ensure the rightful security of the Soviet Union. It had been generous with its Communist ally and had tried to win Moscow's adherence to the principles of the United Nations Charter in order to attain peace and freedom. But Stalin's insatiable ambition and utter contempt for democratic values had given the United States only one realistic option: containment of Soviet aggression. Second, American diplomatic historians, especially those who wrote college textbooks, disseminated the essence of this consensus to several generations of students. Not only did these texts blame the Cold War on the Soviets and defend containment as the "essential response of free men to Communist aggression," the simplicity with which they did so often paralleled the rhetorical excesses indulged in by American officials to win public and Congressional approval for initiatives like the Truman Doctrine, the Marshall Plan, and aid to Indochina. For almost two decades these textbooks functioned as "recruitment tools" whereby future members of the foreign policy establishment (or, at least, the attentive public) were initially and systematically exposed to postwar American diplomacy. Third, even in its heyday the Cold War consensus was threatened by those who wished to move "beyond containment" in order to win back territories lost (or "surrendered") to the Communists. A conservative revisionism, well-represented in the American press but largely rejected by academe, argued that grievous errors committed by U.S. policy-makers during World War II had led to the loss of Eastern Europe and China. The Truman Administration, in particular, was hard-pressed to counter these claims, and Dean Acheson invited his old friend Herbert Feis to examine the State Department's files in order to write "objective" histories of these controversial episodes. Although the resulting monographs did not silence revisionist critics of Yalta (McCarthyism proved a more effective antidote), they vividly demonstrated the intimate relationship between the orthodox interpretation of Cold War origins and official American Cold War policy. And while it is true that the Feis affair was an extreme case—even by the standards of the 1950s—it also indicates not only the political implications of Cold War historiography but its political *intentions* as well. In short, the nature of Cold War orthodoxy was obviously affected by the prevailing climate of opinion, but at the same time, at least some of these orthodox works were designed, in turn, to alter that climate. That books like THE CHINA TANGLE failed to end the divisive public debate about "Who lost China?" should not obscure the fact that they were written out of something more than simple scholarly curiosity.

If there were certain journalists, interest groups like the China Lobby, and some Eastern European emigrées and "ethnics" who would have gone beyond containment, there was an element in the foreign policy establishment during the high Cold War who wanted to make containment something *less* than it had evidently become. These realist revisionists had no real quarrel with the orthodox rendition of events up to 1947, but they parted company with historians who defended the apparently open-ended goals of the Truman Doctrine and NSC-68. Kennan, Lippmann, and Morgenthau also tended to blame the Soviet Union for causing the Cold War (though they placed more emphasis on structural than ideological elements), but they rejected the orthodox claim that the official policy of containment represented a necessary response to that historical reality. What the realists proposed was a containment policy aimed at Soviet power in Europe and the Middle East that would place less emphasis on an American military commitment and more stress on negotiations with Moscow. In essence they contended that the Truman Doctrine's version of containment threatened to overwhelm American power with enormous and unsustainable responsibilities. The appeal of the realists lay in their sermon of restraint, limits to power, diplomacy, priorities, and balance, but so long as major American foreign policy disasters attributable to overcommitment were avoided, their critique seemingly pushed at an open door. And while it clearly had more impact on Cold War academic historiography than the conservative revisionism of Chamberlin, Flynn, and Burnham, it remained very much a minority interpretation. Until the United States stepped into the Vietnam quagmire, their observations appeared unduly pessimistic. And even after the war lent new relevance to their account of the Cold War, they were overshadowed (at least in the academic community) by radical revisionists urging the abandonment of containment for a drastically restructured diplomacy.

In many respects, the realists offered a sensible, sophisticated analysis of American foreign policy, yet their impact on the scholarly debate about the Cold War remained rather muted for several reasons. First, while all of them wrote about the evolution of the Cold War, Kennan, Lippmann, and even Morgenthau by the 1960s were primarily concerned with changing current U.S. policy. Their recommendations to neutralize Germany, for example, took precedence over their misgivings about the Truman Doctrine. In short, they perceived their real antagonists as American policy-makers dedicated to the further extension of containment and not those diplomatic historians who defended past American conduct. Second, because the realist revisionists more or less accepted the orthodox historians' interpretation of Cold War origins, there was never a full-scale debate between them over "first causes." It was disagreement about the American response to alleged Soviet provocation that divided realist revisionism from orthodoxy, not the fact of Soviet provocation. Though the realists emphasized structure and power in their account of the early Cold War, while orthodox historians focused on the morality of the struggle, their conflict had clear limits and helped prevent the debate from becoming a brawl. Third, the realist revisionists never seized the imagination of the historical community, perhaps because they failed to produce a compelling alternative to orthodoxy. They nibbled at its edges, warned of overcommitment, and urged restraint, but in contrast to the messianism of both orthodoxy and Cold War revisionism, the realists' vision seemed bland and remote. Because it ultimately depended on the distribution of national power and possessed no project grander than the achievement of a balance of American power and interests, it lacked the emotional appeal of its historiographical competitors. Even members of the foreign policy establishment who borrowed from realist revisionism to dissent from the Vietnam War soon abandoned it in favor of a nobler vision: global interdependence and the promise of pluralism.

If the unprecedented expansion of American commitments after World War II provided the initial political environment for realist revisionism's genesis, the relative lessening of Soviet-American tension after 1955 followed by United States military involvement in Southeast Asia formed the backdrop for Cold War revisionism. To put it somewhat crudely, the radical revisionists' ability to offer a plausible and increasingly persuasive interpretation of Cold War origins and their complementary claim that only a drastic domestic transformation could safely terminate the American empire were largely responses to contemporary circumstances. Above all, the Cold War revisionists answered pressing questions that many Americans were asking, particularly on college campuses, in the early 1960s: Why did racism, urban blight, poverty, and injustice persist in America despite the nation's unprecedented material prosperity? Why did the United States require an enormous defense budget to compete with a Soviet Union apparently now dedicated to peaceful coexistence? Was America responsible for perpetuating the Cold War through its dependence on a military-industrial complex? Was Communist China really a threat to American security?

Beyond their willingness to confront these questions, they were also eager to attack virtually every aspect of Cold War orthodox historiography. No doubt the altered political culture of the 1960s was partly to blame for the meanness, even by academic standards, of the ensuing controversy over Cold War origins and responsibility, but it can also be attributed to the chasm that separated these interpretations. So wide was the gulf that in many ways these accounts constituted mirror images of each other. Not since the 1930s had a comparable academic rift appeared over the nature of American foreign policy.

In addition to their substantial historiographical differences which certainly contributed to the sharpness of the debate, orthodoxy and Cold War revisionism also offered apparently contrasting but equally compelling visions of an ideal world. Whereas orthodoxy's appeal rested in part on its portrait of a cosmic struggle waged between two ways of life—the one almost wholly virtuous, the other unspeakably evil—radical revisionists called upon an omnipotent yet deeply-flawed America to withdraw, renew itself, and reenter the world cleansed and purified. Moreover, both visions were drawn from their respective historical theories. Needless to say, the serious domestic divisions, both caused and reflected by Vietnam, exacerbated the gap between these preferred worlds. Maddox's critique of Cold War revisionism constituted the historiographical counterpart to the no-holds-barred tactics used by domestic supporters and opponents of the Vietnam War, for it attacked the personal integrity of "New Left" historians.

The lack of an historiographical consensus about the Cold War since the late 1960s and the resulting interpretive eclecticism known as "post-revisionism" has persisted into the 1980s. Yet despite the significant differences among the interpretations of Gaddis, Herring, Davis, Yergin, and Kuniholm, all of these accounts had one rather obvious element in common: They emphasized the domestic and bureaucratic constraints that limited the options available to American policy-makers during the early Cold War. For Gaddis, public opinion imposed on FDR and Truman shackles that did not encumber Stalin; for Herring, the ability of U.S. officials to employ Lend-lease aid as a diplomatic tool was seriously crippled by Congressional skepticism about foreign economic assistance; for Davis, the widespread public popularity of the Atlantic Charter principles made it extremely difficult for American policy-makers to conduct a flexible Eastern European diplomacy; for Yergin, the "Riga axioms," reinforced by bureaucratic maneuvering and popular prejudices, prematurely locked the United States government into an anti-Soviet posture; and for Kuniholm, McCarthyism and its legacy of fear weakened the incentive of American officials to reevaluate their policy premises in the light of changed circumstances. Orthodox historians and Cold War revisionists had, of course, scarcely ignored domestic constraints on American diplomacy (though the bureaucracy did not much concern them), for Bailey and his colleagues feared that defects in the American national character would damage the United States' ability to wage the Cold War, while the radicals claimed that capitalism had placed American policy in a straight-jacket. The post-revisionists, though not oblivious to economic factors, focused on other, more tangible, institutional realities. These predilections, we would suggest, reflected the political environment of 1970s' America, wherein Vietnam and Watergate raised troubling questions about the vitality of domestic political institutions. Furthermore, the lack of an historiographical consensus about the origins of the Cold War found its public counterpart in the continuing absence of a consensus regarding the purposes and limits of American power in the aftermath of Vietnam.

In large measure it was the neo-conservatives' desire to shape a new liberal internationalist foreign policy consensus that begot Vietnam revisionism. Podhoretz and his allies realized that their hopes for a truly reasservative American diplomacy would probably go unfulfilled so long as the orthodox lessons of Vietnam remained widely persuasive. Despite evident public frustration by the late 1970s about America's fall from "number one," the neo-conservatives recognized that unless a new understanding of Vietnam was achieved, it would be difficult for even a Reagan Administration to translate this public anger into concrete action. While an altered memory of the war might not be essential to the revitalization of containment, it would surely facilitate that task.

This brief review leads to a few final conclusions about the historiography of the Cold War and Vietnam. First, it substantiates the observation that American diplomatic history, "more than any other historical specialty in this country, has an agenda determined not so much by the dynamics of evolving methodology and contacts with other research fields but by major developments in the world around us."[1] Such "presentism" is "reinforced by the unusually large constituency, made up of policy-makers and the informed public that diplomacy history attracts," and it has, as we have seen, "defined the field's central controversies, from the debate over involvement in World War I, through internationalist and Cold War apologetics, to New Left revisionism,"[2] and most recently to the neo-conservative revisionism of Vietnam. Second, it follows from these circumstances that historical investigations of the Cold War and Vietnam, whatever the intentions of their authors, could not help but possess implications for current policies and public attitudes toward them. Historical judgments about living memories like Yalta, Stalin, Hiroshima, the Truman Doctrine, containment, and Vietnam necessarily commented on the sufficiency of subsequent American foreign policy. If Yalta was a "sell-out," Stalin a defensive-minded nationalist, Hiroshima genocide, the Truman Doctrine a Pandora's box, containment provocative, and Vietnam a "noble cause," then significant changes in current United States policy might be required to reflect those historical "truths." Third, we have discovered that many historians of the Cold War and Vietnam, whether orthodox or revisionist, wrote from something more than purely scholarly curiosity, for they clearly *intended* to influence the course of American foreign policy. While not all or, perhaps, even most of this historiography was primarily political in purpose, the best-known works—THE CHINA TANGLE, THE TRAGEDY OF AMERICAN DIPLOMACY, WHY WE WERE IN VIETNAM—did aim to change or defend contemporary American foreign policy. A few writers, such as Gar Alperovitz and David Horowitz, abandoned diplomatic history altogether after concluding that it could not speak directly enough to urgent current social and economic problems. Like Charles Beard and his compatriots in the interwar period who used the "lessons" of World War I to argue for neutrality legislation in the 1930s, the realist, Cold War, and Vietnam revisionists employed the lessons of the past in support of limited containment, radical domestic change, and anti-Communist containment respectively.

* * * * *

Did these revisionists succeed in actually influencing American policy-makers? According to Michael H. Hunt, diplomatic historiographical controversies have "to a degree, spilled back over into the public domain, influencing policy and ultimately further deepening the historian's presentism. The recent concern with the lessons of Vietnam constitutes only the latest instance of this persistent pattern of reciprocal influence between policymakers and historians."[3] It must also be emphasized, however, that the issue of influence is maddeningly complex, and our discussion of it must remain tentative. Warren I. Cohen, for example, correctly warned that "it would be foolish . . . to credit or blame five revisionists, or the ten or twenty revisionists others might call to mind, for the state of American opinion on matters of foreign policy between 1919 and 1939. Until the historian or social scientist perfects better methods of demonstrating influence than have been exhibited to date, it is wisest to view the revisionists as men who reflected and gave voice to the general intellectual background of the day."[4] Similarly, it would be silly to claim that the realist revisionists were responsible for détente, that the Cold War revisionists provided the Carter Administration with its "global agenda," or that the Vietnam revisionists revitalized anti-Communist containment for the Reagan Administration. Nor can it be proven that these historical interpretations decisively affected the public opinion that more or less supported the Nixon, Carter, and Reagan foreign policies. The sources of policy and opinion are hard to identify and impossible to measure precisely. Major unanticipated international events, the print and broadcast media, literature, the personality of leaders, bureaucratic factors, the national "style," and even such symbols of popular culture as films and contemporary music feed this complex process, but the degrees of influence each exerts can only be surmised. Furthermore, while we and others have shown that presumed "lessons of the past" can often function as one source of policy and opinion, it is much more dangerous to claim that such lessons serve as the primary determinants of policy and public opinion. Thus even if it could be demonstrated that the historical analogies used by officials of, say, the Carter Administration were heavily informed by revisionist understandings of the Cold War, it still requires a large leap to suggest that this change in historical thinking determined specific Administration decisions. In short, we must be careful not to exaggerate the influence exerted by these historical revisionisms on recent American foreign policy.

On the other hand, it would be fatuous to contend that realist, Cold War, and Vietnam revisionism and the historical controversies they helped to produce, were nothing more than obscure donnish quarrels wholly removed from the policy arena. While it may be true that American policy-makers use historical analogies neither very well nor very often, we cannot thereby conclude that American diplomacy has been entirely unaffected by changing academic and public perceptions of the past. In fact, Ernest R. May has argued persuasively that the Truman, Kennedy, and Johnson administrations' Korean and Vietnam policies were significantly—perhaps decisively—influenced by historical analogies that we have here termed "orthodox."[5] According to his analysis, "Because of the earlier studies and decisions, evaluating Korea as of negligible importance and concluding that warfare there should be avoided, the 1950 decision provides a particularly vivid illustration of the potency of beliefs about history. When events in the peninsula were perceived as analogous to certain events in the recent past, an axiom derived from the analogies came into play, *and all* previous calculations lost their force."[6] These analogies were, of course, drawn from the conventional lessons of the 1930s when the Western failure to resist the piecemeal aggression of the totalitarians had allegedly brought on World War II, and the Kennedy and Johnson administrations subsequently relied on them in Southeast Asia. May concluded that, "Given the assumptions generally shared by Americans in the 1960s, it seems probable that any collection of men or women would have decided as did members of the Kennedy and Johnson administrations. Nevertheless, at the moment I write [1973], almost everyone regards those decisions as mistaken. Many find them incredible."[7] In other words, by the mid-1970s those historical analogies that had for twenty years reflected and strengthened the premises of the Cold War consensus had evidently lost their force and had been replaced by others.

Since the shattering of this consensus in the late sixties American policy-makers have invoked historical lessons that have at times been significantly different from those of their Cold War predecessors, and these analogies have been informed, albeit frequently indirectly, by revisionist interpretations of American diplomacy. At the same time, however, our review of recent American foreign policy suggests that none of these revisionisms—realist, Cold War, or Vietnam—has gained the unchallenged policy status enjoyed by Cold War orthodoxy from the late forties to the late sixties. Put differently, the absence of an academic historiographical consensus about postwar American diplomacy has been reflected in the absence of a firm public consensus for more than a decade about the purposes of American power.

The precepts of the realist revisionists were, as we saw in chapter five, broadly compatible with the Nixon-Kissinger reformulation. Their analysis of the Truman Doctrine and Asian containment appealed to anti-war liberals who concluded in the late 1960s that the American intervention in Vietnam constituted a dangerous and imprudent overcommitment. Although these establishment liberal internationalists borrowed selectively from the realist revisionists and soon forsook them for a nobler cause—the "global agenda"—few objected to Kissinger's pursuit of Soviet-American détente. Détente, after all, presumed that the Soviet Union could be dealt with rationally by enmeshing it in a complex system of rewards and punishments, and this premise underlay much of the realist revisionist account of the Cold War. Even at the height of U.S.-Soviet tension in the late forties and fifties, first Lippmann and then Kennan urged that negotiations to remove the Red Army from Central Europe and to neutralize Germany be undertaken with Moscow. Because the realist revisionists claimed that global containment effectively ruled out diplomatic solutions, they welcomed the Nixon-Kissinger initiatives as attempts to invest American diplomacy with flexibility and restraint.

The Reagan Administration, as we discovered in chapter seven, has not yet embraced the neo-conservative explanation of Vietnam. While its policy advice is certainly compatible with the Administration goal of a significant revitalization of containment, the public memory of Vietnam has thus far proven to be a formidable obstacle to the realization of that aim. And during its first two years the Reagan Administration refused to offer a revised account of the Vietnam War. Perhaps future events such as the fall of the Saudi monarchy, an intensified growth in West German neutralist sentiment, or the accession to power of several pro-Cuban Central American regimes will drastically alter the public's perception of the "lessons of Vietnam." Comparable shifts have occurred before in American history and may again. Thus far, however, the Vietnam revisionists have failed to provide the catalyst for such a change.

It must be emphasized that neither realist revisionism nor the neo-conservative revisionism of Vietnam began as academic historiographical interpretations of American foreign policy. Their chief architects—Lippmann, Kennan, and Podhoretz—were public figures who wished to (and sometimes could) affect opinion and policy. These revisionisms certainly had formidable academic articulators—Morgenthau, Graebner, Kenneth Thompson, Berger, Novak—but from the outset both interpretations received primary expression in newspaper columns and magazine articles.

Cold War revisionism, on the other hand, sprang entirely from the academic community, and it clearly exerted much more influence on American diplomatic historiography than either realist or Vietnam revisionism. Perhaps for this reason its policy impact has been considerably less obvious. Its chief academic spokesmen—Williams, Alperovitz,[8] and Kolko—have enjoyed little public visibility—certainly less than their World War I counterparts in the 1930s. Nevertheless, Cold War revisionism has spilled over into the wider arena in at least three important ways. First, its portrayal of the United States as an aggressive, exploitative empire reflected a public mood evident as early as the late 1950s that was expressed in a fear of the economic, social, and political consequences of the "military-industrial complex." The civil rights movement, increasing dissent against the Vietnam War, the conviction that America's priorities had become dangerously distorted, and the simultaneous belief that the Cold War was now an anachronism were all facets of a mood which by the late 1960s had emerged as a significant political factor. Second, the project of Cold War revisionism—a radical restructuring of domestic socio-political institutions as the prerequisite for a new American foreign policy—was supported by the New Left, and Cold War revisionists lent to this movement an historical rationale for its goals. While Maddox erred in suggesting that the Cold War revisionists had fabricated history in order to justify their politics, many of these historians clearly smiled on the goals of the New Left. In short, Cold War revisionism supplied American radicalism, 1960s' style, with an important dimension. Third, the enormous popularity of Cold War revisionist works on college and university campuses—a popularity that has persisted into the 1980s—has doubtless played a role in articulating the foreign policy outlooks of several generations of students. To paraphrase Warren I. Cohen's assessment of the 1930s, novelists like Vonnegut, Kesey, and Hesse reached a wider audience than a handful of Cold War revisionists and reflected the same disenchantment with power and institutions, but Williams and his allies certainly had a profound impact on many students in search of specific reasons for the Cold War and Vietnam.

Finally, did Cold War revisionism have a direct impact on the actual conduct of American foreign policy, particularly during the Carter Administration? Although our interviews of Carter officials failed to turn up any unreconstructed Cold War revisionists, Brzezinski's rather contemptuous judgment of Cold War revisionism as merely a sociological phenomenon of the sixties cannot be fully accepted. Many younger Carter advisers had at one time been deeply impressed with the arguments of Williams, Kolko, and other radical diplomatic historians and only gradually concluded that their Cold War theories were exceedingly difficult to translate into policy or had seemingly been contradicted by intervening events. In addition, we discovered that the early, "world order politics" orientation of the Administration derived from a curious amalgam of liberal internationalism, realist revisionism, and Cold War revisionism. But it cannot be claimed that the Carter Administration turned to Cold War revisionism for its historical analogies. At most, we found that several Carter officials, including most prominently PPS Director Anthony Lake, admired the post-revisionist account of Daniel Yergin and tried to interpret Soviet behavior with the assistance of the "Yalta axioms." Indeed, we discovered that until late 1978 Administration officials generally discounted the continued relevance of the Cold War. While

Cold War revisionism was certainly compatible with early Carter initiatives—e.g., the determination to downgrade the centrality of Soviet-American relations, recommendations to cut from five to seven billion dollars from the defense budget, the search for a more just international economic order, and the attempt to normalize relations with Vietnam and Cuba—it cannot be said that Cold War revisionism was responsible for them. Richard J. Barnet, in particular, proposed specific reforms designed to prevent a "new" Cold War and future Vietnams. Of all the radical revisionists he came closest to playing the role fulfilled by Charles Beard in the 1930s. But Barnet's appeal remained confined primarily to the left-wing of the Democratic Party, and, as we saw, Administration officials viewed him with ambivalence at best. In sum, we would suggest that although certain aspects of Cold War revisionism—e.g., its mistrust (even dislike) of American power—were present among some in the Carter Administration, neither the socio-economic project nor the historical arguments of the Cold War revisionists formed significant components of that approach.

* * * * *

For more than two decades beginning after World War II successive administrations consistently relied on a rather limited set of historical "lessons" to justify the policy of anti-Communist containment. In some cases—e.g., the decision to intervene quickly and massively in Korea—they may have played a decisive role in determining policy. These lessons, as we know, were originally drawn from the experience of the 1930s and provided U.S. officials with apparently dependable historical analogies with which to interpret and respond to Soviet behavior. Then, after the Truman Administration's decisive actions in the eastern Mediterranean and Iran evidently deterred further Soviet aggression, the "lessons of Greece" (ultimately derived from the "lessons of Munich") were invoked to support the extension of containment to other regions. Until the late 1960s their validity and continued relevance seemed unassailable. Mavericks like Lippmann had immediate misgivings about their applicability, but until Vietnam very few American policy-makers shared his doubts. Subsequently, of course, it became fashionable to dismiss the lessons of Munich as the illusions of fools and knaves, but such retrospective judgments suffered from the same myopia as the analogy they ridiculed.

Ernest May and Bruce Kuniholm, however, offered more helpful evaluations of American policy-makers' use of history during the

Cold War. On balance, May concluded that in planning for the postwar world, framing the Truman Doctrine, responding to the North Korean invasion, and deciding to send troops to Vietnam, senior United States officials selected historical analogies very narrowly and subjected them to no deliberate scrutiny or analysis. While he by no means believed that all of these decisions had been wrong, May criticized the manner in which they were reached: "Here one can see men who would have been scandalized by an inelegant economic model or a poorly prepared legal brief making significant use of historical parallels, analogies, and trends with utter disregard for expertise or even the inherent logic of their assertions."[9] In order to help U.S. policy-makers make better use of history he presented several concrete proposals. First, although admitting that imprudent advisers are as frequently found among historians as among any other group and cautioning that history is not an arcanum requiring a priesthood comparable to the Council of Economic Advisers, May suggssted that "historians ought to be asked to supply perspective on events in foreign countries."[10] Second, "people in government should also look to historians for some information about past policies of the United States,"[11] so that new administrations, in particular, will have accurate information about the exact nature of American commitments to other governments. May argued, for example, that Kennedy appointees mistakenly presumed that the Eisenhower Administration had given an iron-clad guarantee to protect South Vietnam from the Communists. Third, government officials should rely on historians to analyze and challenge, if necessary, those parallels, analogies, and precedents which pass for historical "lessons." Fourth, increased funding should be made available to train scholars in the history of non-Western areas so that future American policy-makers will have more information about these regions than past officials had about Southeast Asia.[12] And finally, May urged that the government might commission studies comparable to Herbert Feis' THE CHINA TANGLE to enhance the public's (and its own) education about past policies.[13] To this end he further recommended a drastic acceleration in the declassification process, and, if that proved not feasible, he suggested that special research privileges be granted to a limited number of qualified historians.[14]

Kuniholm's analysis pointed in a somewhat different direction. Unlike May he argued that in framing a response to the Near Eastern crises of the late 1940s American policy-makers made a realistic assessment of the national interest by correctly understanding the nature of the historical balance-of-power in the region. In short, they used history well in helping to define the contemporary regional responsibilities of the United States. The "lessons" of Greece and Iran, which did have limited applicability to other parts of the Near East, were, however, subsequently ripped from their geographical and historical contexts and employed abstractly and indiscriminately in Berlin, Korea, and Vietnam.[15] Thus was history abused, but Kuniholm blamed this circumstance on the inflated if necessary rhetoric of U.S. officials and on the rather paranoid political environment that this rhetoric helped to produce. In contrast to May, however, he offered no suggestions to assist people in government make better use of history except to emphasize that the validity of historical models must be constantly reexamined in order to prevent rigidity and dogmatism.

Did the Carter Administration use history any more effectively than its Cold War predecessors? In view of the large number of academic specialists—including historians—among Carter's foreign policy advisers we might have expected a more systematic and self-conscious search for historical parallels, analogies, and trends than was evident when American diplomacy was the bailiwick of lawyers, bankers, and industrialists. The "lessons" of Munich and Greece no longer commanded unquestioning allegiance. Indeed, relatively few Carter officials had lived through these events as adults. Many advisers had read rather extensively in the literature of the Cold War and were aware of conflicting historical interpretations. Its "world order politics" enthusiasts spoke of the inexorable forces of change. The "legacy of Vietnam" evidently hung heavy in the atmosphere at the White House and the State Department. Notwithstanding these circumstances, however, members of the Carter Administration selected historical analogies about as narrowly and subjected them to about as little deliberate scrutiny as those policy-makers described by May. In a few instances, as with Brzezinski's attempt to liken the Persian Gulf of 1980 to the eastern Mediterranean situation in the 1940s, explicit reference was made to apparently compelling analogies, but, in fact, this equation was made with the help of very little expert advice and was primarily designed to wrap President Carter in the mantle of Harry Truman in an election year.[16] And, to be sure, historically-oriented background studies occasionally reached the President, as, for example, Bruce Kuniholm's one-hundred page history of U.S.-Iranian relations written in the aftermath of the embassy seizure,[17] although their impact is difficult to evaluate.

What was disturbing, however, was the fact that the "lessons of Vietnam" attained for much of the Carter Administration the same sort of tacit allegiance that the lessons of Munich and Greece had previously enjoyed. The lessons of Vietnam deserved to be taken seriously, but they also deserved to be explicitly examined and, if necessary, debated by the Administration. Just as the lessons of Munich meant that the option to avoid military force in Korea and Vietnam was never seriously considered by the Truman and Kennedy administrations, so the lessons of Vietnam meant that the option to employ military force in Iran and Nicaragua to save American clients was never seriously considered by Carter.

Almost everyone we interviewed agreed that Vietnam had preoccupied the Administration, yet these officials had rarely addressed the war's legacy directly. If during the Cold War successive administrations had evinced a determination to avoid another Munich, the Carter Administration was equally determined to avoid another Vietnam. If previous administrations had concluded that unchallenged piecemeal aggression would inevitably lead to a major war, this Administration firmly believed that the use of American combat troops would almost as inevitably run the risk of another Vietnam. As PPS member Robert Gallucci put it, "We had a great respect for the difficulty of pulling back from something like that, and that undoubtedly was a feeling that was impressed on us by Vietnam."[18] If other administrations had used the experience of the 1930s as the touchstone against which contemporary crises were measured, Carter and his advisers asked, "How likely was this situation to get us involved in another Vietnam?". This question was, of course, asked tacitly, because the Carter Administration prided itself on its alleged ability to deal with each case on its own merits.[19] In short, fears of another Vietnam consumed the Administration, but they rarely surfaced in policy debates.

Brzezinski, we know, did by the end of 1978 begin to mutter that the lessons of Vietnam had been overlearned by some of his colleagues, and his annoyance became louder after the 1980 election. But he failed to challenge these lessons directly. Instead, he offered another, equally unexamined, historical analogy—the Truman Doctrine—to articulate his Persian Gulf strategy. By the end of the Carter Administration two sets of analogies, one drawn from the sixties and the other taken from the forties, vied with each other, but neither had been deliberately and carefully scrutinized. For those future Carter officials who had helped to formulate the orthodox understanding of Vietnam in FOREIGN POLICY, its "lessons" soon became a dogma whose self-evident good sense required no further examination. And for those officials who began to doubt the sufficiency of this explanation of Vietnam, the older lessons of the Cold War, derived from the "lessons of Greece," were embraced without debate.

Can anything be done to improve the manner in which American policy-makers use diplomatic history, or is it inevitable that they fix on one or two apparently compelling "lessons" that are then indiscriminately applied to a wide variety of situations? Here our study leads to a rather pessimistic conclusion, for several formidable obstacles stand in the way of improved performance. First, most policy-makers simply do not have time to hear or read much history. Bombarded as they are with cables, memoranda, and urgent requests for action, policy-makers, even if they had the inclination to gather extensive historical information, would find it difficult to digest in any detail. Even those advisers with academic backgrounds that we interviewed ruefully noted that they had not been able to read serious history since they joined the government.[20] Lynn E. Davis recalled that she was sometimes asked to recommend "one good book" to non-academic policy-makers interested in learning about the history of the Cold War,[21] and William Quandt observed that in those rare instances when senior officials read history, they opted for slightly dramatized narratives yielding rather simple lessons.[22] For example, apparently both Secretary Vance and President Carter read Alastair Horne's A SAVAGE WAR OF PEACE[23] about Algeria and from it concluded that it was dangerous to frustrate Arab nationalism. This "lesson" was then used to justify a new Palestinian policy and even played a role in the Administration's handling of the (non-Arab) Iranian revolution. The "one good book" syndrome constitutes an important barrier to improving the systematic historical knowledge of policy-makers. Second, although the outlook and priorities of policy-makers are informed by historical judgments, however unacknowledged, some officials doubt the practical usefulness of historians in the policy process. May correctly suggested that "most historians by training and temperament tend to err on the side of giving too much detail and introducing too many qualifications," and he interviewed one State Department officer who remarked that " 'Historians refuse to generalize . . . to give up detail and to give up shadings.' "[24] Davis noted that while she could often use history to "win debating points," most officials—and especially the lawyers—felt that this sort of thinking was "too academic"[25] to be very useful. Bruce Kuniholm admitted that he was never sure how or if the historical information that he provided about Iran and the Persian Gulf was employed by senior officials.[26] The ambiguity of the policy environment can erode the clarity of even the most precise historical analogy. Finally, the presentism of historians does not inspire confidence in their ability to instruct policy-makers. *Perhaps* area specialists can provide "objective" information about non-Western regions, but we have seen that American diplomatic historians, at least, have been prime participants in political disputes about American foreign policy. Furthermore, as we noted in our discussion of Maddox's critique, "facts" cannot be easily separated from "interpretations," and even the most dispassionate recounting of postwar American foreign policy carries with it certain interpretive implications. In sum, it is not clear that diplomatic historians can deepen the historical knowledge of policy-makers without simultaneously providing them with implicit "lessons." Taken together these factors help to explain why it is unlikely that future American policy-makers will employ history with more deliberateness, scrutiny, or self-consciousness than past officials. Those who write history and those who make policy will probably remain locked in their reciprocal, but frustrating, relationship.

NOTES

Introduction

1. Robert Darnton, "Poland Rewrites History," *New York Review of Books,* July 16, 1981, 6, 10.
2. *Washington Post,* January 14, 1982, 16.
3. Walter Laqueur, "Rewriting History," *Commentary,* March 1973, 53.
4. *Ibid.*
5. Franklin D. Roosevelt, "Peace," *Vital Speeches of the Day,* September 1, 1936, 732.
6. Warren I. Cohen, *The American Revisionists* (Chicago, 1967), 6.
7. Quoted in Cohen, *The American Revisionists,* x.
8. Quoted in Francis Loewenheim, review of Robert James Maddox, *The New Left and the Origins of the Cold War, The New York Times Book Review,* June 17, 1973, 10.
9. Robert J. Skotheim, ed., *The Historian and the Climate of Opinion* (Reading, MA, 1969), 5.
10. Ernest R. May, *"Lessons" of the Past: The Use and Abuse of History in American Foreign Policy* (New York, 1973).

Chapter I

1. For a more detailed defense of this proposition see Godfrey Hodgson, "The Establishment," *Foreign Policy,* 10 (Spring 1973), 3-40.
2. *Ibid.*, 8.
3. X [George F. Kennan], "The Sources of Soviet Conduct," *Foreign Affairs.* XXV (July 1947), 566-82.
4. Quoted in Martin F. Herz, *Beginnings of the Cold War* (Bloomington, 1966), 192.
5. *Ibid.*, 200.

6. See Thomas Etzold, and John Lewis Gaddis (eds.), *Containment: Documents on American Policy and Strategy, 1945-1950* (New York, 1978); Fred M. Kaplan, "Our Cold War Policy, Circa '50," *New York Times Magazine,* May 18, 1980, 34, 88-94.
7. Charles Gati (ed.), *Caging the Bear: Containment and the Cold War* (Indianapolis, 1974).
8. Etzold and Gaddis, *Containment,* 25-37.
9. Kaplan, "Our Cold War Policy," 88.
10. *Ibid.*
11. U.S. Department of State, *Foreign Relations of the United States, Diplomatic Papers,* Vol. I, National Security Affairs; Foreign Economic Policy (Washington, D.C., 1976), 271-77.
12. Bohlen memorandum, April 14, 1949. Ibid., 277-78.
13. Kennan to Acheson, April 14, 1949. Ibid., 282.
14. Kaplan, "Our Cold War Policy," 91.
15. U.S. Department of State, *Foreign Relations of the United States, Diplomatic Papers,* Vol. I (Washington, D.C., 1977), 432.
16. Kaplan, "Our Cold War Policy," 92.
17. *Ibid.*, 93.
18. *Foreign Relations of the United States, I, 1950,* 468-69.
19. *Ibid.*, 427-31.
20. These terms were coined and used somewhat differently by William Welch, *American Images of Soviet Foreign Policy: An Inquiry into Recent Appraisals from the Academic Community* (New Haven, 1970).
21. Particularly in the State Department.
22. Frances Fitzgerald, "Rewriting American History, Part II," *New Yorker,* March 5, 1980, 80.
23. Arthur M. Schlesinger, Jr., "Origins of the Cold War," *Foreign Affairs,* L (October 1967), 22.
24. Cf. John T. Flynn, *The Roosevelt Myth* (New York, 1948); William Henry Chamberlin, *Beyond Containment* (Chicago, 1953); James Burnham, *Containment or Liberation?* (New York, 1953) and *The Struggle for the World* (New York, 1947); and George N. Crocker, *Roosevelt's Road to Russia* (Chicago, 1959).
25. George C. Herring, Jr., *Aid to Russia,* 1941-1946: *Strategy, Diplomacy, and the Origins of the Cold War* (New York, 1973), x.
26. *Ibid.*
27. Quoted in Herz, *Beginnings of the Cold War,* 191.
28. Quoted in Herring, *Aid to Russia,* xvi.

29. *Ibid.* The official was George Racey Jordan.
30. Cf. Townsend Hoopes, *The Devil and John Foster Dulles* (Boston, 1973), 114-23.
31. Herbert Feis to Dean Acheson, January 16, 1950, in Herbert Feis Papers, Library of Congress, Washington, D.C.
32. Thomas A. Bailey, *A Diplomatic History of the American People* (New York, 1940 and rev. eds.); Dexter Perkins, *The Evolution of American Foreign Policy* (New York, 1948, 1954); John W. Spanier, *American Foreign Policy Since World War II* (New York, 1960 and rev. eds.); Richard W. Leopold, *The Growth of American Foreign Policy* (New York, 1962); Julius Pratt, *A History of United States Foreign Policy* (New York, 1954); Foster Rhea Dulles, *America's Rise to World Power* (New York, 1954); Samuel Flagg Bemis, *A Diplomatic History of the United States* (New York, 1936 and rev. eds.).
33. Dulles, *America's Rise to World Power,* 227.
34. *Ibid.,* 231.
35. *Ibid.,* 276.
36. Pratt, *A History of United States Foreign Policy, passim.*
37. *Ibid.,* 780.
38. *Ibid.*
39. *Ibid.,* 781.
40. Bailey, *A Diplomatic History of the American People, passim.*
41. *Ibid.,* 852-53.
42. John W. Spanier, *American Foreign Policy Since World War II* (New York, 1960, 1962, 1965, 1968, 1971, 1974, 1977, 1980, 1983).
43. Spanier, *American Foreign Policy,* 2nd ed., 1-2.
44. Spanier, *American Foreign Policy,* 6th ed., 3.
45. Spanier, *American Foreign Policy,* 6th and 8th eds., 2O.
46. Spanier, *American Foreign Policy,* 6th ed., 20.
47. Spanier, *American Foreign Policy,* 8th ed., 13.
48. Spanier, *American Foreign Policy,* 2nd ed., 30.
49. Spanier, *American Foreign Policy,* 6th ed., 39, 8th ed., 27.
50. Spanier, *American Foreign Policy,* 2nd ed., 30.
51. Spanier, *American Foreign Policy,* 6th ed., 39, 8th ed., 27-28.
52. Spanier, *American Foreign Policy,* 2nd ed., 31.
53. Spanier, *American Foreign Policy,* 6th ed., 40.
54. Spanier, *American Foreign Policy,* 8th ed., 28.
55. Spanier, *American Foreign Policy,* 2nd ed., 33.
56. Spanier, *American Foreign Policy,* 6th ed., 41, 42, 41, 42.
57. *Ibid.*, 42.
58. *Ibid.*

59. *Ibid.*, 43.
60. *Ibid.*, 43-44.
61. Spanier, *American Foreign Policy,* 8th ed., 30.
62. *Ibid.,* 30-31.
63. *Ibid.*, 31.
64. Cf. Gar Alperovitz, *Cold War Essays* (New York, 1970), 133-36.
65. *Current Biography 1961,* 158.
66. Papers of Herbert Feis, Library of Congress.
67. *Ibid.*
68. Herbert Feis to Dean Acheson, September 17, 1948. *Ibid.*
69. Herbert Feis notes, October 20, 1954 and October 21, 1954. Four pages of documents and photographs sent by Feis to W. Averell Harriman, October 21, 1954. *Ibid.*
70. John Paton Davies to Herbert Feis, February 12, 1954. Memo of talk with Davies, February 12, 1954. *Ibid.*
71. Interview with William Franklin, Washington, D.C., March 16, 1982.
72. Herbert Feis, *As Seen From E.A.* (New York, 1947).
73. William L. Langer, *Our Vichy Gamble* (New York, 1947).
74. Franklin interview.
75. William L. Langer and S. Everett Gleason, *The Challenge to Isolation* (New York, 1952) and *The Undeclared War, 1940-1941* (New York, 1953).
76. Herbert Feis, *The Road to Pearl Harbor* (Princeton, 1950).
77. The same was true as well of Herbert Feis, *The Spanish Story,* (New York, 1948).
78. Telephone interview with William Z. Slany, March 12, 1982. In *The China Tangle: The American Effort in China from Pearl Harbor to the Marshall Mission* (Princeton, 1953), Feis explained it as follows "This work was made possible only by the wish of the State Department to have this historical experience as fully explored and objectively told as it could be at this time while the meaning of so much of it is still hard to grasp. For this reason the former Secretary of State, Dean G. Acheson, encouraged the enterprise, and the competent Departmental Committee authorized me to consult the official files" (p. vi).
79. Herbert Feis, *The China Tangle* (Princeton, 1953).
80. Franklin interview.
81. Herbert Feis, *Between War and Peace: The Potsdam Conference* (Princeton, 1960).
82. Slany interview.

83. Herbert Feis to Dean Rusk, December 13, 1960. Papers of Herbert Feis, Library of Congress.
84. The "restricted" designation had been ended by Franklin in the early 1960s.
85. Herbert Feis to Dean Rusk, July 15, 1966. Papers of Herbert Feis, Library of Congress.
86. Herbert Feis, *From Trust to Terror: The Onset of the Cold War, 1945-1950* (New York, 1970).
87. Herbert Feis to Dean Rusk, August 4, 1967. Papers of Herbert Feis, Library of Congress.
88. This is William Franklin's term for Feis, Langer, and Gleason.
89. Franklin interview.
90. See chapter 3, 70-2.
91. Feis, *The China Tangle,* 429.
92. *Ibid.*
93. *Ibid.,* 252.
94. *Ibid.,* 253.
95. *Ibid.*
96. *Ibid.*, 254.
97. *Ibid.*
98. *Ibid.*
99. Herbert Feis, *Churchill, Roosevelt, Stalin: The War They Waged and the Peace They Sought* (Princeton, 1957), 550.
100. *Ibid.*
101. *Ibid.,* 557.
102. See, for example, his discussion of Yalta in *Churchill, Roosevelt, Stalin.*
103. Feis, *Churchill, Roosevelt, Stalin,* 655.
104. See, for example, Feis' references to the atomic bomb "revisionists" in *From Trust to Terror,* 93.
105. Cf. Herbert Feis to Eugene Dooman, April 28, 1954. Papers of Herbert Feis, Library of Congress.
106. Robert Strausz-Hupé, William R. Kintner, James E. Doughterty, Alvin J. Cottrell, *Protracted Conflict* (New York, 1959).
107. Elliot R. Goodman, *The Soviet Design for a World State* (New York, 1960); Anthony T. Bouscaren, *Soviet Foreign Policy: A Pattern of Persistence* (New York, 1962); and Bertram D. Wolfe, *Communist Totalitarianism: Keys to the Soviet System* (Boston, 1961).
108. Strausz-Hupé, *et al., Protracted Conflict,* 148.

109. *Ibid.*, 148-49.
110. For a sketch of Bemis' work see John Higham, *et al., History* (Englewood Cliffs, 1965), 188-90.
111. Samuel Flagg Bemis, "American Foreign Policy and the Blessings of Liberty," in *American Foreign Policy and the Blessings of Liberty and Other Essays* (New Haven, 1962), 10.
112. *Ibid.*, 45.
113. *Ibid.*, 14.
114. Reprinted in Department of State Bulletin, 46 (January 15, 1962).
115. *Ibid.*, 83.
116. Walt Whitman Rostow, *The United States in the World Arena: An Essay in Recent History* (New York, 1959).
117. *Ibid.*, 145.
118. *Ibid.*, 166.
119. *Ibid.*, 224.
120. *Ibid.*, 229.
121. *Ibid.*, 258.

Chapter II

1. Quoted in Fitzgerald, "Rewriting American History," 80.
2. William Hardy McNeill, *America, Britain, and Russia: Their Cooperation and Conflict* (London, 1953). See also Louis J. Halle, *The Cold War as History* (New York, 1967).
3. McNeill, *America, Britain, and Russia,* 406-08.
4. *Ibid.,* 408.
5. *Ibid.,* 761-62.
6. Introduction, 1970 reprint of *ibid.,* 1.
7. *Ibid.*
8. Cf. Walter Lippmann, *Isolation and Alliances* (Boston, 1952), *passim.*
9. Robert W. Tucker, *The Purposes of American Power* (New York, 1981) and James Chace, *Solvency: The Price of Survival* (New York, 1981).
10. Gati, *Caging the Bear,* 49.
11. Walter Lippmann, *U.S. Foreign Policy: Shield of the Republic* (Boston, 1943), 6-7.
12. *Ibid.*, 7.
13. *Ibid.*, 149.
14. Lippmann, *Isolation and Alliances,* 40.

15. Hans J. Morgenthau, *Politics Among Nations* (New York, 1948).
16. *Ibid.*, 17.
17. Kenneth W. Thompson, *Masters of International Thought* (Baton Rouge, 1980), 85.
18. Hans J. Morgenthau, *In Defense of the National Interest* (New York, 1951), 34.
19. *Ibid.,* 117.
20. *Ibid.,* 116.
21. *Ibid,*, 121.
22. Reprinted as Appendix II in *ibid.*
23. *Ibid.,* 121.
24. *Ibid.,* 75.
25. Joseph M. Jones quoted in Gati, *Caging the Bear,* 10.
26. Louis J. Halle quoted in Thompson, *Masters of International Thought,* 146.
27. Quoted in *ibid.,* 146.
28. George F. Kennan, *Memoirs: 1925-1950* (Boston, 1967), 482.
29. Cf. George F. Kennan, *American Diplomacy, 1900-1950* (Chicago, 1951), *passim.*
30. George F. Kennan, *Realities of American Foreign Policy* (Princeton, 1954), 12.
31. *Ibid.,* 115.
32. Gati, *Caging the Bear,* 51.
33. Lippmann, *Isolation and Alliances,* 25.
34. Quoted in Charles Gati, "Another Grand Debate? The Limitationist Critique of American Foreign Policy," *World Politics,* 21 (October 1968), 140.
35. Norman A. Graebner, *Cold War Diplomacy, 1945-1960* (New York, 1962); Norman A. Graebner, *Cold War Diplomacy, 1945-1975* (New York, 1977).
36. Graebner, *Cold War Diplomacy, 1945-1975,* iv.
37. *Ibid.*
38. *Ibid.,* iv-v. Emphasis added.
39. *Ibid.,* v.

Chapter III

1. Carl Marzani, *We Can Be Friends* (New York, 1952).

2. Among the most prominent of those who we will not specifically consider are Lloyd C. Gardner, Thomas G. Paterson, Ronald Radosh, Diane Shaver Clemens, and David Horowitz.
3. William Appleman Williams, *American-Russian Relations, 1789-1947.*
4. William Appleman Williams, *The Tragedy of American Diplomacy* (Cleveland, 1959).
5. William Appleman Williams, *The Contours of American History* (Cleveland, 1961).
6. William Appleman Williams, *The Great Evasion* (Chicago, 1964).
7. William Appleman Williams, *The Roots of the Modern American Empire* (New York, 1969).
8. See my article, "The Social and Political Thought of William Appleman Williams," *Western Political Quarterly,* 31 (September 1978), 392-409, for a fuller discussion of this theme.
9. Williams, *The Contours of American History,* 145.
10. Williams, *The Great Evasion,* 136.
11. Williams, *The Contours of American History,* 428.
12. William Appleman Williams, *Some Presidents* (New York, 1972).
13. Cf. Thomas G. Paterson, ed., *Cold War Critics: Alternatives to American Foreign Policy in the Truman Years* (Chicago, 1971) and Ronald Radosh, *Prophets on the Right: Conservative Critics of American Globalism* (New York, 1975).
14. William Appleman Williams, "Rise of an American World Power Complex," in Neal D. Houghton, ed., *Struggle Against History* (New York, 1968), 17.
15. *Ibid.*, 3.
16. Williams, *The Great Evasion, 31.*
17. *Williams, "Rise of an American Complex," 11.*
18. Williams, *The Contours of American History,* Foreword to the 1966 edition.
19. Williams assumed that the decision-maker was fully aware of the elements which made up his *Weltanschauung.* Furthermore, he ignored such factors as internalized beliefs, a "cognitively dissonant" world-view, or misperception of one's own or one's adversary's perspective.
20. William Appleman Williams, "The American Century: 1941-1957," in *Nation,* November 2, 1957, reprinted in Williams, *History as a Way of Learning* (New York, 1974), 215.

21. *Ibid.*
22. *Ibid.*, 216.
23. *Ibid.*
24. *Ibid.*, 221.
25. *Ibid.*, 223.
26. *Ibid.*, 225.
27. *Ibid.*, 225-26.
28. Williams, *The Tragedy of American Diplomacy,* 308.
29. *Ibid.*, 307.
30. *Ibid.*, 306.
31. *Ibid.*
32. *Ibid.*
33. *Ibid.*, 308.
34. *Ibid.*, 308-09. Emphasis in the original.
35. *Ibid.*, 309. It is interesting to note that for Graebner and other realist revisionists, conservatism held the key to the *long-term* rehabilitation of American foreign policy. See chapter two, 55.
36. Staughton Lynd, review of *The Contours of American History, Science & Society,* 26 (Summer 1962), 243.
37. Robert L. Heilbroner, *The New York Review of Books,* January 21, 1965, 21.
38. Eugene Genovese, "Williams on Marx and America," *Studies on the Left,* 6 (January-February 1966), 81.
39. This book proved to be Williams' last (to date) excursion into extended research.
40. Howard Zinn, "America II," *Partisan Review* (April 1971), 524.
41. Michael Harrington, "America II," *Partisan Review* (April 1971), 504.
42. Arthur M. Schlesinger, Jr., "America II," *Partisan Review* (April 1971), 505.
43. Walter LaFeber, *America, Russia, and the Cold War* (New York, 1967, 1972, 1976, 1981).
44. Cf. Lloyd C. Gardner, *Economic Aspects of New Deal Diplomacy* (Madison, 1964) and Gar Alperovitz, *Atomic Diplomacy: Hiroshima to Potsdam* (New York, 1965).
45. Lloyd C. Gardner, "Truman Era Foreign Policy: Recent Historical Trends," in Richard S. Kirkendall, ed., *The Truman Period as a Research Field: A Reappraisal* (Columbia, Mo., 1974), 47.

46. Herbert Feis' treatment of this theme had long typified the orthodox position on this issue. Cf. Herbert Feis, *Japan Subdued* (Princeton, 1961).
47. Cf. P.M.S. Blackett, *Fear, War, and the Bomb* (New York, 1949).
48. Alperovitz, *Atomic Diplomacy,* 28.
49. Feis, *Japan Subdued, passim.*
50. Gar Alperovitz, "The Use of the Atomic Bomb," in *Cold War Essays* (New York, 1970). Most of these essays originally appeared in the *New York Review of Books* during the mid-60s.
51. Ibid., 73.
52. Alperovitz, *Cold War Essays,* introduction, 4.
53. Alperovitz, "The United States, Revolutions, and the Cold War: Perspective and Prospect," in *Cold War Essays,* 121-22.
54. Ibid., 122.
55. Gabriel Kolko, *The Politics of War: The World and United States Foreign Policy,* 1943-1945 (New York, 1968); Joyce and Gabriel Kolko, *The Limits of Power: The World and United States Foreign Policy, 1945-1954* (New York, 1972); and Gabriel Kolko, *The Roots of American Foreign Policy* (Boston, 1969).
56. Kolko, *The Politics of War,* 3.
57. *Ibid.,* 620.
58. *Ibid.*
59. *Ibid.*
60. *Ibid.,* 625.
61. Kolko and Kolko, *The Limits of Power,* 716.
62. For an elaboration of these differences see Barton J. Bernstein, "Commentaries," in Kirkendall, *The Truman Period: A Reappraisal,* 162-71.
63. *Ibid.,* 164.
64. Richard J. Barnet, *The Giants* (New York, 1977).
65. Cf. Richard J. Barnet, *Roots of War* (New York, 1972).
66. Barnet, *The Giants,* 15.
67. *Ibid.,* 168-69.
68. *Ibid.,* 169.
69. *Ibid.,* 170.
70. Barnet, *Roots of War,* 338.
71. *Ibid.,* 339.
72. *Ibid.,* 340.
73. *Ibid.,* 341.
74. *Ibid.,* 339.

75. *Ibid.*
76. *Ibid.*
77. *Ibid.*
78. *Ibid.*, 340
79. *Ibid.*
80. *Ibid.*
81. *Ibid.*, 340-41.
82. *Ibid.*, 341.
83. *Ibid.*
84. Walter LaFeber, *The New Empire* (Ithaca, 1963).
85. Robert L. Beisner, "*The New Empire* and American Historians: A Report on a Survey," Paper delivered to the annual meeting of the Organization of American Historians, New Orleans, La., April 16, 1971.
86. The book's phenomenonal sales, at least, would seem to support this contention.
87. In this regard Norman A. Graebner recalls a letter that he once received from LaFeber. In it LaFeber wrote that "the New Left without purely economic motivation is like Paris without a brothel." Letter from Graebner to author, January 4, 1981.
88. LaFeber, *America, Russia, and the Cold War* (1967 ed.), 6, 7. All quotations are from this edition.
89. *Ibid.*, 14.
90. *Ibid.*, 15.
91. *Ibid.*, 21.
92. *Ibid.*
93. *Ibid.*, 22.
94. *Ibid.*, 23.

Chapter IV

1. Letters reprinted in Alperovitz, *Cold War Essays,* 133-36.
2. Arthur M. Schlesinger, Jr., letter to *New York Review of Books,* October 20, 1966, where he suggested that it was "time to blow the whistle" on Cold War revisionism.
3. Eugene V. Rostow, *Peace in the Balance* (New York, 1972), 128.
4. Alperovitz, *Cold War Essays*, 135.
5. William Appleman Williams, "The Cold War Revisionists," *Nation,* November 13, 1967, reprinted in Williams, *History as a Way of Learning.* 378.

6. Robert W. Tucker, *The Radical Left and American Foreign Policy* (Baltimore, 1971).
7. Charles S. Maier, "Revisionism and the Interpretation of Cold War Origins," in Richard M. Abrams and Lawrence W. Levine, eds., *The Shaping of Twentieth-Century America: Interpretive Essays* (Cambridge, 1971).
8. Tucker, *The Radical Left,* 9.
9. *Ibid.,* 148.
10. *Ibid.*
11. Maier, "Revisionism," 346.
12. Ibid., 347.
13. Robert James Maddox, *The New Left and the Origins of the Cold War* (Princeton, 1973).
14. Maddox analyzed these revisionist works: William Appleman Williams, *The Tragedy of American Diplomacy;* D.F. Fleming, *The Cold War and Its Origins, vol. I* (New York, 1961); Gar Alperovitz, *Atomic Diplomacy: Hiroshima and Potsdam;* David Horowitz, *Free World Colossus* (New York, 1965); Gabriel Kolko, *The Politics of War: The World and United States Foreign Policy, 1943-1945;* Diane Shaver Clemens, *Yalta* (New York, 1970); and Lloyd C. Gardner, *Architects of Illusion* (Chicago, 1970).
15. Maddox, *The New Left,* 10.
16. Ibid.
17. *Ibid.,* 10-11.
18. *Ibid.,* 10.
19. *Ibid.*
20. *Ibid.*, 159-60.
21. *Ibid.*, 160.
22. *Ibid.*
23. *Ibid.*
24. *Ibid.,* 163-64. Emphasis in the original.
25. Gar Alperovitz, "Communication to the Editor," *Journal of American History,* 59 (March 1973), 1062-67.
26. David Horowitz, *Ramparts,* September-October 1973, 37-40, 58-60, 62.
27. *Ibid.,* 60.
28. *Ibid.,* 62.
29. *Daily Princetonian*, Ootober 18, 1973, 3.
30. *Daily Princetonian,* October, 1973, 1.
31. *Ibid.*

32. *Daily Princetonian,* October 25, 1973, 2. Princeton University Press social sciences editor Sanford Thatcher suggested that "I have no reason to believe that any boycott has been mounted against us as Professor Kolko once threatened," (Letter to the author. December 10, 1976) Maddox was not quite so sure, however, for he observed that the question about " 'pressures' being applied against is difficult to answer. I have heard that there were, but have no substantial evidence on it. . . ." (Letter to the author, October 11, 1976).
33. For a fuller discussion of these practices see my "Revisionism Subdued? Robert James Maddox and the Origins of the Cold War," *Political Science Reviewer,* 7 (Fall 1977), 229-71.
34. Maddox, *The New Left*, 142.
35. *Ibid.,* 158.
36. *Ibid.,* 14. Emphasis added.
37. Lloyd C. Gardner, "On Robert James Maddox's *The New Left and the Origins of the Cold War:* A Reply Intended for the Persistent and the Patient," (unpublished paper, May 1973), 31-32.
38. Gardner, *Architects of Illusion,* 180-81.
39. Harry S. Truman, *Memoirs, vol. I* (New York, 1955), 87. Emphasis added.
40. Another factor· to consider is the "unconditional surrender" doctrine. If the "Big Three" were in agreement that Japan must ultimately surrender unconditionally in any case (bomb or not), what could Byrnes have meant by his statement that "the bomb might well put us in a position to dictate our own terms at the end of the war"? To dictate terms to an unconditionally defeated power would seem redundant.
41. Maddox, *The New Left,* 10.
42. Robert James Maddox, "Response to Professor Warren Kimball," (unpublished paper, nd.), 7. Emphasis in the original.
43. Maddox, *The New Left,* 142.
44. *Ibid.,* 16.
45. John J. Rumbarger, "Robert James Maddox and the Use of Evidence," (unpublished paper, nd.), 1.
46. *Ibid.,* 3.
47. *Ibid.,* 4.
48. *Maddox, The New Left,* 162.
49. Robert H. Ferrell, "Truman Foreign Policy: A Traditional View," in Kirkendall, *The Truman Period, 1972,* 14.

50. Letter from Charles S. Maier, January 16, 1981.
51. Barton J. Bernstein, "Commentaries," in Kirkendall, *The Truman Period, 1972,* 161.
52. Cf. Tucker, *The Radical Left,* 153.
53. Cf. Robert W. Tucker, *Nation or Empire?* (Baltimore, 1968), *passim.*
54. Harry Magdoff, *The Age of Imperialism* (New York, 1969), *passim.*
55. Lloyd C. Gardner, "Truman Era Foreign Policy," in Kirkendall, *The Truman Period,* 1972, 47.
56. Tucker, *The Radical Left*, 154.
57. *Ibid.*
58. For a more detailed treatment of this theme, see Maier, "Revisionism."
59. Lloyd C. Gardner, "Truman Era Foreign Policy," 48.
60. Letter from Robert A. Divine, January 12, 1981.
61. Letter from Walter LaFeber, March 20, 1981.
62. *Ibid.*
63. John Lewis Gaddis, *The United States and the Origins of the Cold War, 1941-1947* (New York, 1972); George C, Herring, *Aid to Russia;* Lynn E. Davis, *The Cold War Begins: Soviet-American Conflict Over Eastern Europe* (Princeton, 1974); Daniel Yergin, *Shattered Peace: The Origins of the Cold War and the National Security State* (Boston, 1977); and Bruce R. Kuniholm, *The Origins of the Cold War in the Near East* (Princeton, 1980).
64. Gaddis, *The United States,* 358.
65. *Ibid.*, 355-56.
66. *Ibid.*, 352.
67. *Ibid.*, 360-61.
68. *Ibid.*, 358.
69. *Ibid.*, 358-59.
70. *Ibid.*, 361.
71. Herring, *Aid to Russia,* xix.
72. *Ibid.*, xx.
73. *Ibid.*
74. *Ibid.*, 279.
75. *Ibid.*
76. *Ibid.*, 280.
77. *Ibid.*
78. *Ibid.*
79. *Ibid.*, 281.

80. *Ibid.*
81. *Ibid.*, 282.
82. *Ibid.*
83. *Ibid.*, 285.
84. *Ibid.*, 287.
85. *Ibid.*
86. *Ibid.*
87. *Ibid.*
88. *Ibid.*, 288.
89. *Ibid.*, 292.
90. *Ibid.*, 292-93.
91. *Ibid.*, 290.
92. *Ibid.*, 293.
94. Davis, *The Cold War Begins,* 4-5.
95. *Ibid.*, 8.
96. *Ibid.*, 376.
97. *Ibid.*
98. *Ibid.*, 376-77.
99. *Ibid.*, 377.
100. *Ibid.*, 379.
101. *Ibid.*, 384.
102. *Ibid.*
103. *Ibid.*, 384-85.
104. *Ibid.*, 385.
105. *Ibid.*, 387.
106. *Ibid.*, 392. Emphasis added.
107. *Ibid.*, 393.
108. *Ibid.*, 394,
109. We have reached this conclusion on the basis of interviews with former Carter Administration officials. See chapter 6, 153-67.
110. Daniel Yergin and Martin Hillenbrand, eds., *World Energy: The Crisis and What We Can Do About It* (Boston, 1982).
111. Yergin, *Shattered Peace,* 13.
112. *Ibid.*
113. *Ibid.*, 35.
114. *Ibid.*, 37.
115. *Ibid.*, 37-38.
116. *Ibid.*, 39.
117. *Ibid.*, 36.
118. *Ibid.*. 43.
119. *Ibid.*, 44.
120. *Ibid.*, 45.

121. *Ibid.*, 48.
122. *Ibid.*, 57.
123. *Ibid.*, 68.
124. *Ibid.*, 336.
125. *Ibid.*, 408.
126. *Ibid.*, 409.
127. *Ibid.*
128. Joseph M. Jones, *The Fifteen Weeks* (New York, 1955).
129. Kuniholm, *The Origins of the Cold War,* xx.
130. *Ibid.*, 415.
131. *Ibid.*
132. *Ibid.*, 416.
133. *Ibid.*
134. *Ibid.*, 419.
135. *Ibid.*
136. *Ibid.*
137. *Ibid.*, 421. See also John Lewis Gaddis, "Containment: A Reassessment," *Foreign Affairs,* 57 (July 1977), 873-887.
138. *Ibid.*, 427.
139. *Ibid.*, 428.
140. *Ibid.*
141. *Ibid.*, 429.
142. *Ibid.*
143. Interview with Bruce R. Kuniholm, Durham N.C., February 16, 1982.
144. *New York Times*, February 8, 1980, 10.
145. Ronald Radosh, *Prophets on the Right: Conservative Critics of American Globalism* (New York, 1975).
146. Blanche W. Cook, *The Declassified Eisenhower: A Divided Legacy* (New York, 1981).
147. Robert L. Messer, *The End of an Alliance: James F. Byrnes, Roosevelt, Truman, and the Origins of the Cold War* (Chapel Hill, 1981).
148. Martin J. Sherwin, *A World Destroyed: The Atomic Bomb and the Grand Alliance* (New York, 1975).
149. Davis, *The Cold War Begins,* ix.
150. Sherwin, *A World Destroyed,* 238.
151. *Ibid.*, 3-4.
152. *Ibid.*, 5.
153. *Ibid.*, 6.
154. *Ibid.*
155. *Ibid.*, 6, 7.

156. *Ibid.*, 7.
157. *Ibid.*, 238.
158. *Ibid.*, 8.
159. *Ibid.*
160. *Ibid.*
161. *Ibid.*, 238.

Chapter V

1. J. William Fulbright, *The Arrogance of Power* (New York, 1966).
2. Arthur M. Schlesinger, Jr., *The Bitter Heritage* (Boston, 1966).
3. Ronald Steel, *Pax Americana* (New York, 1967).
4. Edmund Stillman and William Pfaff, *Power and Impotence* (New York, 1966).
5. George W. Ball, *The Discipline of Power* (Boston, 1968).
6. Robert W. Tucker, *Nation or Empire?* (Baltimore, 1968).
7. Steel, *Pax Americana,* 329-30.
8. Ball, *The Discipline of Power,* 301.
9. *Ibid.*, 306.
10. Quoted in Earl M. Ravenal, *Never Again: Learning From America's Foreign Policy Failures* (Philadelphia, 1978), 25.
11. *Ibid.,* 26.
12. Fulbright, *The Arrogance of Power,* 14.
13. Early indications of this phenomenon can be detected in Steel, *Pax Americana* and Fulbright, *The Arrogance of Power.*
14. Telephone interview, Seth Tillman (former aide to Fulbright), April 9, 1981.
15. Cf. Kolko, *The Roots of American Foreign Policy.*
16. Cf. Magdoff, *The Age of Imperialism.*
17. The Cold War revisionists contended, of course, that this circumstance was but further proof of their arguments about the real nature of the foreign policy establishment. That is, even dissenting members were, above all, capitalists.
18. See chapter 3, 76-81.
19. Various interviews, Washington, D.C., Spring 1981.
20. Letter from Schlesinger to author, November 26, 1979.
21. Robert E. Osgood, *Ideals and Self-Interest in American Foreign Policy* (Chicago, 1953).
22. Interview with Osgood, Washington, D.C., May 11, 1981.
23. Interview with Sonnenfeldt, Washington, D.C., April 28, 1981.
24. *Ibid.*

25. *Ibid.*
26. *Ibid.*
27. *Ibid.*
28. Henry A. Kissinger, *Nuclear Weapons and Foreign Policy* (New York, 1957); Henry A. Kissinger, *The Necessity for Choice: Prospects of American Foreign Policy* (New York, 1961); Henry A. Kissinger, "Reflections on American Diplomacy," *Foreign Affairs,* XXXIX (October 1956), and Henry A. Kissinger, "Missiles and the Western Alliance," *Foreign Affairs,* XL (April 1958), plus several others.
29. Henry A. Kissinger, *A World Restored: Metternich, Castlereagh, and the Problems of Peace, 1812-1822* (Boston, 1957); Henry A. Kissinger, "The White Revolutionary: Reflections on Bismarck," *Daedalus,* (Summer 1968).
30. Henry A. Kissinger, *White House Years* (Boston, 1979).
31. *Ibid.*, 58, 59, 60.
32. *Ibid.*, 61.
33. *Ibid.*, 62.
34. *Ibid.*
35. *Ibid.*
36. *Ibid.*
37. *Ibid.*
38. *Ibid.*, 55.
39. *Ibid.*, 65.
40. Stanley Hoffmann, *Primacy or World Order: American Foreign Policy Since the Cold War* (New York, 1978), 35.
41. *Ibid.*, 36.
42. This term is Robert W. Tucker's. See his "America in Decline: The Foreign Policy of 'Maturity'," *America and the World, 1979, Foreign Affairs,* LVIII (1979), 459.

Chapter VI

1. Hoffmann, *Primacy or World Order,* 199.
2. Carl Gershman, "The Rise and Fall of the New Foreign-Policy Establishment," *Commentary,* July 1980, 24.
3. *Ibid.*, 20.
4. "Suetonius" (Roger Morris), "The Junior Varsity," *New Republic,* February 19, 1977, 13.
5. Graham T. Allison, "Cool It: The Foreign Policy of Young America," *Foreign Policy,* 1 (Winter 1970-71), 147.
6. *Ibid.*
7. *Ibid.*, 156-57.

8. *Ibid.*, 159.
9. Interview with W. Anthony Lake, Washington, D.C., June 2, 1981.
10. These conclusions were reached on the basis of our interviews with Carter officials in 1981.
11. *Washington Post,* October 12, 1981, A2.
12. Hoffmann, *Primacy or World Order.*
13. *Ibid.*, 7.
14. *Ibid.*, 8.
15. *Ibid.*, 8-9.
16. *Ibid.*, 9.
17. *Ibid.*, 10.
18. *Ibid.*, 23.
19. *Ibid.*, 47.
20. *Ibid.*, 92.
21. *Ibid.*, 94.
22. *Ibid.*, 95.
23. *Ibid.*
24. *Ibid.*, 88.
25. See *ibid.,* 162-82.
26. *Ibid.*, 111.
27. *Ibid.*, 112.
28. *Ibid.*, 113.
29. *Ibid.*, 114.
30. *Ibid.*
31. *Ibid.*, 111.
32. *Ibid.*, 118.
33. *Ibid.*
34. *Ibid.*, 120.
35. *Ibid.*
36. *Ibid.*, 122.
37. *Ibid.*, 125, 126.
38. *Ibid.*, 131-32.
39. *Ibid.*, 135.
40. *Ibid.*
41. *Ibid.*, 209
42. *Ibid.*, 213.
43. *Ibid.*, 224.
44. *Ibid.*
45. *Ibid.*, 186-87.
46. Interview with Colonel L.G. Denend, Washington, D.C., May 14, 1981.

47. W. Anthony Lake, "Pragmatism and Principle in U.S. Foreign Policy," Boston, Massachusetts, June 13, 1977.
48. *Ibid.*
49. *Ibid.*
50. *Ibid.*
51. *Ibid.*
52. Zbigniew Brzezinski, "American Power and the Global Challenge," Washington, D.C., August 2, 1979.
53. *Ibid.*
54. Interview with Robert A. Pastor, Washington, D.C., April 20, 1981.
55. This book was published in the United States as *Free World Colossus* and was, it will be recalled, one of the works lambasted by Robert James Maddox in *The New Left and the Origins of the Cold War.*
56. Interview with Pastor.
57. *Ibid.*
58. *Ibid.*
59. *Ibid.*
60. Interview with Samuel R. (Sandy) Berger, Washington, D.C., May 29, 1981.
61. *Ibid.*
62. *Ibid.*
63. *Ibid.*
64. *Ibid.*
65. *Ibid.*
66. Background interview, Washington, D.C., Spring 1981.
67. Interview with F. Stephen Larrabee, Washington, D.C., May 11, 1981.
68. *Ibid.*
69. *Ibid.*
70. *Ibid.*
71. *Ibid.*
72. Interview with Madeleine Albright, Washington, D.C., May 29, 1981.
73. *Ibid.*
74. *Ibid.*
75. *Ibid.*
76. Interview with Fritz Ermarth, Washington, D.C., May 22, 1981.
77. *Ibid.*
78. *Ibid.*

79. *Ibid.*
80. *Ibid.*
81. Letter from Zbigniew Brzezinski to author, May 27, 1981.
82. *Ibid.*
83. Daniel Yergin, *Shattered Peace,* see chapter 4, 109-14.
84. Interview with Roger C. Molander, Washington, D.C., June 19, 1981.
85. Robert Gallucci, *Neither Peace Nor Honor* (Baltimore, 1975).
86. Interview with Robert Gallucci, Washington, D.C., May 21, 1981.
87. Hoffmann, *Primacy or World Order, passim.*
88. Background interview, Washington, D.C., Spring 1981.
89. Interview with Robert E. Hunter, Washington, D.C., May 5, 1981.
90. *Wall Street Journal,* January 21, 1980.
91. *Ibid.*
92. *Ibid.*
93. Albright interview.
94. Hunter interview.
95. *Wall Street Journal,* January 21, 1980.
96. *Ibid.*
97. Interview with John Holum, Washington, D.C., May 27, 1981.
98. *Ibid.*
99. Background interviews, Washington, D.C., Spring 1981.
100. Edward Friedman and Mark Selden, eds., *America's Asia* (New York, 1969).
101. *Ibid.*, xviii.
102. Walter Mondale, speech at Peking, China, August 27, 1979.
103. John K. Fairbank, *The United States and China* (Cambridge, 1948 and rev. eds.).
104. Michel Oksenberg and Robert B. Oxnam, *China and America* (New York, 1977), Headline Series no, 235.
105. Telephone interview with Michel Oksenberg, April 21, 1981.
106. *Ibid.*
107. It only threatened that understanding which contended that the United States should maintain hostility toward all Communist regimes regardless of foreign policy conduct. To do otherwise would be immoral. Norman Podhoretz, as we will see in the next chapter, adopted this outlook and incorporated it into a "neo-conservative" Vietnam revisionism.
108. William Appleman Williams, *The United States, Castro, and Cuba* (New York, 1962).

109. Richard J. Barnet, *Intervention and Revolution* (New York, 1968).
110. The literature of "dependencia" is vast, but cf. Andre Gunder Frank, *Capitalism and Underdevelopment in Latin America* (New York, 1967) and *Latin America: Underdevelopment or Revolution* (New York, 1969).
111. Background interview, Washington, D.C., Spring 1981.
112. *Ibid.*
113. Richard R. Fagen, "The End of the Affair," *Foreign Policy,* 36 (Fall 1979), 189.
114. Jeane Kirkpatrick, "Dictatorships and Double Standards," *Commentary,* November 1979, 45.
115. *Ibid.*, 36.
116. *Ibid.*, 40.
117. Background interview, Washington, D.C., Spring 1981.
118. Interview with Richard Feinberg, Washington, D.C., May 28, 1981.
119. Holum interview.
120. Gallucci interview.

Chapter VII

1. Leslie H. Gelb with Richard Betts, *The Iron of Vietnam: The System Worked* (Washington, D.C., 1978).
2. Cyrus Vance, "Meeting the Challenges of a Changing World," Chicago, Illinois, May 1, 1979.
3. Background interview, Washington, D.C., Spring 1981.
4. Jimmy Carter, "Humane Purposes in Foreign Policy," South Bend, Indiana, May 22, 1977.
5. Interview with Paul Kreisberg, Washington, D.C., June 13, 1981.
6. *Ibid.*
7. Three weeks after the 1980 election Brzezinski publicly denounced "do-gooders" in the Administration and the Democratic Party who had been "traumatized by the experience of Vietnam because their party 'was responsible for the policies that produced the debacle.' " (*New York Times,* November 29, 1980, 1) Although critical of Ronald Reagan for his alleged desire to achieve military superiority, Brzezinski "asserted that his attempts to expand military strength had encountered 'a great deal of opposition within the Administration' and within 'a party which was automatically fearful that any emphasis on com-

petition meant you were wanting to revive the Cold War.' " (*Ibid.,* 20)

8. Background interview, Washington, D.C., Spring 1981.
9. Gelb with Betts, *The Irony of Vietnam,* 24.
10. Leslie H. Gelb, "Dissenting on Consensus," in W. Anthony Lake, ed., *The Legacy of Vietnam* (New York, 1976), 115.
11. *Ibid.,*113.
12. *Ibid.*
13. *Ibid.,* 116.
14. *Ibid.,* 116-17. Gelb's notion of a changing consensus which would lend legitimacy to specific policies formed, in effect, the domestic analogue to Lake's "shifting global coalitions" which America was to encourage and help manage.
15. Leslie H. Gelb, "Beyond the Carter Doctrine," *New York Times Magazine,* February 10, 1980, 40.
16. *Ibid.,* 19.
17. *Ibid.,* 40.
18. *Ibid.*
19. Interview with Leslie H. Gelb, Washington, D.C., June 10, 1981.
20. This, at least, was the consensus of the two dozen PPS and NSC staffers we interviewed. Indeed, Reagan's PPS Director, Paul Wolfowitz, invited several of the more conservative Lake appointees to remain after January 20, 1981.
21. Background interview, Washington, D.C., Spring 1981.
22. Background interview, Washington, D.C., Spring 1981.
23. Hoffmann, *Primacy or World Order,* 42.
24. Carter, "Humane Purposes in Foreign Policy."
25. Holum interview.
26. Earl C. Ravenal, *Never Again: Learning from America's Foreign Policy Failures* (Philadelphia, 1978).
27. Robert W. Tucker, *A New Isolationism?* (Washington, D.C., 1972).
28. Feinberg interview.
29. Background interview, Washington, D.C., Spring 1981.
30. Hoffmann, *Primacy of World Order,* 202, 204.
31. Norman Podhoretz, *Why We Were in Vietnam* (New York, 1982).
32. Guenther Lewy's *America in Vietnam* is a notable exception.
33. Podhoretz apparently prefers this term.
34. Norman Podhoretz, "The New American Majority" *Commentary,* January 1981, 21.

35. Peter L. Berger, in "America Now: A Failure of Nerve?" *Commentary,* July 1975, 21.
36. *Ibid.*
37. *Ibid.*
38. Michael Novak, in "America Now: A Failure of Nerve?", *Commentary,* July 1975, 69.
39. Peter L. Berger, "Indochina and the American Conscience," *Commentary,* February 1980, 33-34.
40. Guenther Lewy, *America in Vietnam* (New York, 1978).
41. Daniel Ellsberg, *Papers on the War* (New York, 1972).
42. Richard A. Falk, *The Vietnam War and International Law,* 4 vols. (Princeton, 1969-1976).
43. Charles Horner, "America Five Years After Defeat," *Commentary,* April 1980, 50.
44. Norman Podhoretz, "The Future Danger," *Commentary,* April 1981, 29.
45. Carl Gershman, "After the Dominoes Fell," *Commentary,* May 1978, 47-54.
46. Horner, "America Five Years After Defeat," 56.
47. *Ibid.*
48. See, for example, Gershman, "The Rise and Fall of the New Foreign-Policy Establishment," 13-24.
49. Irving Kristol, "The Trilateral Commission Factor," *Wall Street Journal,* April 16, 1980, 24.
50. Norman Podhoretz, *The Present Danger* (New York, 1980), 90.
51. Norman Podhoretz, "The New Nationalism and the 1980 Elections," *Public Opinion,* February/March 1980, 5.
52. Kristol, "The Trilateral Commission Factor."
53. Podhoretz, "The New American Majority," *passim.*
54. Podhoretz, "The Future Danger," 38-39.
55. *Ibid.*, 39.
56. *Ibid.*
57. *Ibid.*
58. *Ibid.*
59. Irving Kristol, in "America Now: A Failure of Nerve?", 54.
60. Podhoretz, *Why We Were in Vietnam.*
61. Podhoretz, "The Future Danger," 41-42.
62. Podhoretz, in fact, has revealed a good deal of ambivalence on this point, an ambivalence that has been heightened by his most recent writing on Vietnam. He now seems to conclude that the U.S. could never have won in Vietnam, despite noble intentions.

63. William Schneider, "The Public and Foreign Policy," *Wall Street Journal,* November 7, 1979, 26.
64. Robert E. Osgood, "The Revitalization of Containment," *America and the World, 1981, Foreign Affairs,* 60 (1981), 471.
65. *Ibid.*, 475.
66. Jeffrey Record, "A 3-War Strategy?", *Washington Post,* March 22, 1982, 28.
67. *Washington Post,* December 14, 1981, A1, A10.
68. Osgood, "The Revitalization of Containment," 476.
69. Cf. Tucker, *The Purposes of American Power.*
70. Ronald Reagan, "Caribbean Basin Initiative," Washington, D.C., February 24, 1982.
71. *Ibid.*
72. Alexander Haig, "A New Direction in U.S. Foreign Policy," Washington, D.C., April 24, 1981.
73. Alexander Haig, "Overview of Recent Foreign Policy," Washington, D.C., November 12, 1981, U.S. Department of State, Bureau of Public Affairs.
74. Podhoretz, "The Future Danger," 46.
75. *Ibid.*
76. *Ibid.*
77. *Ibid.*
78. *Ibid.*, 47.
79. Ibid.
80. The term is Joseph Kraft's. See his "Of Arms and Men," *Washington Post,* May 24, 1981.
81. *New York Times,* August 19, 1980, D17.
82. Ronald Reagan, "The New Spirit That Is Abroad: Patriotism," West Point, New York, May 27, 1981.
83. *New York Times,* February 21, 1982, IV, 2.
84. *Newsweek,* March 1, 1982, 19.
85. *New York Times,* March 21, 1982, 22.
86. *Washington Post,* March 24, 1982, A8.
87. *Washington Post,* March 7, 1982, A1.
88. *The Economist,* February 13, 1982, 26.
89. Robert G. Kaiser, "Is El Salvador Vietnam?", *Washington Post,* March 7, 1982, C5.
90. *Washington Post,* March 7, 1982, A1.
91. Cf. Norman Podhoretz, "The Neo-Conservative Anguish Over Reagan's Foreign Policy," *New York Times Magazine,* May 2, 1982.

Chapter VIII

1. Michael H. Hunt, "Responses to Charles S. Maier, 'Marking Time: The Historiography of International Relations,' " *Diplomatic History* 5 (Fall 1981), 354.
2. *Ibid.*
3. *Ibid.*, 354-55.
4. Warren I. Cohen, *The American Revisionists,* 233-34.
5. Ernest R. May, *"Lessons" of the Past,* 83. Emphasis added.
6. *Ibid.*
7. Ibid., 120-21.
8. Alperovitz has, no doubt, received more public exposure since he left diplomatic history. Indeed, he appeared on *Meet the Press* in 1978 as an economic expert.
9. Ernest R. May, *"Lessons" of the Past,* 121. Although May leveled this particular charge at the Vietnam decisions, he reached similar conclusions about others as well.
10. *Ibid.*, 173, 174.
11. *Ibid.*, 175.
12. *Ibid.*, 180, 181.
13. *Ibid.*, 185.
14. *Ibid.*, 185, 186.
15. Bruce R. Kuniholm, *The Origins of the Cold War in the Near East,* 416.
16. Background interviews, Washington, D.C., Spring 1981.
17. Kuniholm interview.
18. Gallucci interview.
19. Kreisberg interview.
20. These, at least, were the experiences of Robert Gallucci and Robert A. Pastor.
21. Davis interview.
22. Quandt interview.
23. Alastair Horne, *A Savage War of Peace: Algeria, 1954-1962* (New York, 1978).
24. Ernest R. May, *"Lessons" of the Past,* 189.
25. Davis interview.
26. Kuniholm interview.

APPENDIX: INTERVIEWS

Historians:

In person—	
Lynn E. Davis	March 5, 1982
William Franklin	March 16, 1982
John Lewis Gaddis	February 19, 1979
John Higham	November 12, 1980
Bruce R. Kuniholm	February 16, 1982
Walter LaFeber	August 8, 1979
By telephone—	
Gar Alperovitz	May 1, 1982
William Z. Slany	March 12, 1982
Ronald Steel	April 9, 1981
By letter—	
Robert A. Divine	January 12, 1981
Robert H. Ferrell	January 8, 1981
Norman A. Graebner	January 4, 1981
Warren F. Kimball	February 23, 1981
Walter LaFeber	March 20, 1981
Richard W. Leopold	January 12, 1981
Charles S. Maier	January 16, 1981
Arno J. Mayer	January 20, 1981
Robert James Maddox	October 11, 1976 and October 22, 1976
Thomas G. Paterson	January 19, 1981
Ronald Radosh	January 15, 1981
John J. Rumbarger	November 15, 1976
Arthur M. Schlesinger, Jr.	November 26, 1979

Carter Administration Officials:

In person—

Madeleine Albright	May 29, 1981 and February 18, 1982
Samuel R. Berger	May 29, 1981
Zbigniew Brzezinski	February 18, 1982
Lynn E. Davis	March 5, 1982
Leslie G. Denend	May 14, 1981 and February 18, 1982
Guy F. Erb	May 26, 1981
Fritz Ermarth	May 22, 1981
Richard Feinberg	May 28, 1981
Robert Gallucci	May 21, 1981
Leslie H. Gelb	June 10, 1981
John Holum	May 27, 1981
Robert E. Hunter	May 5, 1981
Paul H. Kreisberg	June 13, 1981
Bruce R. Kuniholm	February 16, 1982
W. Anthony Lake	June 2, 1981
F. Stephen Larrabee	May 11, 1981
Jessica Tuchman Mathews	June 10, 1981
Roger C. Molander	June 19, 1981
William Odom	February 18, 1982
Robert A. Pastor	April 20, 1981
William Quandt	April 16, 1981
Marianne Spiegel	June 4, 1981
Sandra.Vogelgesang	May 9, 1981

By telephone—

Michel Oksenberg	April 21, 1981

By letter—

Zbigniew Brzezinski	May 27, 1981

Other interviews:

In person—

Robert E. Osgood	May 11, 1981
Helmut Sonnenfeldt	April 28, 1981

By telephone—

Seth Tillman	April 17, 1981

By letter—

Sanford Thatcher	December 10, 1976